Chic on a Shoestring

Chic on a Shoestring

Annette Swanberg and Leigh Charlton

Photography by Leigh Charlton

DOUBLEDAY & COMPANY, INC. ○ GARDEN CITY, NEW YORK ○ 1984

Library of Congress Cataloging in Publication Data

Swanberg, Annette.
Chic on a shoestring.

Includes index.
1. Fashion.   2. Clothing and dress.   3. Shopping.
I. Charlton, Leigh.   II. Title.
TT507.S98   1984   646′.34   82–45284
ISBN 0–385–17689–9

Copyright © 1984 by Annette Swanberg and Leigh Charlton
Photography by Leigh Charlton
All rights reserved
Printed in the United States of America

Designed by Judith Neuman

First Edition

To Gloria, Mildred, Ora, Janelle, Lesley, Nike, Laura, Viki and Tris.

To each for her own unique sense of style.

Acknowledgments

We would like to thank our family and friends for their encouragement throughout the research and writing of this book, especially Maureen Strange, Deborah Ashin, Viki King, Deborah Reinberg, and Jim Bickhart. Special appreciation goes to Patrick O'Connor and Carole Garland for their heartening confidence in this book early on; and to our indefatigable agent, Connie Clausen; to our understanding editor, Louise Gault and to our friend and legal advisor, Fred Bernstein.

In addition to our appreciation for the time each of the *Chic* experts took for an in-depth interview, we would like to express our gratitude to Rick Cutler for the generous use of his photography studio, to Hugh Munro Neely for his consistently excellent photographic prints and to Millard of California for the loan of coats and jackets. Thanks, too, to the fashion and marketing officials at Spiegel, JC Penney, and Sears. The Cunningham and Icon International modeling agencies deserve our appreciation, too.

And, finally, we'd like to specially thank Charles Allen and Mason Buck.

NOTE: *Chic on a Shoestring* correspondence should be addressed to: Annette Swanberg and Leigh Charlton, P.O. Box 25060, Los Angeles, CA 90025.

Contents

1 The Gospel According to *Chic on a Shoestring* 1

Section I Develop Your Chic Fashion Eye

2 Express Your Chic Self 7
Stretch Your Imagination • How to Use Fashion Magazines • Meet a Fashion Journalist with Personal Style—Fashion Editor Gwen Jones

3 Color Is Chic 19
How to Easily Determine Your Own Best Colors • KEY 1 and 2 COLORS • Color Advice from an Expert, Professor Mary Kefgen

4 Proportionately Yours 27
Body Self-Knowledge • Proportion Tools • A Self-Taught Lesson in Proportion • Proportion Advice from Designer Liz Claiborne • General Proportion Tips • How to Look Taller and Slimmer • Talking About Body Know-How and Attitude with Designer Harriet Selwyn

Section II How to Build Your Chic Wardrobe (On the Cheap)

5 Discover a Chic Wardrobe 47
What Is a Wardrobe? How to Make the Shift from a Collection of Clothes to a Wardrobe That Works • Excavating a Wardrobe • Honing In on Your Chic Wardrobe Colors • Organizing Your Chic Wardrobe • Wardrobe Advice from Designer Irene Tsu

6 Conquering Your Closet 55
Rethink Your Closet • Recipe for an Organized Closet: Ingredients and Method • Closet Tips

x • Contents

7 Chic Feet *61*
Proportion • Color • Style • Quality Is Chic • General Price Category Guidelines and Best Buys • Shoe Tips • Shopping for Shoes • Where to Buy Chic Shoes

8 Chic Accoutrements *67*
Creative Essentials • A Wardrobe of Accessories: Belts, Scarves, Handbags, Jewelry, Hosiery, Hats and Gloves • Where to Buy

9 Menswear to *Your*-Wear *73*
Shop Smart in the Boys' Department • Equivalent Size Chart • Out of His Closet—What to Borrow from a Man • Menswear Tips • Where to Buy

Section III Stretch Your Chic Wardrobe (And Thereby Your Dollars)

10 Transseasonal Chic *81*
The Three Principles of Seasonless Dressing: Silhouette, Color and Fabrics • Transseasonal Pieces • Tips from Designers • Seasonless Shopping

11 Travel Chic-ly *85*
Wardrobe Guidelines • A Chic Travel Wardrobe • Travel Planning • Packing and Packing Tips • Travel Advice from Top Designers

12 Chic from A.M. to P.M. *91*
A Simple Metamorphosis • Around-the-Clock Clothes • The Added Difference • Day-into-Evening Tips

13 Cheap Jock Chic *97*
Survival Dressing for the 1980s • How to Get Double Duty from Your Active Wear and Sports Gear • Where to Buy Your Jock Chic Cheaply

14 Chic Cover-ups *101*
The Three Basics • Figure Considerations • A Laundry List of Coat Styles • Shopping for a Coat • Coat "Collecting"—Building a Coat Wardrobe • A Chic Coat Wardrobe—Examples from Our Closets

15 Maternity Chic *105*
   How to Save Money on a Maternity Wardrobe • Maternity Wardrobe Tips • Where to Shop • Special Clothing Needs for Postpartum and Nursing • Maternity Wear Advice from an Expert, Designer Elke Lesso

Section IV Smarter Than Fashion

16 Basically Chic *113*
   An Interview on Timeless Chic with Professor Mary Kefgen • Basic Classics • Classics, the Fashion Perennials • Basic Secrets • Best Buys on Basics • Fads, Trends and Classics • Spot Trends Early • The Flow of Fashion—Interview with Fashion Editor Genevieve Buck

17 Quality: More Value for Your Chic Dollar *127*
   Quality Components: Construction, Fabric and Fit • An Insider's Views on Quality: Interview with Designer A'lone Alakazia

18 Tender Loving Care *137*
   Dry Cleaning • Laundering • Individual Fiber Care • Maintaining Leather and Suede • Protecting Furs • Commonsense Guidelines for Leathers and Furs • Stain Removal • Care for Shoes and Accessories • Storage Tips

Section V When the Going Gets Tough, the Tough Go Shopping

19 A Chic Shopping Primer *149*
   The Zen of Shopping • Your Shopping Style • Planning Your Shopping Trip • Tips on Special Needs and Where to Fill Them • Complete Size Comparison Chart for Clothes and Shoes • Tips for the Hunt, or "Inner Shopping"

20 You, Too, Can Be Chic at Retail *159*
   Pros and Cons of Retail Shopping • Shopping Tips • Guerrilla Tactics for Retail Sales Shopping • Sales and Selection Chart • Shopping Chic Tips from Fashion Director Patti Fox • Linking into Chain Stores

21 Discount Glad Rags *169*
Discount Myths • Decoding Labels • Advantages and Disadvantages of Discount Shopping • Less-than-Retail Options • Discount Shopping Tips • How to Spot Fashion Forgeries • When to Think of Seconds First • How to Find Discount Stores

22 Secondhand Chic *177*
The Glories of Secondhand Shopping • Secondhand Shopping Tips • Resale and Consignment Stores • Resale Shopping Tips • Best Buys • Antique and Vintage Clothing Stores • Best Buys • Thrift Shops • Best Buys • Garage Sales, Church Rummage Sales, Charity Bazaars, Swap Meets and Flea Markets • Best Buys

23 Armchair Chic *185*
The Convenience of Mail-Order Shopping • Pros and Cons • Mail-Order Shopping Tips • What to Do if There's a Snafu • How to Get Catalogs • A List of Catalogs by Categories: General Merchandise, Department and Specialty Stores, Classic and Traditional, Boutiques, Fashion Forward, Sports and Outdoor, Western, Discount and Specialty

Recommended Reading 195

Index 199

Chic on a Shoestring

1
The Gospel According to Chic on a Shoestring

Investment dressing meets the discount decade is the *Chic on a Shoestring* attitude toward clothing in the 1980s. *Chic* is a practical how-to book written for women like your authors, who find ourselves caught between a rock and a hard place. We have less time and money to spend on clothing, shoes and accessories, but more need to dress better in all areas of our lives and increased sophistication about our image as a communication tool.

Chic on a Shoestring has evolved out of solving our own wardrobe needs and responding to the questions from several thousand women we have spoken to since the publication of our first book in 1979. As authors of two (and soon-to-be three) directories to discount stores in Southern California—*Glad Rags* and *Glad Rags II*—plus being television fashion experts and writers of a biweekly fashion column, we have discovered that saving money without sacrificing quality or style is the number-one clothing concern of women today.

The *Chic* attitude is: *you don't have to sacrifice quality to save money.* The challenge of this decade in fashion is to take more individual responsibility for our image and not rely on designers to dictate to us what is or is not in fashion. The plus side of this equation is the newfound freedom and exciting opportunities we now have for our own individual styles and personalities to come through in our glad rags.

Chic on a Shoestring will take you on a voyage of self-discovery and show you the wonders of discount shopping. We'll help you analyze your clothing needs, reshuffle your closet and assemble a creative, dynamic wardrobe in the most time- and cost-efficient manner. We'll take you on a discount wardrobe odyssey we've been enjoying ourselves and continue to benefit from daily. Living *Chic*-ly is a twenty-four-hour, seven-day-a-week adventure.

We think of *Chic* as a clothing cookbook—equal parts inspiration and method. As with any recipe, there's plenty of margin for seasoning to suit your own fashion tastes and needs. In contrast to other wardrobe and fashion books, we don't believe in dictating any *one* type or style of dress as gospel. Instead we hope to be able to help you assert your own fashion voice and save money in the process.

Chic on a Shoestring is easy, quick, fun and cheap to read and execute. The extensive lists of tips and hints in each chapter are the keys to reevaluating and rebuilding your wardrobe and your image on a budget. We'll start with the essential you, develop an understanding of your needs and wants and take that knowledge out into the shopping world, where you'll learn to save money daily.

2 • *Chic on a Shoestring*

PHOTO 1 A

PHOTO 1 B

Chic on a Shoestring is a fun, easy-to-read, step-by-step process.

In Section I, Develop Your *Chic* Fashion Eye, you will learn how to quickly, easily and inexpensively discover and maximize your *Chic* personal style. Rather than tell you to spend $200 on a color consultation, we'll show you how to hone in on your most skin flattering colors for only $12.50.

In Section II, How to Build Your *Chic* Wardrobe (On the Cheap), we graphically point out how you already own the basis of your *Chic* wardrobe. We'll help you unearth the hidden gems in your closet and reprogram your attitude and your apparel for maximum *Chic* effectiveness and cost efficiency.

Section III, Stretch Your *Chic* Wardrobe (And Thereby Your Dollars), leads you through recipes for saving money on all the courses of a gourmet fashion meal (at fast-food prices). We'll demystify and simplify fashion phobias such as travel and maternity wardrobes and show you how to think *Chic*.

Section IV, Smarter Than Fashion, details the *Chic* fashion survival strategy for the 1980s. Learn how to save money by understanding the basics in your wardrobe and learning where and how to buy them cheaply. We'll take you from amateur to professional status as a judge of apparel quality and clothing care, so you'll be able to judge for yourself whether a purchase is a true bargain.

Section V, When the Going Gets Tough, the Tough Go Shopping, offers a correspondence course in *Chic* shopping covering best buys from retail, chain, secondhand and discount stores plus catalogs. At the end of this crash course, award yourself a Ph.D. in bargain hunting.

Read on! We promise to take the expense out and put the enjoyment back in wearing and buying clothes.

Chic on a Shoestring *is style on a budget without compromising quality or fashion savvy. These two outfits (Photos A and B) were found in the same store on the same day.*

Photo A:		Photo B:	
Emanuel Ungaro dress	$ 795.00	Private label dress	$ 75.00
Ralph Lauren leather pumps	205.00	Leather-look pumps	30.00
Pearl necklace	500.00	Faux pearl necklace	15.00
Pearl earrings	250.00	Faux pearl earrings	8.00
Leather gloves	55.00	Nylon gloves	5.00
Leather clutch	125.00	Vinyl clutch	27.00
Straw hat	30.00	Straw hat	30.00
Grand Total	$1,970.00	Grand Total	$190.00

$1,780.00—The *Chic on a Shoestring* difference

SECTION I
Develop Your Chic Fashion Eye

2
Express Your Chic Self

Fashion is an act of freedom. One can still choose to look the way one wants to look. It's one of the few creative decisions we make every day.
Mariuccia Mandelli, *designer for Krizia*

Fashion; what do we mean when we say "fashion"? Most of the time we think of it as the world of next season's runway looks and the latest items hanging from the racks in stores. Often fashion is a vague term relating to the way other stylish women (not ourselves) dress or to the entire clothing industry, which seems to tantalize us relentlessly into buying yet more new things, just for the sake of their newness or their "fashion."

But, ultimately, fashion must come home to roost, so to speak, with each of us. Our definition of fashion must be expanded to include *us*—how we view fashion, how we feel about it, how we use it and how we wear it. Fashion is, finally, one of the most important ways we express ourselves, our personalities, our own sense of style. Some of us may say we don't really care about fashion, that we're not interested in keeping up with the latest. But no one really gets off the hook with this excuse, since each of us, whether or not we claim to be interested in clothes or fashion, still has to get dressed every morning.

Each time we change clothes we make a decision, conscious or unconscious, about what kind of clothes to wear and thus what kind of image we want to project.

So fashion then comes down to personal style—how each one of us manifests her own personality through her clothes and accessories, taking into account, of course, where she works and what she does for a living, where she lives, the climate, her hobbies and interests, travel, family, social occasions—in short, every part and parcel of her lifestyle.

Most of the time we admire *other* women, who seem to us to have a highly developed, individual sense of style, while we think of ourselves as merely wearers of clothes. We don't feel we have a personal sense of style, but of course each of us does, no matter what it is or how much we have to spend on it.

So the issue at hand is not *whether* we have a sense of style, but rather *how* we nurture and develop that style, hidden or unconscious though it may be, on a budget?

Developing your own sense of style involves some active looking and trying, some experimenting. Think of it as one of your hobbies or interests, something intriguing and fun, not something you *have* to do or yet another item for your weekend "to do" list.

As we launch into this, it's important to remember that there are no rules here, only options: no right or wrong ways to put ourselves together, only effective and ineffective ways to do it.

If we had to zero in on the single most important aspect of style, we would probably have to say that it is self-confidence: knowing who you are so that you can express this through your clothes. As designer Perry Ellis says, "Women will discover their own personal style as their guidelines rather than a dictate from a specific store or a specific designer. All that comes from self-knowledge. Knowing who the hell you are looking at when you confront a mirror!" One of the nicest things about fashion confidence is that once achieved, it becomes a way of life. How do you get this fashion self-confidence? With the looking and "tasting" we're about to describe.

Stretch Your Imagination

The best way to learn more about your own sense of style is to experiment. Sample the various fashion options, try different colors and looks, and then edit them down to the ones that you really like and that work for you. Notice we said *try,* not *buy.* There's a *Chic on a Shoestring* method for easing yourself out of your usual, predictable (even boring?) ways of putting yourself together and moving into expressing your own sense of style. The following tips are all designed to be low investment (they're all free or very inexpensive) and high return (lots of fashion and clothing information plus knowledge of what you like and feel comfortable in).

Stretch your imagination:

- Window shop. A perfect sunny or rainy day or even evening activity. Note the season's predominant shapes and silhouettes, popular colors and how outfits are put together. Is there a new proportion, such as long tops over short skirts, you might want to try for yourself? What are the different skirt and pants lengths being shown? Is layering the look of the season? How are outfits accessorized? Maybe one new wide belt would be just the thing to bring your classics up to date. Along with colors, look at fabrics and textures and how they're combined.
- Take a day for recreational shopping. Leave your checkbook and credit cards at home, pack up your energy and sense of adventure and head off for a day of sampling. You might visit a favorite store or two plus one a cut or so above what you ordinarily consider to be your price range. You'll see a wide variety of forward designer looks you don't

Having fun with your personal style need not cost more than $5.00, the sum total of each of these "rock and roll" outfits.

usually run across and thus expose yourself to a broader array of fashions. Who knows, you may even find a look you fall in love with and can turn around and create from your own closet or with less-than-retail purchases. This no-cost shopping spree is best timed at the beginning of a season, when store selections are at their peak. Try everything. Looking and experimenting costs you nothing. Besides, you never really know until you *try*.

As designer Carol Horn puts it, "Practice. You have to think a lot, look around a lot and experiment. Try everything on. The trick is to find out which style fits the image of how you feel and how you want to look. Try them all, then cross off the ones that are wrong."

- Style- and fashion-watch. This is a variation of the ever-popular people watching. Where to style-watch? Anyplace well-dressed people congregate or pass through: airports, restaurants, the theater, conventions and even the office. Television and movies can offer inspiration, because actors and celebrities are paid to look good (though we all know not all succeed). Travel is the best excuse for people and style-watching. Notice what women in other parts of your city, state, country or the world are wearing and note your reaction. Observe and make a mental note of those women whose sense of style especially appeals to you. What was it about them and how they put themselves together that you liked and would like to emulate? The key to using the copycat method is to *adapt*, not blindly imitate, the parts or aspects of another woman's style you think would also work for you.
- Experiment with your own wardrobe. Before you run out and buy even one single garment or accessory to express the new you, take a *Chic* tip and use what you already have in new ways to create the looks you liked (1) in the window displays, (2) at the stores, and (3) on the women you saw last week in the hotel lobby. Maybe you never thought to wear your three-quarter-length sweater coat with pants until you saw it in Marshall Field's window. Perhaps you can combine your own khaki and red pieces and accessories as did the stylish woman you saw on the street corner yesterday.

By the way, there's an important shift here from mental to visual. Don't just stay locked in to the usual way you combine your glen plaid suit jacket with the matching skirt. You can't rely solely on your mind here. Use your eyes to tell you if the glen plaid skirt also works with your green velvet blazer. Once again, you'll never know how big and current your wardrobe is until you try pieces—different pieces—together. Likewise, you'll never know all the interesting, fun and stylish aspects of your personality until you experiment with them.

You'll get fashion ideas and entertainment to boot at Liz Claiborne's traveling designer fashion shows.

10 ● *Chic on a Shoestring*

- Attend fashion shows. Check the women's or fashion section of your newspaper or your favorite fashion magazine and make it a point to attend a fashion show or two at the beginning of a season. There's something special and exhilarating about seeing all those great new clothes on the models as they move and show off the latest fashions. Make this fun—take along a friend or two. You can also attend trunk showings at which the designer shows his or her entire line, including the special, pricey, made-to-order garments. Talk to the designer and ask questions. You'll be surprised what you'll learn.
- Make a collage of your favorite looks. This is the most fun personal style discovery tip of all. Gather newspaper ads and clippings from magazines and catalogs featuring clothes and accessories you really like: colors, textures, proportions, fabrics and silhouettes that you would like to wear. You might even include a few snapshots of yourself in your favorite outfits. These visuals can include outfits and pieces similar to ones you already have plus some design ideas you'd like to try. Add the fantasy parts of yourself, too. Why not top off your wardrobe collage with a picture of a full length red fox coat or a diamond necklace?

Now take a roll of white or brown wrapping paper (from the dime store or stationery store) and tape it to a door; the bedroom, bathroom or kitchen door will do fine. Arrange all your favorite pictures and ads on it. What do you see? What recurring themes appear? Do you find yourself drawn to lacy collars and blouses, yet you've always thought of yourself as a tailored person? Maybe it's time to add a little touch of feminine glamour to all your classics. Again, which colors, textures, proportions and lines are you drawn to? This little project may strike you as a juvenile, "Cut-and-Paste 101" exercise, but trust us on this one. It works. You'll be amazed at what you'll discover about yourself and your style. Best of all, it costs next to nothing.

Annette learned a lot about her own personal style while creating this collage.

How to Use Fashion Magazines

One of the best and most reasonably priced ways you can gather the latest fashion information and stretch your imagination is to subscribe to one or more of the popular fashion magazines. Your local newspaper also runs fashion reports from time to time; some large metropolitan papers even run special weekly fashion sections. Use printed fashion information as you would the other suggestions we've just outlined. Make notes on the garments, accessories and total looks you especially like. Pay attention to individual pieces and how they're put together. Read the copy for general trends and highlights each season.

Not surprisingly, we've found that many women avoid reading fashion magazines because they are intimidated by the styles and/or prices of the clothing featured. Why look and lust after something you can't afford or couldn't fit into? The important thing to remember is that these magazines are meant to inspire and inform, not to dictate. Instead of rejecting the latest exaggerated silhouettes you see, select the *parts* of an outfit or trend that may pertain to you. Rather than thinking to yourself that you couldn't possibly wear an outfit that you saw in *Harper's Bazaar* (especially not in the bizarre pose of the model), note that you might like a pair of lizard boots like those featured in the photo. Your job is to interpret these fashion messages for yourself and integrate them selectively into your own style. The *Chic* approach is to create the same high-dollar look for less.

Remember, any new message or visual image must be overstated to be understood. As Calvin Klein explains, "When we show clothes on the runway, we always exaggerate to make our point. The important thing today is that there is no right or wrong in fashion—just a lot of possibilities." Another way to view all those seemingly crazy and off-putting outfits is to regard fashion as an art form, as you would painting or sculpture, for example, and allow the artists room to experiment. Just as you wouldn't want to hang every painting you see in your own home, you naturally won't like every style you see. By expanding the way you use fashion information, particularly by familiarizing yourself with designers and looking at a variety of fashion statements, you will gradually come to better understand your own fashion tastes and preferences.

As painful as it may be, note the prices and study the looks created by the top European and American designers. In order to be *Chic on a Shoestring,* you must know quality, be able to recognize a bargain and invent your own low cost/high fashion looks. Remember, all it takes is money to buy designer clothes at expensive stores. To dress rich without being rich requires a little added imagination, creativity and effort. Once you get the hang of it, it's more fun to be *Chic on a Shoestring.*

While you're working on all this, don't forget the key ingredient: comfort. The latest looks or the most pulled together ensembles fail if you're not comfortable. "Modern dressing means, above all, comfort—that old sweatshirt attitude that's so American," says the king of comfort, designer Geoffrey Beene. What clothes make *you* feel comfortable? Are these same clothes appropriate for *your* lifestyle?

The following publications, divided into broad market categories, will give you much food for fashion thought. Fashion magazines also include features on health, the arts, beauty, travel and psychology. In magazines and newspapers, look at the advertisements for ideas as well as the editorial photo layouts and features. Frequently the most advanced ideas are pictured in ads. In local papers, this will give you instant information on price so you can comparison shop from your living room.

- Leading American fashion and beauty magazines: *Vogue* and *Harper's Bazaar.* Both feature the latest current-season fashions plus preview photos and information on the upcoming season. Both have excellent one-page summaries on current

National and international fashion publications bring the latest looks into our living rooms.

trends and how to keep your own wardrobe up to date.
- Fashion and beauty magazines for the younger woman (18 to mid-30s): *Glamour* and *Mademoiselle*. Both are produced by the leading publisher in the field, Condé Nast, as is *Vogue*. Look for the terrific how-to's in *Glamour*'s regular "Fashion Workshop" section. *Mademoiselle* features several top women writers' fashion and style columns each month.
- Other general interest women's magazines run the gamut from *Cosmopolitan* and *Self* to *McCall's* and *Ladies' Home Journal* to *Good Housekeeping* and *Family Circle*, to name a few. Each offers regular—in some cases monthly—fashion features with a point of view in keeping with the magazine's overall editorial slant. *Cosmopolitan* might do a layout on femme-fatale vacation looks, while *Woman's Day* might do a feature on how to sew a wardrobe of six mix-and-match pieces for under $150. Watch the newsstands for all kinds of specialty women's magazines that also include fashion information. You can choose from magazines for executive women *(Savvy)*, working women and working mothers (with magazines by the same names), black women *(Essence)* and large-size women *(It's Me* and *Big, Beautiful Woman)*.

If you have access to them, you might want to take a glance through the fashion trade publications for the most advanced fashion data. Fairchild Publications' famous (and infamous) *Women's Wear Daily (WWD)* is the best known. *WWD* will inundate you with fashion information, business stories, detailed analyses of European and American collections each season plus profiles of designers, fashion makers and the fashionable BPs. California Fashion Publications also produces a number of regional weeklies, including *California Apparel News*. A nice alternative is Fairchild's four-color mag-paper *W,* a biweekly condensed form of *WWD* that is consumer rather than trade oriented. You'll be six months ahead with fashion information and be able to spot trends and make additions to your wardrobe well in advance of mass market acceptance.

Finally, what would something as personal as style be without a sense of panache, a touch of the unexpected, a note of humor now and then? Think of all the aspects of your personality, including an occasional flight of fancy or fantasy, a bit of whimsy, something clever or downright cute. How about a "casual surprise" in the way you combine pieces or colors? It's okay to let yourself express the more playful, more outrageously feminine and clever, witty sides of yourself. Take a tip from French designer Thierry Mugler, "When I look at the clothes in today's big stores, they all seem so serious. To be really chic today, you need to be snappy, to have energy and to express it with a sense of humor."

We're encouraging you to loosen up a bit, not to go overboard and come up with outfits that are inappropriate for your work or social occasions. For instance, if the unwritten dress code at your office is suits, then of course you'll continue to wear them to work. But you don't have to adhere strictly to the rigid and boring dictates of the "dress for upward mobility" rules. You can dress conservatively yet imaginatively. Perhaps your navy wool suit would look terrific with a bright red or brilliant jade silk pocket square.

Remember, too, that our own sense of style, like ourselves, is constantly changing. At first the idea of change can be scary, and we might have a tendency to view it in absolute terms. We might think to ourselves that if we're uncovering our own sense of style, we have to change our wardrobes radically. But it's not all that black and white. Changing one's wardrobe to reflect an awakened sense of style is best accomplished by gradually (and inexpensively) adding a piece here or there and likewise recycling a few pieces now and then that are no longer needed. The key is subtle, gradual change.

The more you explore your personal style, the more you'll learn to rely on yourself and your own growing self-confidence. The input from girlfriends, your mother, your sister, your favorite store's saleswoman, your husband or boyfriend coupled with all the latest fashion information is, of course, helpful, but the final decisions rest with you. Only you can decide if a particular item works, but if you have a good sense of yourself, you'll find the right balance.

Meet a Fashion Journalist with Personal Style—Fashion Editor Gwen Jones
To further explore the world of fashion journalism, *Chic* interviewed Gwen Jones, fashion editor of the Los Angeles *Herald Examiner*. Ms. Jones inspired us with her *Chic on a Shoestring* personal style and first-rate fashion reporting.

CHIC: What would you say your own personal sense of style is? How would you describe your own personal style now?
G.J.: It's classic with a flair. We can start, for example, by talking about this suit. This suit is a little oversized, but personally I like to wear a look that's not so fitted. I just feel more comfortable in it, and comfort is very important to me. I bought the jacket portion of it four years ago and then a year later I bought the pants. Fortunately, I have a fairly good eye for color and I'm able to do that. But the important thing about this suit is that because I'm working, I'm able to wear parts of this suit three or four days a week and I do that. It's just a matter of changing the blouse. Or I have several skirts that I can wear with the jacket. I have found that this one navy suit has worked so well for me and I still get compliments on it every time I put it on. It's as if it's something new. But it works. And that is kind of the way I

Gwen Jones, fashion editor of the Los Angeles Herald Examiner.

view fashion and clothes that I buy. The only time that I really get into more really high fashion things is for evening wear. That's where I just feel I want to be a little more exciting, a little more glamorous, and I don't tend to buy with that "how many times can I wear it" mentality.

I talk about this navy suit but I also would not just wear navy to wear navy. I have come to learn what colors work best for me, too. I wear this suit with a bright green blouse, for example. It's taken me awhile; it didn't happen overnight, but I looked at myself and watched other people's reactions to things I would wear and came to my own conclusions about which colors work best. I've never had a color consultation. What I found is that when I look in the mirror there's almost a glow you get from certain colors that work.

CHIC: Have you always had this sort of sense of classics with style, or has that definition of your personal style evolved over time? Have you made some mistakes in the past?

G.J.: Absolutely! [laughing] I used to have the quantity mentality and I've changed that considerably. A lot of that has come with my exposure to the best designs in the world through this job. I cover the collections in Europe and New York and have experienced firsthand the finest fashion now created. Although I am still not in the income bracket of couture by any means, I still look for the best quality I am able to afford at any given time. I have steadily traded up. With each year I have been able to go for a little bit better quality—one piece, two pieces; not a whole closetful of clothes. It has happened steadily, but it has been the exposure to the clothes that made me change.

CHIC: What is your advice for a woman just getting started in a job or just getting out of school and starting to job hunt? We know we can't afford an entirely new wardrobe all at once, so where do we begin?

G.J.: Okay. I would say it's not a bad idea to look at fashion magazines to get a feel for what look you would like to have and then translate that expensive look into clothes you can afford either on sale, at discount or in a less expensive make. And I would say it is very important for a person entering the work force to buy carefully and buy separates that can be interchanged to expand a wardrobe. That's extremely important, and often we don't do it because we start a job and want to wear great clothes and wind up buying a bunch of dresses you wear once a week and you don't want to wear again.

CHIC: Would you say your wardrobe is much smaller than it used to be?

G.J.: It's definitely narrower than it used to be. There is nothing in my day wardrobe that I don't wear. Evening is a different story.

CHIC: How do you know you're going to choose a look that's not going to be totally dated next year? How can you think and plan ahead? Is there a rule that someone can use in choosing a style to invest in, keeping in mind that it's not going to be just for this year?

G.J.: The general rule is not to go for any extremes. Let's take hemlines, for example. You'd never want to invest a lot of money in miniskirts, nor would you want to invest a lot of money in ankle lengths or longer. To the knee or mid-knee is always a very safe look. A good way to do this would be to go to a library and look at fashion magazines over a few years and you can see which styles have lasted.

CHIC: What about, for example, the suit you're wearing. You say it's four years old now. What makes that suit as good now as when you bought it? Why is that style still good? Is it because the garment suits you or because intrinsically it has no time element to it?

G.J.: It's not exaggerated. It's versatile. And it's a classic color. You don't get more classic than navy blue.

CHIC: Is personal style timeless? If you feel and look good wearing something, will it always be in style?

G.J.: If it's something that isn't extreme and you do feel good about wearing it, I don't see why not. I think that how you feel and look in clothes has a lot to do with how you felt when you bought it. I felt great when I bought this suit and I still feel great every time I pull it out. You know, it's a funny thing, I don't even stop to think whether it's out of style or if it doesn't look right because it *feels* right. It did when I bought it and does now.

CHIC: What about fashion information? How does one learn about styles or trends from what you read? How can we take that information and interpret it for ourselves? When you write a story or when you report on the collections or when you do a feature story, what do you hope the reader gets from that?

G.J.: What I do, first of all, is definitely look for trends in anything I cover. With the background I have now, I'm able to spot what is different or common among collections, what they're all doing and what that portends. What I then do, though, is interpret for the average consumer. For example, the emphasis was on the waist one season. Okay, the silhouette had been slimmed and trimmed. I looked at that and said, "Aha, okay, a woman doesn't necessarily have to go out and buy any of these more fitted looks; she can do it with accessories—a great belt." But within that context, the designers were showing so many very uncomfortable, huge belts. I talked about that, too. The fact is if a belt is four inches wide and stiff, it's going to hurt. Those are the kinds of things I think anybody in this business has to point out to the readers, and I always do that. Also, I had mentioned in a column that if you are short waisted, by no means do you wear these belts.

CHIC: I think that's what is lacking in fashion information—any commentary on what you're seeing. There's no interpretation of a style or a trend for the average person. And I think that's why it turns people off, because they look at these clothes and they say, "Who's going to wear that?" If consumers don't get down-to-earth fashion information from journalists, how can they be expected to learn it? We can't expect the average woman to look at high fashion, which is exaggerated for runway purposes, and understand it for her own life.

G.J.: Then I'd say they have to go back to the very beginning. You really have to look at yourself honestly and if possible even go to a clothing consultant, someone who is going to be objective. It is very, very important to know what your figure problems are in order to, if possible, correct them and not to wear things that don't fit properly just because they're in style.

CHIC: Do you differentiate between fads and trends? Can you also tell the consumer the difference between the two and where money should be spent?

G.J.: That is difficult to say at times, because we have had, in the history of fashion, fads that turned out to be trends that are still going on—jeans being one example. Predicting trends is hard for the so-called fashion experts. As a general rule, I like to see a look show up at least four seasons, meaning two years. Then you can safely say it is a trend; it is part of the fashion fabric. But fads typically don't last more than a couple of seasons. They're here and gone. It's usually, but not always, a very young look. Often it starts as street fashion, and sometimes the design world will pick it up and reinterpret it.

CHIC: Do you have projections at this point, fads that are going to become trends in the future? Do you see any significant trends developing?

G.J.: I believe that we will continue to see more fitted clothes and that, I believe, is in direct response to the physical fitness boom. There are more women in shape now and able to show off their bodies. I believe very strongly that dance wear is here to stay. I thought initially that that had to be the fad of all time, but I think it's only going to become bigger because it is just now really becoming a mass idea. People are more body-conscious, and I think that's only going to increase.

CHIC: Also, body wear is so comfortable; and lower shoes—that's another trend we would like to see continue.

G.J.: But the bottom line is that there isn't going to be one look. We hear over and over how designers are no longer dictating, and I really believe that. You see it in New York. You find people more casually dressed there than ever before. I think that times have really changed. The last years in particular have shown us there are going to be a lot of looks, and this may be more difficult for the consumer. At least before, when there was one look and you were told to wear it, you didn't have to make any decisions. Now it may be a little more difficult because there's so many options. I think that's why there's so much confusion now. There was a time when you *knew* what black tie meant. Now, nobody knows. It has changed so much and it varies from region to region. I don't know. Maybe it was better in those times when you knew black tie meant a woman wore a gown and a man a tuxedo.

CHIC: Whose suit are you wearing?

G.J.: Calvin Klein's.

CHIC: What about looking at designers. I happen to adore Norma Kamali's clothes. I would buy anything she designs because it happens to work on me. I like it; it feels good. Like you said, it doesn't matter if it's in or out of fashion.

G.J.: It's interesting. I bought some of her pieces and ended up giving them to my sister because they worked on her and not on me. I think it has a lot to do with attitude and spirit and all of those things. And I guess I'm basically an uptight suit person.

CHIC: That's my question. Each designer is developing his or her signature. Amid all this fashion confusion, should you find a designer you like and focus your fashion information and wardrobe that way?

G.J.: I think for someone who has trouble creating or finding her look, that *can* work, but sometimes you have designers who change direction. Calvin Klein, for example, just did a major change in direction. He has gone so European now.

I'm investing in the European designers now because I like the fabric and quality and I can afford it now. My last two purchases have been St. Laurent—a skirt and a jacket I got on sale. St. Laurent hasn't changed in fifteen years. I want a designer I can add to from year to year, and, interestingly, St. Laurent uses the same dye lot and you can go back and practically identically match something you bought last year with a new purchase this season. I really want to be able to wear clothes for a while.

I try to buy things that aren't so mass produced. As I have been able to buy better, I have slowly traded up. I used to be an Evan Picone girl. Of course, I could have five or six Evan Picone suits, but that doesn't bother me. I would rather have that one St. Laurent suit I can wear so often and it's so wonderful. And it holds up so well. That's not to say that Evan Picone doesn't hold up. But there is a quality, a luxuriousness in the fabric and the fit that is so important, and it's taken a long, long time to get to the point where I said, "Okay, Gwen, there's this amount you've got to spend and you're not going to buy three. You're going to buy one." But I'm so much happier for it.

CHIC: You also don't see yourself coming and going.

G.J.: I do not.

CHIC: What about certain designers like Liz Claiborne? Are there other designers you would recommend for people who are not in the St. Laurent price category yet?

G.J.: Evan Picone, Jones New York, Finity. In most major cities, fortunately, there are discount stores and a number of places a woman can turn for value. I still run over to Los Angeles Street in the garment district.

CHIC: What about saving money on clothes nationwide?

G.J.: You know, what's very interesting is that I have found my best buys in out-of-the-way places. You wouldn't think a certain place would be a hotbed for fashion, but almost anyplace you go, you're going to find some well-dressed women, and there are always shops that cater to these women. Here in L.A. you're going to find the best sales—the *best sales* possible. When we were on vacation last summer in Charleston, South Carolina, we went to a little shopping center and they had a Loehmann's there. I was astounded at all the incredible clothes! I was telling you I love St. Laurent. I was in New York and everything was pretty picked over. I shop the sales in Beverly Hills, too. But I was in Washington, D.C., and at the Watergate Hotel I found a little shop having the *best* sale and there were still things left to buy. That's why when you travel, don't rule anything out. You know, if you have a look, you should always be on the hunt. You're always going to find at least one store in every city or town that has the very best sales. Ask around, find out where the best dressed shop.

My favorite sale of all is the Lina Lee "last call" sale in Beverly Hills. I saved some money just for that sale. My advice is to always have some money stashed away for a good sale and good buys. That's usually at the end of the season, so you have to resist temptation.

CHIC: These better lines and designer fashions are at least a season or two ahead of the regular mainstream American fashion.

G.J.: At least. That's why they're going to be great and give you a lot of return on your investment.

CHIC: How do you get over being intimidated at these fancy designer stores with their high price tags and haughty sales help?

G.J.: I was intimidated, too, initially, but think about this: Most of the women who work in these stores are the same as you and me (they might even make less than we do), so you don't have to be intimidated. Also, when a saleswoman comes up to you, you can just say you're looking. You have a perfect right to just look. No one can *make* you buy. You might be surprised by the reception you receive. Part of it may have to do with the economy, but on Rodeo Drive they all but hug you when you walk in. That has at least helped me get over the hurdle of being a little bit reticent about going in to some of these posh stores. Remember, even if you're not going to buy anything, you might want to get ideas in some of these high-fashion stores. *You are good enough to shop anywhere!* You know, what I have found, too, is that in the smaller stores, you truly do get service and I think that is intimidating at first, because we're not used to it. But I think it's a whole lot better than going into most stores and yelling all over the place and not getting any help.

Fashion is one of the most important tools we have for expressing ourselves. Each of us has a unique personal style.

3
Color is Chic

Much has been written on personal coloring and how to choose the color palette most flattering to your skin tone, hair and eye coloring. More often than not, the information we read limits the colors we should wear and types us into one of four "seasons" as if we were plants, not people. In this chapter we will explore the concept of warm and cool colors and explain how you can simply and inexpensively discover for yourself which colors enhance your appearance.

THE COLOR KEY PROGRAM®, devised by Ameritone Paint Corp.,* is the most straightforward and easily adaptable tool for selectively combining and identifying colors. THE COLOR KEY PROGRAM divides all colors of the spectrum into two categories:

* KEY 1 COLORS—blue undertone cool colors
* KEY 2 COLORS—yellow (or golden) undertone warm colors

The beauty of this system is that KEY 1 COLORS are technically and visually harmonious for use in combination with each other. The same is true of KEY 2 COLORS. Thus with the exception of only one color in each key, we can wear colors from an entire spectrum as long as we choose the correct hue (warm or cool base) of each color.

How to Easily Determine Your Own Best Colors
To be *Chic on a Shoestring*, it's essential to understand in which group of colors you belong. Selecting garments in one color group will not only improve your appearance and make every purchase a wardrobe plus, but will enable you to mix and match effortlessly among all the pieces in your closet. Once you get a handle on your most flattering colors and learn to distinguish a KEY 1 COLOR from a KEY 2 COLOR, you'll be well on your way to building a coordinated wardrobe that will work overtime for you and enhance your feeling of well-being.

Without investing $60 or more in a private color consultation, how can we discover our personal coloring? The determining factor is skin tone. Skin coloration for all people is a combination of three pigments: carotene (yellow), hemoglobin (red) and melanin (brown). Each of us has a varying degree of each pigment. To identify our underlying skin tone, it's best to look at the skin on the wrist and underside of the forearm or, even better, the naked body where

---

* THE COLOR KEY PROGRAM is owned by Color Key Corporation and distributed by Ameritone Paint Corp. and Devoe and Raynolds Co., Inc., subsidiaries of Grow Group, Inc. THE COLOR KEY PROGRAM, COLOR KEY, KEY 1 COLORS and KEY 2 COLORS are registered trademarks.

20 • Chic on a Shoestring

No matter what our race or ethnic background, the warmth or coolness of our underlying skin tone determines THE COLOR KEY PROGRAM most flattering to us.

skin hasn't been exposed to sun and is its "pure" color. Suntans don't change our color group but sometimes make it more difficult to distinguish our true skin tone because the epidermis acts as a filter.

Look at your underarm. Do you see a blueish or reddish cast, or is the color slightly yellow or golden? It's best to lay your arm on a white sheet or piece of paper and, of course, perform this test in natural light. If you're with a friend, have her or him do the same and compare your coloration (this usually makes it much easier to decide which color group you're in).

If you can't determine your underlying skin tone by simply looking at yourself, here are some other tactics:

- Take advantage of a free makeup consultation at your local drugstore or department store. A second party trained in analyzing skin color and working with complementary makeup colors will give you useful information that can be applied to wardrobe colors as well. Get several opinions if possible and ask questions about which colors heighten your natural coloration. Be wary about sales promotions geared exclusively to sell this season's latest colors—they may or may not work for you.
- Visit a fabric store, with a friend if possible, and drape fabric around your shoulders or hold swatches to your face (you can also do this with pieces of colored paper at an art supply store if you're brave enough to withstand the stares). Notice what the various colors do to your face. Remember, we can all wear almost every color. It's the *variation* or *hue* of the color that makes a difference. For example, compare blues. Electric blue is a cool color and will flatter skin types in the KEY 1 COLOR group; teal is warm and will bring out the yellow undertone of a complexion in the KEY 2 COLOR group.

A piece of fabric or a towel draped around the face is an easy method to determine whether you're KEY 1 or 2. The color from the fabric reflected into the face will either flatter or fight your own underlying skin tone.

- The colors you feel best wearing, receive compliments on and gravitate to in stores will give you a clue to your personal palette. We instinctively know which colors look best on us; we're just not sure why or how to maximize their usefulness. Without looking in your closet or drawers, list your favorite colors and star the ones that get you compliments.
- In the KEY 1 COLOR grouping all colors are represented except orange; in the KEY 2 COLOR grouping the missing color is magenta (blueish red). Putting these two colors up to your skin will determine whether you belong in KEY 1 COLOR or KEY 2 COLOR. First, drape an orange towel or piece of fabric over your shoulders and under your chin. Notice what the color does for your coloring. Next, do the same with the magenta towel or swatch. If you belong in KEY 1 COLORS, the magenta towel will be most flattering because the blue undertones match your personal coloring. The orange drape will be kindest to the KEY 2 COLORS type because it will compliment the underlying yellowish/orange tint. Be sure to do this test in natural light, with your face devoid of makeup. If your hair is tinted or colored, cover your head with a white scarf or towel.
- You may order a Pocket Dictionary paint chip sample case from Ameritone Paint Corp. for $12.50 postpaid. Both KEY 1 COLORS and KEY 2 COLORS are included. When you discover which group you belong in, you can select from among hundreds of colors when you go shopping and be assured that the colors will enhance your appearance and compliment each other. Write to:

(Western Region)
Beaux Monde
P.O. Box 1125
Covina, CA 91723
(CA residents add 6% sales tax)

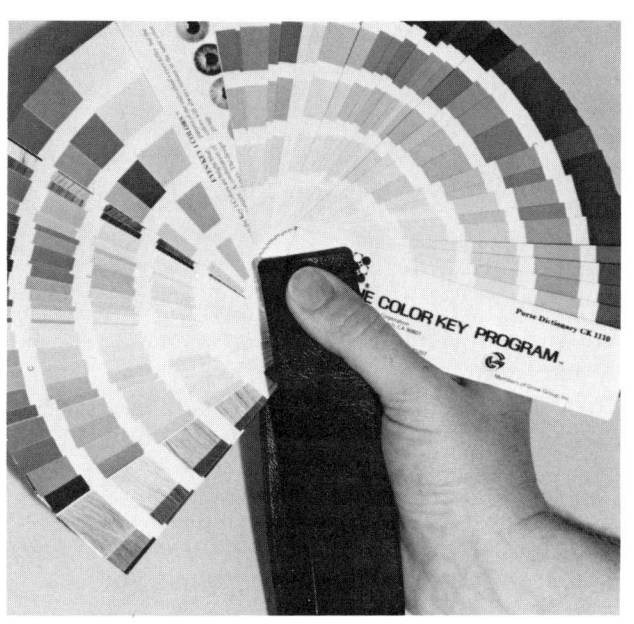

THE COLOR KEY PROGRAM Pocket Dictionary.

(Colorado and east of the Rockies)
Devoe & Raynolds Company
P.O. Box 7600
Louisville, KY 40207
(KY residents add 5% sales tax)

- If you're confused about accent colors to add to your wardrobe and how to select one from your color group, look into your eyes. Wear your eye color and we guarantee you'll receive compliments. Your appearance will be enhanced because your eyes will appear brighter and more prominent.
- Grey has a tendency to sap color from the skin, so to offset this, wear grey with rose or peach next to your skin to put the life back into your complexion.
- As we age, the dramatic contrast between hair and skin color diminishes as hair loses the intensity of youth and turns grey. We don't change color

groups, but we may want to wear less contrasting colors which soften our look slightly and don't overpower or harshen our appearance. Let your eyes and your attitude be the judge—if you still feel good in black, white and red or orange and teal, by all means continue wearing strong, vibrant colors.

- Both color groups can wear black and white, but KEY 1 COLOR types will look best in white-white and KEY 2 COLOR types should wear an ivory, or warmer white. Black is a good color for a high-contrast KEY 1 COLOR person to wear, but anyone can wear black *with* another color in the right color group. Black with silver would be a KEY 1 COLOR choice for evening wear, and black with gold would be KEY 2 COLOR smart.

When a woman buys something, she sees color even before she sees style.   Designer Carole Little

- A good, safe way to start experimenting with color (especially if you are rethinking your colors and rebuilding your wardrobe) is to avoid prints and stick to a few solid colors. This technique is economical because everything you buy can be worn with everything else.

KEY 1 and 2 COLORS

KEY 1 COLORS	KEY 2 COLORS
(Cool)	*(Warm)*
rose pink	peach
French blue	teal
grey-beige	camel
chalk white	cream
blue-red	orange-red
hunter green	moss green (pine)
mint green	chartreuse
blue-violet	red-violet
magenta	orange
ash brown	chestnut
silver	gold
wine	Indian red
taupe	khaki
sky blue	aquamarine
pale yellow	lemon yellow

THE COLOR KEY PROGRAM works for all races. For example:

white: KEY 1 COLORS—
rose-pink complexion
KEY 2 COLORS—
peach-pink complexion

yellow, red, brown & black: KEY 1 COLORS—
umber cast
KEY 2 COLORS—
golden cast

Age doesn't change your color group, and generally your natural hair color is in the same group. (Take your color group into consideration when tinting or streaking your hair.) KEY 1 COLORS include: platinum blonde, auburn red, jet black, snow white and smoky blue or purple tints. These colors all share a blue undertone. KEY 2 COLORS have golden undertones and include: honey blonde, rust red, chestnut, off-black and cream white. When your hair greys it will do so in your color group.

The simple logic of THE COLOR KEY PROGRAM is that colors in your correct group are most flattering because they are related to and therefore enhance your natural coloring. Once you become comfortable identifying colors in your group, you'll be able to coordinate your wardrobe, jewelry, shoes and accessories confidently. You'll also be able to resist trendy fashion colors we're told to buy each season whether or not they look good on us. In this way color truly becomes a major *Chic on a Shoestring* tool.

As with every rule, there are exceptions, and some people are "cross-keyed" so that they can wear either KEY 1 COLORS or KEY 2 COLORS. Our advice here is to choose the group you feel best in and stick with it so that everything you buy will go with everything else. This way you'll save money and present a more pulled together look.

Professor Mary Kefgen, co-author of *Individuality in Clothing Selection and Personal Appearance: A Guide for the Consumer* (4th ed.; New York: Macmillan), teaches fashion at California State University, Long Beach. Her book, co-authored with Phyllis Touchie-Specht, is in its fourth edition. It is a comprehensive textbook dealing with the psychological and sociological influences of dress and the importance and impact of dress as a form of communication. Their chapter on "Color" inspired the *Chic on a Shoestring* approach. We talked to Ms. Kefgen about her color discoveries.

Professor and author Mary Kefgen.

Color Advice from an Expert, Professor Mary Kefgen

CHIC: Why has interest in color become so widespread?

M.K.: I think people like to be told what they look best in rather than figure it out for themselves. They'd rather not have to think about it or try it out. Anyone can go into a yard-goods store and hold up different colors in front of them and see what looks best, or call over several friends and try on different colors among themselves to see which hues are most flattering. Remember the clothes people compliment you on wearing and start with those.

Also, people are bored; they're looking for some new form of self-improvement. Another reason could be the highly competitive job market. Studies have proved that attractive people have more opportunities—they get the job, the handsome man, whatever. Personal color theory isn't new; it's just been simplified for the general public now and therefore has received mass attention.

CHIC: What is your opinion of color theories?

M.K.: Most of the theories are too limiting. We've discussed color in apparel selection in each of the four editions of our book, and with each writing, we've become less dogmatic. We work with THE COLOR KEY PROGRAM. There are hundreds of colors in each group; in fact, every color except orange and magenta is represented in both groups, which means you only eliminate one color from your wardrobe. THE COLOR KEY PROGRAM is the easiest for people to grasp. It was one of the first systems developed and it doesn't conflict with any other theory.

CHIC: How do you demonstrate THE COLOR KEY PROGRAM?

M.K.: I drape students with a magenta towel (KEY 1 COLOR or cool) and then an orange towel (KEY 2 COLOR or warm). The most desirable color should make your skin look less tired and your eyes more bright, less sunken. If you're wearing an outfit in one group, it's best to keep your shoes, makeup, nail polish, lipstick, and so on in the same group. Also, it's more economical to keep your entire wardrobe in one group because then you can mix and match all the pieces to make more outfits.

The warm KEY 2 COLORS have an orangish or yellowish undertone. KEY 1 COLORS, the cool group, have a blue undertone. I carry my dictionary from Ameritone Paint Corp. whenever I go shopping for anything for myself or for the house. Once you know which group you belong to, which group is most flattering to you, you can choose from among four hundred colors. Before I buy anything, I get as near a window as possible and look at how the fabric affects me. I hold the garment up to my face and see whether it will make me look aged or wrinkled; whether it makes my eyes look tired; whether it makes me look *alive* and *healthy*.

CHIC: Is there such a thing as a cross-keyed person?

M.K.: If you have hair in one group and skin in another, you might be cross-keyed. In this case, either choose colors from one group and stick to them to save money, or stay with some of the darker colors that can more easily be worn by either group (for example, navy). Another factor to consider is *contrast* in your personal coloring. Do you have dark hair and fair skin, or are your skin and hair color of similar intensity? A high-contrast person generally looks good in black and white; if your personal coloring is more subdued, you might feel more comfortable in khaki and cream. On the other hand, a low-contrast person can benefit from the added punch of a bright color.

CHIC: Should certain people stay away from high-contrast colors?

M.K.: It's largely a matter of personal taste, personality and mood. I might suggest to a student that she would look good in red, but she wouldn't feel comfortable wearing such a bright color. She could choose a shade of pink instead that would be equally flattering but more suitable to her shy, retiring personality.

CHIC: What makes skin a KEY 1 or KEY 2 COLOR?

M.K.: If your blood vessels are close to the surface, you tend to have a blueish-pinkish skin (KEY 1 COLOR). Skin of this color group also will flush easily when embarrassed or is exposed to the sun. Everyone has carotene in their skin, which produces the yellowish/orange cast. People who harmonize with KEY 2 COLORS simply have more, and thus it dominates the skin color. So you see there's a scientific reason why one skin has the rose and one the peach undertone. You look at skin first, then hair, eyes and teeth in that order to judge your color group.

We recommend THE COLOR KEY PROGRAM because it is the least expensive, most practical and useful tool generally available to help educate ourselves about color. The Pocket Dictionaries now include color chips in each color group for hair, eye, skin (makeup), lipstick and nail colors most flattering to KEY 1 COLOR and KEY 2 COLOR groups.

A word of caution: once you determine your most flattering group of colors, don't go off on a binge and start throwing out everything in your closet that's not in that group. You can subtly shift your color emphasis by accessorizing with colors from your palette. For example, if you are a KEY 2 COLOR person with a closetful of refrigerator-white oxford-cloth shirts, warm up the look and enhance your appearance with a peach or teal scarf tied around your neck. As the blouses wear out, you might consider shifting to a cream white.

A word about uniforms and dress codes: again, when possible and within the confines of company codes, choose accessories in colors from your color group to individualize a uniform and make it flattering to you. If brown suits are suggested attire, choose a shade of brown that compliments your skin tone and doesn't make you look washed out and tired. If you don't have this flexibility, then your only alternative is to key your makeup with your uniform even if it is not in your color group. You might have to change your makeup base slightly and wear a different lipstick to work, but this is better than using yourself as a COLOR KEY PROGRAM battleground.

Personal color histories and regional color preferences also play a part in our color choices. Colors we were dressed in as children find their way into our adult wardrobes in spite of our best judgment. One of us, a high-contrast KEY 1 COLOR person, wore unflattering orange for years before she realized it was because she wanted to look like her KEY 2 COLOR mother.

Light, climate and lifestyle in different parts of the country directly affect our color choices. Bright, clear "summer" colors are worn year-round in Southern California and the Southwest but would be inappropriate for winter in the East or Midwest. A *Chic* tip: if you're planning a move or awaiting a job transfer, postpone major wardrobe purchases until you get a sense of the area. A suit that feels and looks right in San Diego might be out of place in Washington, D.C.

Color is the first thing people see when they look at us. The impact of color, plus its strong influence on moods and behavior, makes our "plumage" one of our most powerful and creative fashion tools.

4
Proportionately Yours

Proportion. It's one of the single most important tools, along with color, that we can use to look and dress terrific, yet most of us (1) don't know that much about proportion, or (2) are intimidated by the subject, or (3) both of the above. Why? Because proportion has to do with our bodies, bringing the various parts of our bodies into balance with each other through the artful use of different types of clothes. Most of us would probably admit that we're not all that good at working with our own body's particular proportions. Most of us know our bodies, especially our "faults," all too well. Every time we look in the mirror we're reminded of how wide our hips are, for instance, or how our legs are too short for the rest of our body. We're frankly too hard on ourselves. We don't remind ourselves of our good points, which is essential to the self-knowledge and body self-esteem, if you will, required for dressing in proportion. In this chapter we'll tackle body know-how and proportion tips first and then get into some hints and advice from designers Liz Claiborne and Harriet Selwyn.

Body Self-Knowledge
The first step is to take some measurements so that you can get an accurate, objective look at yourself and what you have to work with. The key areas are shoulders, bust, waist, hips and torso.

To measure your shoulder width, stand with your back against a wall or door. Have a friend mark the sides of your shoulders with a yardstick and a pencil. Do the same with the widest point of your hips, usually seven or eight inches below the waist.

Simple measurements, taken with the aid of a friend, will give you a sense of your own proportions.

You can also do this yourself by marking your shoulders one side at a time with a pencil. Now step away from the wall and measure (with a yardstick or tape measure) the distances between the shoulder and hip marks. Which are wider, your shoulders or your hips? Or are they the same, in balance or in proportion? If your hips are wider, you'll need to work on widening your shoulder line in order to balance your hips. The converse, shoulders wider than hips, is usually not considered a problem by most of us.

Waist

Stand in front of a full length mirror and squint at your figure. Do you see an indentation at your waistline, or is your midriff straight up and down? This will tell you whether you have a thin or thick waist. Also, take a piece of string three and a half feet long or so, circle your waist with it and mark your waist circumference on the string with a colored pen.

Bust and Hips

Take the same piece of string and measure your bustline with a different colored pen. Do the same with your hips. How do your bust, waist and hips compare? Are the bust and hip measurements about the same—within an inch or two of each other—and is your waist ten or twelve inches smaller? Or is the hip measurement larger than the bust measurement? Or is your bust larger in proportion to your hips?

Now take some body lengths. Sit on a hard-seat chair. Have a friend take a yardstick or piece of string (18 inches or so long) and mark the length from your waist to the bottom of your buttocks and also the length from your armpit to your waist. If the former length is greater, you are short waisted; if the latter is longer, you're long waisted; and if they're the same, you're in balance or average.

Stand and make a mark at the top of a shoulder, at a hip and at your feet. Is the distance from your shoulders to hips the same as, shorter than or longer than the distance from your hips to your feet? In other words, are your legs in proportion to or shorter or longer than your torso?

These are the major body points and measurements you need to be aware of. Notice we didn't use a tape measure and compare the actual inch lengths, say 38-inch bust, 27-inch waist and 39-inch hips. The actual numbers of our measurements are not important. It's the *relationship* of various parts of the body and to the whole that we're concerned about; those relationships determine whether the parts of the body are in balance or need to be brought into proportion through the tips and hints we're about to give you.

In going through this measuring exercise, we hope you discovered some pluses about your body that may have pleasantly surprised you. As we said before, most of us don't give ourselves a break when it comes to our bodies, and thus we don't do a good job of maximizing our assets because we don't have a clear sense of exactly what our assets are. When we did this little exercise, we were delighted to discover that our hips and shoulders are the same width, for instance. The by-product of this is a little boost in body self-esteem.

Take a look at yourself in the mirror from a side view. Your eye will tell you if you have a flat or protruding tummy; slender or heavier arms; thinner or thicker thighs, calves and ankles.

Proportion Tools

Rather than give you the usual laundry list of do's and don'ts for each specific type of figure "flaw," we feel that it is more positive and helpful to discuss the different aspects of clothing and how you can use them to bring parts of your body into balance. You can use any of these aspects or tools for any part of you from your shoulders down to your ankles. Our goal here is to make the most of our assets while deemphasizing our liabilities, or the areas we don't want to draw attention to, so that the end result—our outfit or look—is a balanced, pleasing whole.

Proportionately Yours • 29

Dark colors are more slenderizing to the figure and can be used effectively to balance your proportions.

Color

Basically all you need to know about the effect of color on proportion is that dark and neutral colors do not attract the eye, while light and bright colors do. That's why we always hear the advice that black is slimming. You might experiment with a bright orange or pink top and brown or navy pants or skirt if you'd like to visually balance your smaller bust with hips that are more generous than you'd like.

Texture

Dull, flat textures are good for areas you want to draw the eye *away* from, while bright, shiny or bulky textured surfaces *attract* attention. A fluffy angora sweater is a good idea if you want to visually add a little weight to your top and bustline. If you don't want to call attention to your hips or waistline, you won't want to wear a fuzzy mohair–wool blend skirt. Nubby, fuzzy textures fill out an area, while smooth, flat fabrics simply cover without calling attention to it.

Line

You probably already know the rule about vertical stripes making the body look taller and horizontal lines widening the body. You *do* need to let your own eye be the final judge, however. Once in a while the opposite and undesired effect can result. For instance, lots of narrow vertical stripes can sometimes widen the body because the eye repeatedly measures the spaces between the stripes and moves from stripe to stripe across the body. Diagonal lines can take on the characteristics of vertical or horizontal lines, depending on the degree of slant. The lines of a V neckline are flattering to most of us, since this line lengthens the upper body and draws attention to the neck, face and bustline.

Shape or Silhouette

This is one of the most important tools at your disposal; you can go a long way toward achieving a well-proportioned look by using the shape of cer-

The fluffy angora sweater on the left adds visual weight to the upper body—a useful technique for small-busted women—while the flat knit on the right minimizes the body dimensions.

Proportionately Yours • 31

In these examples, the horizontal stripes lead the eye outward and widen the body, while the diagonal lines draw the eye inward and create a slenderizing optical illusion.

tain clothes to your advantage. Generally, extreme silhouettes and very full or very tight, figure-revealing shapes attract attention, while simple, understated shapes merely cover an area without calling undue attention to it. For instance, skintight leather pants look *Wow!* on a woman with terrific legs and hips; form-fitting slacks don't flatter those of us who wish Mother Nature hadn't been so generous in the hip and waist department. We would do better in easy-fitting pleat-front trousers.

In other words, add fabric fullness for a bigger or fuller silhouette where you want to draw attention or "flesh out" part of yourself. Don't use a skirt or blouse with lots of gathers or pleats where you feel your body already has enough of its own fullness or where you don't want to attract attention.

Clingy knits or dresses or blouses with fitted bodices are examples of body-defining silhouettes, while tent and smock dresses typify full shapes that call attention to themselves through their fullness or mass. For many of us a small or moderate amount of fullness, such as a skirt with a few gathers (not a full-fledged dirndl) or a tailored slack with a pleat front (neither snug fitting nor baggy pants) is best.

Extreme silhouettes attract attention and distort the normal body proportions (sometimes with positive results), while simple, understated shapes cover an area without exaggeration.

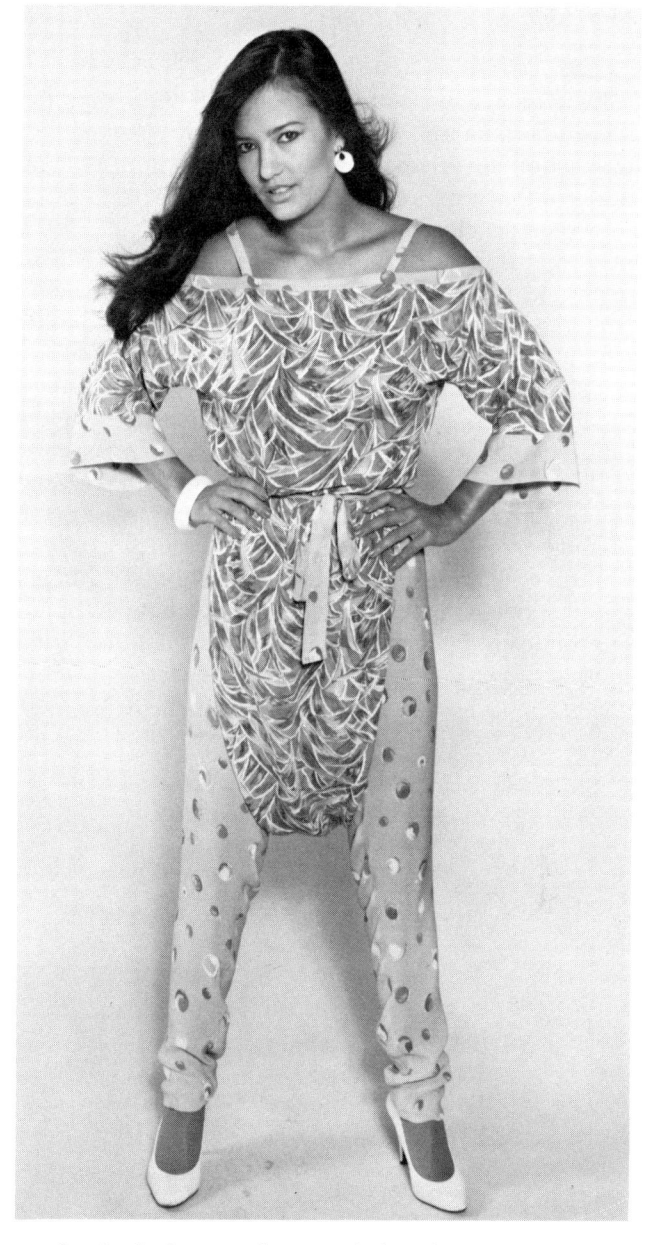

Big, bold, allover patterns such as the example on the left can make the body seem large and shapeless, while an artful mix of patterns and the use of negative space can be dramatic and still flattering to the figure.

Pattern

Usually the bigger and bolder the pattern or design on the fabric, whether plaid or polka dots or print of any kind, the more attention is called to that garment and area of the body. Color influences the visual effect of pattern, too. A high-contrast print, in black and white for instance, will attract the eye more readily than one in muted greys and blues.

34 • *Chic on a Shoestring*

Detail

By now you've gotten the general idea that the more you take any one of these seven principles of proportion to an extreme, the more attention you draw to that area of the body. This is certainly true for *detail* in clothing, which is why a lot of advice on proportion centers on adding details near your neck and face to draw the eye upward (and away from the body). Some examples of how to use details to your advantage: soft pleats or tucks at the shoulder widen the shoulder line and balance the shoulder/hip proportion; a bright, contrasting color belt shows off a slender waist; pretty lace trim on blouse cuffs and collar accents graceful hands and neck. Most of us, unless we're five foot eight and weigh 120 pounds or have a truly avant garde sense of style, will do well to use detail in moderation. Too much detail, like too much of anything, can create an opposite, undesired effect and, in this case, an unflattering look.

Accessories

All these tools or means to balance proportion apply to clothes and to accessories, too. Belts or sashes at the hip are advisable if you like to accent your hips and not your waist. Medium-width (1 inch or so) belts in the same tone as the rest of your outfit are a good idea if you want to keep waist attention to a minimum.

As we said before, all these techniques apply to every kind of garment, from blouses and scarves to slacks and shoes. Your assignment now is to "think proportion" and to be aware of the various shapes, colors, lines, textures, and so on of the clothes and accessories in your closet and in stores when you go shopping.

A Self-Taught Lesson in Proportion

Naturally, rules and tips are only valuable when they're put to use. In terms of proportion, each of us has to learn firsthand which details, lines, patterns

Detail can be used to accent or minimize body areas. Horizontal stripes across the bust give an illusion of fullness; soft tucks at the yoke and shoulder widen the shoulder line and balance the shoulder/hip proportions.

Proportionately Yours • 35

Accessories can easily overpower an outfit and its wearer by being too large or too contrasty in color. Petite women such as our model should keep their accessories small and in the same tones as their clothing to create a long, uninterrupted line.

and silhouettes work for us. How do we do this? By taking some time on a Saturday or Sunday afternoon and experimenting with different pieces in front of a full length mirror. Do your hip length blazers flatter you or does that new fitted Spencer jacket do more for you? Which seems to balance your proportion better? Try on a dress and try raising and lowering the hem. Which hem length does the most for your legs in proportion to the rest of your body? Try belting a jacket or tunic at the waist, slightly above and below and at your hips. Everything doesn't always have to be belted at the waist; you may find another means of belting that's more flattering to you. Experiment with the different shapes and colors of accessories you have. Perhaps your boots look better than pumps with your mid-calf-length skirt, since the boots create one continuous line.

You can do this exercise with a friend whose fashion judgment you trust, or you can do it by yourself, especially if you'd like to build up your proportion self-confidence. The more you try on different combinations of pieces, the better you'll get at zeroing in on just which ones create the best proportions for you. At the same time, you'll feel better about your own sense of your pluses and minuses and gain a bit of that all-important body self-esteem. Learning about your own body's proportions and how to best create looks that make the most of you is actually like a lot of things in life—doing your job, playing the piano, hitting a golf ball: It takes practice. There really aren't any secrets, hard-and-fast rules or short cuts; it just takes a little awareness and effort.

Before long you'll be a real pro at putting yourself together in the best way possible.

Proportion Advice from Designer Liz Claiborne
We talked to well-known designer Liz Claiborne about proportion. Her line of career separates and dresses has become a favorite of working women across the country.

Fashion designer Liz Claiborne.

CHIC: How does proportion factor into your design concept? How do you design with so many different figure types in mind?
L.C.: Two things come into play. First, as a woman, I have an advantage as a designer, because every woman has her own figure faults or specific proportions you have to work with, so I'm conscious of that while designing. Second, it's just a lengthy task to make sure clothes fit the widest audience possible. Even though they fit the ideal size eight, I know there's really no such person. But I always make sure to have different *types* of skirts, pants and jackets that will suit the different proportions. There are certain looks that will work on almost *any* figure, but there are certain looks that can enhance the figure. Pants with inverted pleats, for example, look better on a full-hipped woman than skintight ones. If you're wearing a full skirt, wear a shorter jacket. Don't combine a full skirt and a long jacket. When you get to petites, it's a question of taking that look and really reproportioning the whole thing. We work on a model, and the minute it looks overpowering,

we know we have to do something. We have to modify the shoulders or neck, if it has a huge cowl, for example. All the details have to be brought down to scale. If we use an oversized plaid, we don't make it in petites. We'll use smaller prints, small stripes or plaids.

CHIC: If you can buy clothing in petite sizes, these factors of proportion have been taken care of for you. How do you figure proportion out for yourself either as a petite or average size? How do we learn what looks good on us?

L.C.: Get yourself a full length mirror and really *look* at yourself. Try to be objective. For example, if you have a dress with a belt, look at yourself in the mirror and experiment. Try the belt at the waist and then at the hip or slightly empire if you're full-hipped. Use a hand mirror and look at yourself from the sides and back (especially important with pants). Most important, learn to be comfortable with your body and your style. Good proportion has as much to do with your head (attitude) as your body. Your style really has nothing to do with your physical figure type.

You should never be that aware of what you're wearing. You should put it on, feel great, know you look great and forget about it. If you're wearing something you're a little uncomfortable in, you're conscious of it all day and it's terrible.

General Proportion Tips

The following are tips and bits of advice to think about, proportion-wise.

- Oscar de la Renta: "Generally speaking, if the skirt is narrow, it should be shorter; if it is full, it should be longer, but there are no hard-and-fast rules."
- Junior sizes are cut a bit less full and have a shorter neck-to-waist length than misses sizes. If you're small to medium busted and tend to be a little short waisted, try junior sizes.
- Jacket sleeve lengths usually look best just covering or a half-inch below the wristbone.
- Good posture is a proportion tip many of us forget. Comfortable, erect stature looks and feels best and helps ensure a good fit.
- Try a variety of sizes in shoulder pads from small to large and even oversized if you'd like to extend your shoulder line and/or balance the width of your hips.
- When wearing big shapes or clothes with volumes of fabric such as big blouson jackets or full dirndl skirts, it's best to define the body at some point. Total body camouflage with lots of fullness only calls attention to the big shapes. This is especially true of a voluminous top and full-cut pants. The mass tends to pull the body's center of gravity down visually and you wind up looking short and dumpy.

   Try the blouson jacket with a straight skirt or trim slacks, the skirt with an easy-fitting shirt or soft sweater.
- Always check your rear view when trying anything on. The rear-view perspective on proportion is just as important as the front or sides. Many of us forget to check this, and our sometimes less-than-flattered posteriors show it.
- Pay extraspecial attention to fit. Fit is an underlying aspect of proportion that some of us forget. No matter what our size or shape, clothes have to fit easily and comfortably for us to look and feel our best.

   Don't be afraid to alter your clothes in order to achieve the best fit possible. Find a good tailor or seamstress—the money is well worth it. Even what may seem like minor changes—a half-inch or an inch at seams or hemlines—can make a world of difference in fit and looks. We need to take a tip from our male friends here. They think nothing of having a good share of their clothes altered (suits, jackets, pants) to achieve proper fit.

- Rules for scale of clothing and accessories:
   In general, small women look best in small- and medium-scaled pieces.

38 • Chic on a Shoestring

Medium-sized women can wear small, medium and large garments and accessories.

Large women can wear medium and large things.

How to Look Taller and Slimmer

- Keep your skirt hemlines around the knee. Mid-calf lengths can make legs look shorter and hips appear heavier.
- Dress in colors and accessories in the same tone or color family. Solid fabrics and small-scaled prints work best. This monochromatic palette also lends a rich, classy tone to your look.
- Try vertical stripes. Check the effect on yourself in a full length mirror, though. Lots of slender vertical stripes actually draw the eye across the body, the opposite effect from what you want.
- Observe the two-thirds ratio in combining pieces. This proportion is often more pleasing to the eye than equal halves. Check to see that a dress, for instance, is about two-thirds as long as your entire body or that your pants are about twice the length of your upper body (and thus two-thirds of your outfit).
- If you don't want to keep your entire outfit keyed to a single color, try harmonizing the lower part of your look. Keep skirt, hose and footwear toned to the same shade (navy, for instance) for a longer line.
- Choose lean and slender (not clingy or tight) lines and shapes.
- Uncuffed trousers lengthen the leg, while cuffed pants tend to shorten no matter how long the legs.
- Single-breasted jackets look leaner than double-breasted ones.
- Tunics (make them two-thirds the length of your outfit, whether over a skirt or over pants) elongate the figure.
- Jumpsuits, in easy-fitting, simple cuts and in solid colors, are a good bet.
- Straight, unconstructed jackets or cardigans are usually more slimming than fitted blazers.

This two-thirds-length tunic elongates the body.

- Simple pumps with 1½- to 2½-inch heels are a better shoe choice than anything with a lot of detail or ankle straps.
- The glimpse of skin created by a V neckline or a blouse unbuttoned a couple of buttons draws the eye up and thus lengthens the silhouette.

Talking About Body Know-How and Attitude with Designer Harriet Selwyn

Harriet Selwyn is an innovative designer, an inspiring teacher, an outspoken thinker and a champion of the "real woman." She combined comfort and practicality with high-fashion pizzazz in her one-size-fits-all clothing concept, Fragments. In 1977 she received the first Lord & Taylor Creative Design Award.

CHIC: How do we develop a positive attitude about our bodies and ourselves and learn to look at ourselves objectively?

H.S.: One good method of learning about your own proportion is just standing in front of the mirror and looking, maybe taking two or three pieces of clothing and putting them on. You'll find one or two ways to combine them that make you feel more comfortable, and when you *feel* more comfortable, you have a clue to your own proportion.

CHIC: Could you suggest two or three pieces of clothing to try this with?

H.S.: You could fool around with a blouse and a skirt, for instance. You're going to find that it's trial and error. You've got to try things on. You might find, for example, that a top that comes down two or three inches below your waist and a skirt that comes to just below your knees looks best on you if you're short waisted. Try different lengths of tops and bottoms. You're going to try them on and one of those times you're going to *feel better*. Usually feeling better comes from the fact that you look more slender.

This is a difficult subject because every woman is built so differently. There is no *one* way to be or *one thing* you can say that is true.

Fashion designer Harriet Selwyn.

CHIC: Is there a first step of accepting yourself, or does the self-acceptance come after the attitude step of saying to yourself, "This is what I have to work with. Now, I'm not going to tear myself down here. I'm going to build myself up."

H.S.: That really changes. You know, I've had a mastectomy, and there have been times I've felt fine about that and secure about not even wearing a prosthesis. Then there have been times when I've gained weight and the one breast I do have has gotten large and I really do look lopsided. Then I look at myself and I don't feel comfortable. Now I would probably put a bigger top on, you see. But then if I put a bigger top on, what about the bottom? So, it's trial and error again. You've got to go back to the mirror.

CHIC: So we must keep experimenting. Even once we accept our proportions, we have to keep looking

40 • *Chic on a Shoestring*

at ourselves. We can't accept our shape and then forget about it because of the daily, weekly or monthly changes.

H.S.: Yes, you know, we're always changing. It's just like life, so you've got to keep working at it.

CHIC: As a designer and a woman, you've watched our fetishes with the ideals of Twiggy slimness and Marilyn Monroe curvaceousness. Now we're told the athletic female body is in vogue. Do you find that it's easier now to like our own superstructure or is it again just a matter of changing ideals and we now have to struggle to be seventeen and muscular?

H.S.: The emphasis on youth in the world is rampant. I think once you get a style of dressing that makes you feel good, you can be okay. I mean, if you go out there and you feel you don't look good . . . You know, actually for me, it's more hair and shoes. When my hair doesn't look good, it really doesn't matter what I'm wearing, I don't feel good. Also, I can't get dressed without the right pair of shoes. Sometimes I have a great outfit I want to wear and I put it on and I just don't have the right shoes to wear with it. By *right* I mean probably the height. In other words, I'll put a pair of flats on and it's just wrong; then I put a pair of high heels on. What I really need is a small heel and I don't have it so the whole proportion of the outfit is thrown off and I don't look good. I don't look *terrible,* but definitely something's off. So there are certain basic shoes that one should have for her own body, leg and ankle shape. You see, the minute I put a pair of high heels on, the way I'm built, I look thin, I feel good. Now, that's total vanity but that is really what makes me feel good. We do all want to be skinny.

I think you can tie how you *feel* together with how you're going to *look.* So if you put a pair of shoes on, and if it feels wrong to you with the outfit you have on, probably it *is* wrong. Because when you feel good, you also look good.

CHIC: Is it possible that our ideal of female beauty

Experiment with the same dress worn three different ways and discover which look is most flattering to your figure proportions and fashion personality.

Proportionately Yours • 41

is actually loosening? With a larger part of the clothing audience getting older, are we going to be a little kinder toward our bodies and our sense of what works?

H.S.: I think this tendency toward totally idolizing youth can change as long as each one of us changes our attitude individually. If each person would look at herself and say, "This is how I look. I'm doing the best with it. I feel pretty good about myself," that energy will build up. But if everybody feels negative about herself on an individual level, then collectively it's never going to work. There is such an emphasis on youth everywhere you look that it is hard to be positive about yourself as you get older. All the clichés you hear, like never wear your hair long when you get older—well, you begin to believe them.

We should all take a more positive attitude—there's no place else to go. And I think more women should think about that. All of us have seen older women and reflexively said, "Oh, doesn't she look good for an older woman." Well, you know, I can't stand that. What does that mean, really? In other words, the ideal is youth and unless you're young, forget it. Believe me, I've gone through some changes of my own. I find that I feel that way sometimes also and I really fight the feeling because it doesn't make me feel great.

CHIC: That gets back to our question about attitude—learning to like what we have, whatever that is.

H.S.: Keep your hair looking great and that's going to be a big help.

CHIC: Just as there are no set hemlines in fashion right now, no set looks, are we also freer to accept our own shapes and then go from there to make the most of it? Do you feel there's any more freedom now than before?

H.S.: Absolutely. I think that women have realized that there is no one way to be. I mean a *lot* of women have realized that and I think more will follow. We're like fledglings; we're just beginning to fly.

CHIC: Have you found that there are proportion and style rules that can be successfully broken? Why, for instance, does Diana Vreeland or Dolly Parton look dramatic and terrific by maximizing something that other people might play down? Is it attitude or personality that enables you to carry off an exaggerated look?

H.S.: What it is is *energy*. There are some people who are so magnetic that it even comes through in a photograph. And you know, look at Diana Vreeland—a beautiful and fascinating woman, yet by certain standards she is certainly not a beauty. She's got great style, and she's not afraid to make a statement.

CHIC: Have you found that color can influence proportion?

H.S.: Oh, yes! Color changes proportion. The only thing I can say about color is that if I have a black skirt, I'm safe [laughing]. I'll tell you what I found recently, on the level of getting older. You always hear that cliché about not being able to wear black when you get older. And it's true. I love black, but when I wear black, I always try to have the neckline reveal some of my own skin. Color will definitely change proportion, but there are no hard-and-fast rules. The thing to do is take those pieces I mentioned and try them on in front of a mirror. Take the same types of pieces in different colors and see what happens. You see, the whole thing is to observe yourself. Look at that woman in the mirror. That woman in the mirror is you. Pretend she is a woman on the street you are critiquing. As that woman in the mirror walks toward you, what is it you think about her? What do you think about how she looks?

CHIC: Do you think we can do this for ourselves or do we have to ask someone else's advice? A friend?

H.S.: I think we can do it for ourselves, but I think it's okay to ask someone's advice. If you're feeling very insecure and you have a friend whom you respect, it's fine to do that. Once you get on the right track, then it's trial and error. It's like learning how to drive. Once you get to the place where you cover up or draw attention away from the parts of yourself you can't bear, you can walk out the door feeling great.

CHIC: Sometimes what we would consider a figure flaw or something we'd rather not have is just *there*. Is there a way to maximize what might otherwise be considered a flaw?

H.S.: Absolutely. By emphasizing it. It just depends what it is. I've seen a woman with a big nose and with the right makeup and the right haircut, it looked divine. So there is a way to minimize, let's say, by emphasizing.

CHIC: Does this have something to do with self-*pride* or just saying "This is who I am" and therefore defusing any negativity?

H.S.: Absolutely. People respond to confidence, if you do it with style. And you see, that goes back to feelings. You have to really feel that way; you have to be *real*. If it isn't real, it won't work.

My advice is, take a risk. Put it out there.

SECTION II
How to Build Your Chic Wardrobe (On the Cheap)

5
Discover a Chic Wardrobe

What Is a Wardrobe? How to Make the Shift from a Collection of Clothes to a Wardrobe That Works

Rule number one for living *Chic on a Shoestring:* the best way to save money and build a *Chic* wardrobe is to better utilize the clothes you already own.

Before we get into the actual process of rearranging your closet and building your wardrobe, it's important to pause and reflect on precisely what a wardrobe is and does. Not only are the individual pieces in a wardrobe of importance, but also important is the *concept* of a wardrobe, that is, the way we see and use our collection of clothes.

Most of us have a somewhat random selection of garments that don't really go together well enough to create all the outfits and looks we need. We don't go to the closet each morning and admire the wardrobe we've created. In fact, we may even unconsciously reject this notion and feel that only wealthy clotheshorses or rich socialites can afford the time and money required to build a wardrobe.

Well, what exactly *is* a *wardrobe?* Our working definition: "a coordinated and planned set of garments and accessories in flattering colors and styles that work easily in a number of ways to meet every situation and occasion in our lives." Of consideration here are practicality, ease of care and our emotional needs. A *Chic on a Shoestring* wardrobe is satisfying emotionally, practically and financially. It's understood that these clothes are high-quality garments purchased at the best possible price.

Back to our own closets. Frankly, most of us have too many clothes. Think of all the never- or seldom-worn items that for one reason or another simply don't work for us. The first lesson to learn in building a *Chic on a Shoestring* wardrobe is that less is more, particularly in the beginning stages. It's not the large number of different pieces that counts; it's the optimal group of integrated pieces you want to strive for.

Another important concept in the expansion of the way we conceptualize our wardrobes is that of change and the evolution of our tastes and needs. We're primarily concerned with building the foundation for a cohesive, versatile wardrobe of long-lasting clothes, but remember that no *one* set of clothes at *one* point in time is your wardrobe for all time. Nothing is cast in concrete. Rather, it's helpful to see a wardrobe as analogous to life—constantly changing as we ourselves grow older, change marital status, add families and/or jobs, advance in our careers, shift to new interests and friends. Our personal preferences and tastes are altered as time goes on; indeed, even the way we feel and see ourselves changes over time. Naturally our clothes sense will constantly evolve to reflect all the facets of our lives. Our wardrobes are as fluid as our lives and the times we live in.

Last, a wardrobe can also be viewed as an important and creative avocation or hobby. Instead of thinking merely about the necessity of covering our bodies, we can expand our perception to include clothes as an important and enjoyable means of self-expression and ego satisfaction. Some women might claim they simply don't have the time or inclination for yet another hobby or interest. However, each of us gets dressed every morning whether we like it or not. Something as integral to our lives as clothing ought to be fun. We intend to help you see it that way.

Excavating a Wardrobe
That's right, excavating. You already have, believe it or not, the rudiments of your wardrobe. Our task now is to help you uncover and organize these elements. The reason you don't know you already own a wardrobe is that your wardrobe pieces are hidden among all your clothes, some of which we're going to get rid of soon. It's the syndrome of not being able to see the forest for the trees.

The first step is to tackle your closet with unbridled vigor. On a Saturday when you have enough time and energy, invite over a friend whose taste and clothes sense you trust to help. You'll find the task much less onerous with companionship. Remember, we promised to make this fun. If you feel guilty about asking a friend to help, you can always turn around and return the favor another weekend. Put on the coffeepot or chill the Chablis and begin to empty your closet or closets completely of every single garment you own. The same goes for your drawers full of sweaters, knit dresses, and so on. Sort each item into one of three piles:

A. Keepers. These are clothes that already work for you. You wear them often; they make more than one outfit; the colors flatter you; you receive compliments when you wear them.
B. Ambivalents. The not-sure category. These could be used with a minimum of alteration. You might simply need to test them with other clothes to see if they really do work for you. Maybe you're not sure of the color or shape or fit. Hold these in this in-between pile for now.
C. Definite No-Nos. This group of discards is the good-bye pile. A good rule when deciding what to include here is to ask yourself, "Have I worn this article within the past year?" Possible exceptions to the rule are evening clothes or valuable antiques. More specifically, the clothes you choose to eliminate will most likely be in colors that don't look good on you; unflattering styles and cuts; pieces that don't, never did and never will fit; and all your mistake or impulse purchases that don't go with anything else in your closet. Also included here are the clothes that don't mesh with your clothes-care personality, for instance, the beautiful ruffled silk blouse you received as a gift but don't wear because it requires dry cleaning you can't afford.

We'll come back to these three piles one by one. Separate pile A into types of garments: Sort all the slacks, skirts, sweaters, blouses, jackets and dresses into separate piles. Be sure to split matched outfits such as suits, jacket dresses and pantsuits into their respective garment categories. Now lay out all your accessories, too. Scarves, belts, gloves, hats, shoes, bags and jewelry should all be out of their storage places so that you can see them and have easy access to them. (Remember what we said about feeling energetic today? You might need a B-complex vitamin about now.)

With your friend at hand, start trying on outfits complete with accessories. You'll probably begin with the way you usually pair certain garments. It's a good idea to have a Polaroid loaded with color film (you'll need several packs before the day is out) to record the outfits you'll want to re-create. Now try different jackets with the dress or skirt-and-blouse combination you have on. Try a scarf at the neck or in the breast pocket, maybe one in a totally different color than you would normally wear with this outfit. Pair your blazer jackets and cardigan sweaters with one- and two-piece dresses to create an alternative suit look. Don't be afraid to mix textures and colors, but beware of radical print combinations. Do you like your new look? Take a picture.

Before you change clothes, take off all the accessories you chose and put on different ones. Never tried pearls and black strappy sandals with your grey sweater and navy suit? With this new combination you can effortlessly go from the office to dinner. Take another snapshot.

The old mix and match concept is what we're after. You need to try on every garment in your A pile with several other wardrobe pieces (including shoes and accessories) to discover all the outfits and looks you can make from the clothes in your closet. This "closet search" is one of the keys to *Chic on a Shoestring*. Most of us haven't been through this particular exercise/adventure. We buy a shirt or a suit and then play it safe by only wearing it one or two ways. We rarely experiment to see if that red jacket will work with more than the matching red slacks or the navy skirt. Naturally none of us wants to make a mistake and go out in a mismatched ensemble. But by avoiding risks we also cut off our options and never tap all the resources already in our wardrobes.

Take one Saturday and mix and match in the privacy of your own bedroom. So what if the camel blazer doesn't work with the kelly green plaid kilt? It looks great over a two-piece challis print dress. Some of the trials will turn out to be errors, but you'll have more successes than failures and all you've expended is a little bit of time. Meanwhile you've learned a lot about your wardrobe.

The process of wardrobe building is *visual*. You have to physically try on different, even seemingly

Cleaning out your closet can be fun—all you need is a good (and patient) friend, a bottle of wine and plenty of Polaroid film to record the fashion discoveries buried in your own wardrobe.

crazy combinations to see if they actually work or not. Wearing clothes is more than a mental activity. You don't know if your black suit jacket works with your white-and-red two-piece dress until you try them on together and look at yourself in a full length mirror.

You'll get better at creating new outfits as you go along. Your friend will be a big help, too, in suggesting combinations and accessories you might not think of. Use the Polaroid to record the "keeper" ensembles, or take good notes. If you go the photograph route, you can thumbtack the photos to a piece of poster board or cork mounted on the wall to use as a reference when you are getting dressed in the morning. Bear in mind that by stretching your imagination, you can also stretch your wardrobe.

On to pile C. (Skip B for now.) Look over the clothes and accessories in this pile and analyze why they're here. Are they the wrong color for you? Bad fit? Never really looked good on you? Do you just plain not like this particular blouse or top? An impulse buy or sale item that never worked out? Note the nature of these "mistake" clothes and accessories so that you can best avoid them in the future. In going through this closet-cleaning procedure ourselves, we've each learned a lot about ourselves and our wardrobes.

Pile B now deserves your attention. Once more, with conviction, separate this pile into A and C. Maybe a questionable color will actually work with your A items, or a minor sewing job will bring a skirt or pair of pants up to snuff. On the other hand, the perfectly good taupe cardigan sweater simply doesn't go with anything else you have and really doesn't flatter your skin tone either. Get rid of it.

It may seem that this middle step of sorting and dealing with pile B is an unnecessary waste of time. You might think it best to separate everything at the beginning of this exercise into "keepers" and "discards." Either you keep an article or you don't, right? Well, it's really not quite that simple. As you find out by actually working with all the clothes you've known and loved and worked hard to buy and even hated, merely yeaing or naying doesn't work for everything. Give yourself a little while to make the decisions on this in-between category. It's really done best after exploring and expanding and learning more about your wardrobe by thoroughly working through the A pile first and then going through B.

As for liquidating your cast-offs, you have several options. You can, of course, give things to your friend who generously donated her time and expertise to your wardrobe excavation. You can also give things to other friends or family members. Thrift shops, churches and charitable organizations are always eager to receive clothing donations. You gain the advantage of a tax deduction, too.

We recommend recycling your unwanted clothing and accessories through a local resale or consignment shop. These stores sell recent (within the past season or two) fashions at one-fourth to one-third of their original retail prices. Generally you split the selling price 50-50 with the shop. All types of garments from casual to dressy styles, even furs and accessories, are available. In researching our Southern California discount fashion directories, *Glad Rags* and *Glad Rags II,* we've witnessed a rapid growth in the number of first-rate resale shops throughout the area. We've also seen a similar increase of these stores throughout the rest of the country.

We not only enjoy shopping for ourselves at resale stores—we've picked up some incredible buys on furs and shoes—we also make money by recycling our own clothes through them. Call one or two stores in your area and discuss the possibility of bringing in your clothes, shoes and accessories on consignment. Consult your local discount shopping guide or check the Yellow Pages under "Used Clothing." You can use the money you make by recycling to add needed items to your wardrobe.

Honing In on Your Chic Wardrobe Colors

The crux of your wardrobe is color (we'll get into the other aspects of your wardrobe a little later), and the light and dark neutrals you discover in your closet are the foundation. You will notice as you fill in this chart that you own a number of garments in different neutral tones but that one dark and one light neutral predominate. You need to concentrate on these two colors in building your wardrobe. You may have several other light and dark neutral tones present, which is fine. For instance, you may see mostly beige and navy clothes with a few black, brown, off-white and pearl grey pieces, too. You'll be working on basing your wardrobe on the navy and beige.

As for accent colors, you probably have a range of different shades that serve to liven an outfit or to complete a look. Depending on your skin tone and color preferences, you may have mostly softer pastels or intense brights, or maybe a mixture of both. An accent can be a delicate peach or an electric blue.

Earlier we discussed expanding our concept of a wardrobe and then experimenting with clothes to increase the number of ways they can be worn. It's also helpful to expand our notions about neutrals and accents. Besides the usual neutrals of black, charcoal, navy, brown, wine, grey, beige, off-white and white, other colors can also be considered neutrals. If none of the above particularly interests you, perhaps your basic wardrobe colors are dark moss green and camel, or plum and pale mauve. For some women, mauve or plum might be an accent to the other colors in their wardrobes. You may love these two colors above all others and have lots of both in your closet. For you, they're the basis of your wardrobe; they're your light and dark neutrals.

Even the concept of a "bright" can be stretched a bit. One of Nancy Reagan's favorite colors is red. She has many red outfits and dresses and wears the color often. Since so much of her wardrobe is red, the color isn't really an occasional accent in her case; it is a basic tone for her wardrobe, a "neutral," in a sense.

Organizing Your Chic Wardrobe

Before you return your A clothes to their rightful storage places, complete the following chart by noting each garment and accessory in the proper section.

The purpose of this is to help you see particularly the colors your wardrobe is based on, the relation of the pieces to each other and what you need to acquire to flesh out your wardrobe. Notice that there are no categories for pantsuits or two-piece dresses or suits. Remember, these are to be considered as separate garments that work in a number of ways, not just as one outfit. Also note the detailed accessories listing. The accessories are just as essential to your wardrobe as the clothes themselves.

After you've completed the chart, you'll notice holes. Perhaps you're missing a jacket in your dark neutral, or maybe a pair of tailored slacks in your light neutral would give you three or four more outfits. Perhaps it is now clear that your wardrobe is a little too neutral or accent heavy. Based on this and on your discoveries while trying on clothes, you can begin to make a shopping list of the items you need, both clothes and accessories. In order to get the most for your money, it's best to concentrate on purchases in your light and dark neutrals at first.

The shopping list is a good idea to have on hand at all times. Keep a note card or small pad near your closet so that you can jot down needed items as you're selecting an outfit or getting ready for work. This way you can note that a lacy, romantic-style white blouse would make three different evening looks when teamed with your dark green velvet pants, your plaid tartan floor length skirt and maybe even your black jeans.

Since everything is out of your closet, here's your big chance to rearrange your clothes so that all the options within your wardrobe are more readily ap-

Color

Type of Garment	NEUTRALS DARK	NEUTRALS LIGHT	ACCENTS
Jackets			
Skirts			
Pants, Jeans, Slacks			
Dresses			
Blouses, Tops, Shirts			
Sweaters			
Coats			
Lingerie, Camisoles			
Sports/Action Wear			
At-home wear, caftans, robes			
Sleepwear			
Accessories			
Bags			
Belts			
Gloves			
Hats			
Shoes			
Pumps			
Sandals			
Flats			
Boots			
Casual/Sports			

parent. Hang garments by type (all the skirts in one area, all slacks in the next and so on). Hang all the bottoms in one section and all the tops in the next. We'll go into more detail on the optimal physical aspects of your closet in Chapter 6.

As you are hanging up all your jackets or skirts, arrange them by color, ranging from light to dark or vice versa. Because your wardrobe is essentially based on color, the clothes in your closet also need to be arranged by color.

One last note on the job you've just completed: as you know by now, this has been work, to say the least. You've put in a lot of effort to weed out your clothing deadwood and discover and organize your own wardrobe. Give yourself a gold star. You deserve it. Savor, too, the clean, neat closet you've gained as a by-product. There really is a psychologically cleansed feeling that comes from having weeded out and organized your wardrobe.

Wardrobe Advice from Designer Irene Tsu
Designer Irene Tsu was born in Shanghai, spent her early years in Hong Kong, where she studied classical ballet, and moved to New York with her family in 1957. She gave up dancing to become an actress and has worked on stage, film and television. Ms. Tsu's mother is a well-known textile designer, and clothes have always been important in her life, but she got hooked on designing while on location for the film *Paper Tiger,* starring David Niven. Ms. Tsu fell in love with the batik process in Malaysia during the filming and felt she "just had to make the hand-painted silks into clothes."

Irene Tsu's clothes are, to quote their creator, "contemporary classics," with all the emphasis on color and fabric. She designs for a "young to middle-aged career woman or housewife who's confident enough to be able to resist wearing a big designer name, but appreciates quality and simple good taste."

CHIC: How would you advise women to build a wardrobe?
I.T.: Build a wardrobe from the shoes up, not the

Fashion designer Irene Tsu.

other way around. Fashion follows shoe styles. I've talked to a lot of designers, and we're all shoe freaks. We watch trends in shoe styles, because clothing changes will follow. Remember when we wore platform shoes? They were mostly disguised underneath wide-legged pants and long bell-bottoms. When shoes are flat and heels narrow, pants are narrower and show off the foot and ankle. Skirt lengths, too, are determined by the balance of leg and heel. Longer, fuller skirts generally dictate a higher heel; short, tight skirts look better with a flat or wedge heel.
CHIC: Should a woman decide what heel height she is most comfortable wearing and plan her wardrobe accordingly?
I.T.: Yes. Let's take for example the working woman getting ready for the office each morning. Unless she's

very tall, she will probably wear a shoe with some heel, but not a spike heel unless she wants to be in pain all day. A simple pump with a one-and-a-half- to two-and-a-half-inch heel or a low-heeled (two-inch) mid-calf boot are probably the two most flattering shoes for most skirts and pants and the most comfortable. Building from this point up, you are already going to be fairly conservative because of your shoe choices. What you can do to liven up this "safe" look is wear colored or patterned stockings. Carry through your shoe color or pick up an accent color from your outfit in your hosiery. You can also try a contrasting color if you're that bold. You can be in a very sedate suit or dress and inexpensively jazz up your look with colored hosiery or socks. For casual wear, leg warmers in fashion colors are a great way to salvage boring or dated looks. The sweatpants I'm wearing shrank but they're still in good shape and I'm not ready to throw out the whole sweat-suit outfit, so I just pulled on leg warmers and instantly lengthened the pants and updated the look—all for six dollars. Some of the most interesting innovations in fashion now are in hosiery and accessories. Anyone can incorporate these new ideas into her current wardrobe.

CHIC: Can we be both timeless and current with fashion? I purchased a silk chemise dress of yours in 1979 and I'm still wearing it and getting compliments. This is one of the few pieces I own that will never go out of fashion. What's your secret?

I.T.: I don't think of myself as an on-the-minute fashion person. If I was designing a junior line and under the gun to come up with something trendy four times a year, I would hang out at junior high and high schools and see what the young people are wearing; what they are listening to on the radio; what they are eating and thinking. But my lifestyle isn't like that, and therefore I tend toward classics with a distinctive look in good fabrics. I've always worked in fine silks, cashmeres and other beautiful fabrics that hold their value over time and drape well on the body. I draw my design inspiration from travel, especially the pared-down shapes and utilitarian aspects of Asian clothing, and from draping fabric on myself as I design. Sometimes I drape with a towel as I get out of the bathtub. I've caught a lot of colds standing in front of the mirror draping a towel around myself for ideas. I work out a lot and I used to be a dancer, so I'm very aware of how the body moves and how clothes should work with, not against, movement and form. Body-flattering shapes will never look dated. The secret of the chemise is it can be worn unbelted or belted at the hip or waist, wherever it enhances the body. The fabric is lustrous hand-painted silk crepe that glides over the body and reflects light in a subtle yet dazzling way.

Leigh's timeless silk chemise, purchased from Irene Tsu in 1979, worn by a model.

6
Conquering Your Closet

Rethink Your Closet
What is the point in organizing your closet, anyway? We bring up this question because there's more to a clean, well-laid-out closet than meets the eye. While a messy closet does not necessarily indicate a correspondingly cluttered mind, an organized closet is the first logical step in getting a handle on your *Chic on a Shoestring* wardrobe.

Think of your wardrobe and clothes closet as analogous to a mechanic's tools and equipment. An auto mechanic can fix your car provided he has the proper tools. It will be easier for him to do a good job quickly and efficiently if he has all his tools close at hand in his toolbox rather than spread out all over the garage. You are about to put your own clothing "toolbox" in order.

Closet Management
To start, we'll borrow a concept from sound business practices, namely, management by objective. MBO, as it's known, is accomplished by outlining your objectives or goals, determining the techniques and procedures needed to achieve them and getting to work on them. First, let's define closet organization goals:

- Simplify the decision-making process of getting dressed in the morning in order to save time and effort and eliminate frustration.
- Clearly define your style and taste in clothes.
- Get more use from each item in your wardrobe.
- Pinpoint specifically what needs to be added to your wardrobe in order to avoid mistakes when making future purchases.
- Enjoy the feeling of self-satisfaction and pride that comes from being in control of your wardrobe via a nice clean, organized closet.

In order for your closet to really serve your needs through these objectives, you need to expand the way you think about your closet in terms of both its form (size) and its purpose. If you were asked to visualize your ideal closet, you'd probably conjure a spacious, brightly lit walk-in closet with racks and compartments for every item in your wardrobe. "But," you say, "I don't live in a dream mansion complete with my very own capacious closet." Well, don't despair. We're all in the same predicament, trying to cram too many clothes into too little storage space. But let's not give up on the visualization—and realization—of the perfect closet. We'll use this as the basis for creating a new and more functional wardrobe storage system.

Most of us are hampered by lack of space. Living

quarters, whether old or new, simply don't have enough conventional closet and storage space. The answer, then, is to create more closet space from the room you already have, namely your bedroom. Start to expand your closet out into your bedroom so that the room becomes one big, pleasant, colorful and personal walk-in closet. Here's where the term *coming out of the closet* takes on new meaning. The following "recipe" gives step-by-step instructions for your closet transformation.

Besides gaining much-needed storage space, storing and displaying your garments around your bedroom is a visual delight. Rows of pretty bracelets and necklaces hanging on the wall, hats jauntily arranged on top of a coat tree, a colorful poncho displayed over your bed all illustrate the clothes-as-wearable-art concept. Your clothes and accessories are beautiful body ornaments. Bringing them out into the open is an excellent reminder of their decorative and image-enhancing properties.

Recipe for an Organized Closet:
Ingredients and Method
Ingredients
- Full length mirror—a *must* if there ever was one.
- Hangers: plastic and wooden dress, suit, coat, skirt and pants varieties. Also padded hangers for silks and delicates.
- Plastic boxes: various sizes for sweaters and knits, shoes, belts, gloves, handbags.
- Belt bar.
- Wooden-peg racks.
- Over-the-door racks.
- Tissue paper.
- Pomanders and sachets.
- Moth balls.
- Pen and paper—your wardrobe shopping list to hang inside your closet door.
- Kitchen towel rack.
- Hanging garment and accessory bags.
- Coat rack.

Useful closet tools include (left to right) clear plastic boxes with covers, wooden and satin-covered hangers, sachet, coffee mug rack, tissue paper and tie rack.

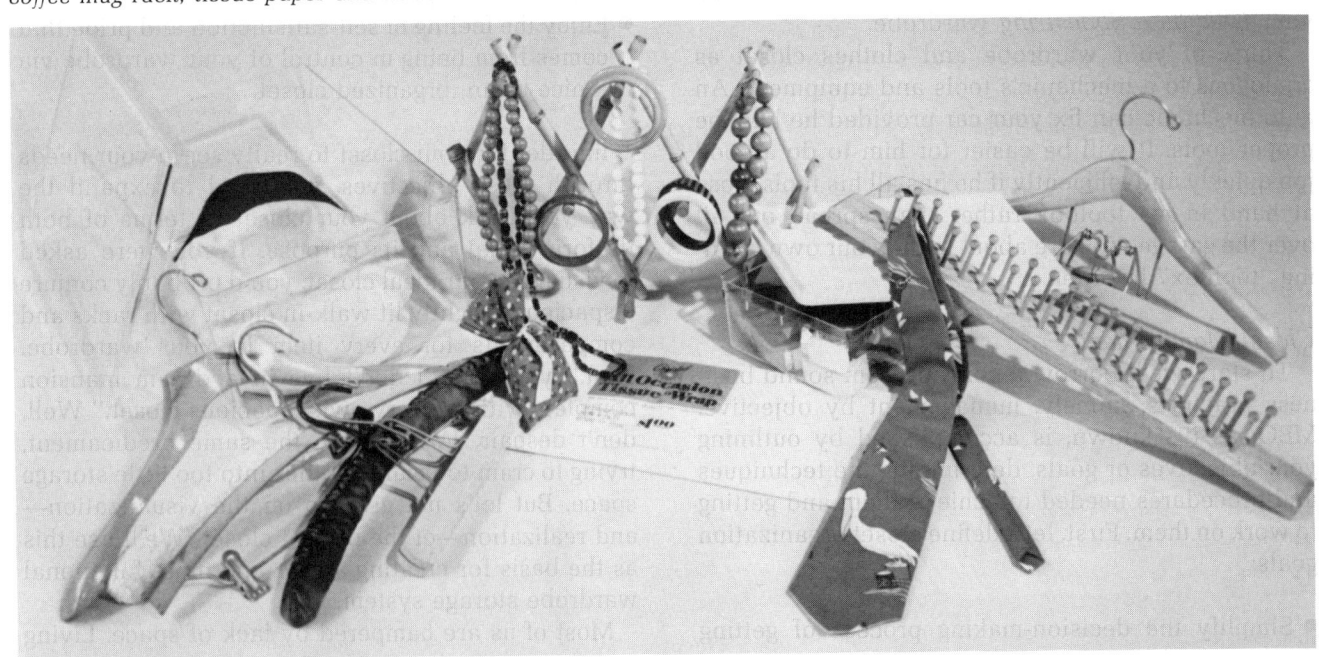

You don't need every single item on this list; it's meant to show you all the optional low-cost equipment, both ordinary and offbeat, you can use to organize and display all the items in your wardrobe. This system will help you quickly and easily find all the ingredients necessary to create just exactly the right look or outfit. For example, if you use several hanging shoe and accessory bags, you might not need stacking plastic boxes to store your shoes and handbags, or vice versa. If you've got more drawer space than closet space, you might not need to store your knits and sweaters in see-through boxes as we recommend.

Method

Let's start with garments. Group your clothes by type and by color, light to dark or the other way around. Just as you discovered and organized your wardrobe according to color, your closet should likewise be arranged by color. Hang all your blouses side by side in one area. Next, tops; then jackets, slacks, jeans, shorts and skirts. Hang items that fit the top half of your body in one area, the garments for the bottom half in the next (or below if there's room). Dresses and coats hang in their own areas. As we recommended earlier when we were experimenting with new wardrobe combinations, don't hang outfits together. Suit jackets and the tops of two-piece dresses belong in their respective categories, as do suit skirts and pants and the skirt portions of two-piece dresses. To gain room, add an expanding rod beneath your original closet bar and hang blouses, tops and jackets on the closet rod and skirts, pants and shorts on the newly added rod below.

Store out-of-season garments in garment bags in the back reaches of your closet, in a hall closet if you're lucky enough to have one, or in storage boxes under your bed. Don't forget to add moth-proofing materials, if needed. Make your seldom-used luggage pieces (you know, the big Samsonite cases you took to college and haven't used since) do double duty as clothes storage. An old trunk or a straw hamper can be both decorative and practical for storage. Remember that most of your clothes can be worn for at least nine months out of twelve. Keep transseasonal pieces like blouses, cotton sweaters, lightweight wools and knits and almost anything made of silk in your closet year round.

Hang the clothes you wear less often, such as evening and dressy garments, in the back of your closet, and keep the front area accessible for the work and casual clothes you wear often. Hang robes and nightwear in a handy place, maybe on hooks on the closet or bathroom door or just inside your closet. We've found over-the-door hangers invaluable for our jumpsuits, caftans, dressing gowns and floor-length dresses. These extralong garments simply don't fit on conventional closet rods. With all your hanging garments, make sure there's enough space between hangers to prevent wrinkling.

Knit garments and sweaters should be stored flat or rolled in drawers or in clear plastic boxes. Hanging them up causes the knit to stretch, and the garment loses its shape in no time. A good tip is to lay or roll items in clear boxes and stack them on your closet shelf so that you can see them and reach them easily. The same gentle loving care is recommended for loosely woven or heavy fabrics such as beaded sweaters and fine, delicate antique garments. You'll want to add a layer of tissue paper between the folds of these special treasures.

The old adage out of sight, out of mind particularly applies to accessories. When shoes, belts, scarves, bags, hats and jewelry are all stashed away or hidden in drawers and shoe boxes, it's difficult to remember what you have, much less make use of all of them. Once you bring your accessories out in the open, you'll be pleasantly surprised by all the different looks made possible by combining them. You'll have more options than you ever imagined and, in true *Chic on a Shoestring* fashion, won't have to spend a lot of money on new accessories. It's a breeze to be well dressed from head to toe and neck to fingertips when all your accessories (or wardrobe "tools") are close at hand and visible.

We suggest hanging as many of your accessories as possible on racks, hooks and nails around the bedroom. When we're coordinating a fashion show and need the perfect bracelet, necklace or hat to complete a look, we simply cast our eyes around the room and pick the right piece off the wall. This system is incredibly time and energy efficient, and a heck of a lot of fun.

Shoes can be kept on shoe racks, in clear shoe boxes, in the original shoe boxes (clearly labeled), or in hanging shoe bags or racks on your closet door. Boots can be stored on the floor of your closet or closet shelf, or hung with special boot clips on hooks. To preserve their shape, make an inexpensive boot tree by stuffing the toes with tissue paper and the calves with tightly rolled newspaper. This will keep the boots standing upright and prevent wrinkles from forming at the ankles.

Belts with buckles should be arranged by color on a belt rack hung on the wall. We made one quickly and inexpensively by nailing $1\frac{1}{4}$-inch finishing nails at 2-inch intervals on an 18-inch board ($1'' \times 4''$ pine works fine). You can make yours any length. Spray paint, dry and install on your wall—all for under five dollars. Sashes, webbed belts, elastic cinches and other nonhanging types can be rolled and kept in clear boxes on shelves or under the bed.

Expandable pegged racks, the kind used in hallways for coats or in kitchens for coffee mugs, are inexpensive and ideal for hanging all sorts of accessories—belts with large buckles, bracelets, necklaces, beads, hats and bags. We've found ourselves adding more and more of these expanding wonders to our walls as our accessory collections grow. It's a great way to keep costume jewelry from getting all tangled.

Hats can be stored on their own individual hooks or on nails on the walls—create your own hat "exhibit." Hat boxes are being sold again, or look for old ones at garage sales, thrift shops or in grandmother's attic (maybe with a hat inside!). Another good bet are large see-through plastic boxes.

Wooden or brass coat trees can be found on sale (new) or in used furniture stores and can serve as a kind of miniature freestanding closet. They can be placed near a door and loaded with jackets, hats and umbrellas, or they can be used as an unusual touch in your bedroom laden with belts, hats, scarves and jewelry.

Another closet stretcher is the addition of a shelf unit or *étagère* to your boudoir. Simply stack those clear plastic sweater boxes, shoe and hat boxes on the shelves and *voilà!* You have cleverly and decoratively expanded your closet.

Gloves and scarves can be arranged by color in drawers or in clear boxes and then stacked on shelves. Plastic Ziploc bags in various sizes are good for keeping pairs of gloves together and clean. This is also a good trick for pantyhose and tights. If your underwear drawer is typical, it will benefit from grouping socks and hosiery together by color and style. Handbags can be stored in hanging compartmentalized garment bags (also good for scarves and sweaters) or hung on hooks.

A special word on fine jewelry: in these days of rising property crimes, law enforcement officials often recommend keeping good jewelry (precious gems, sterling silver and gold) in airtight containers hidden in unexpected places. The exact storage location is up to you; the point is, don't make it easy to steal your precious and irreplaceable jewelry.

Closet Tips
- Fishing tackle boxes make great jewelry boxes, fine for earrings, pins, chains, etc. They're easy to stash in hiding, too.
- Add the olfactory treat of sachets to your drawers and boxes, pomander balls hung in your closet and bowls or baskets of potpourri in your bedroom or closet at large.
- Don't let the space of closet and bedroom doors go to waste. Over-the-door hangers, hooks and pegboard can store clothing and accessories; hanging shoe bags take care of you know what.

- Let us not forget those of you who share your bedroom with a man. Why not enlist his help and enthusiasm for your closet expansion and organization project? For instance, he can display his hats, belts, ties and scarves right alongside your accessories. The two of you can easily follow the recipe as described for a his-and-hers closet.
- Pick up the closet accessories mentioned here in a *Chic on a Shoestring* fashion by shopping at less than retail. Hanging garment and compartmentalized accessory bags can be found on sale frequently at department store notion counters, as can shoe racks, boxes and all manner of hangers. Watch the newspaper ads. These same items are often available for less from mail order companies. Clear plastic boxes of all sizes, hangers, mug racks and belt racks are all readily available at dime stores and discount chains. Pick up your coat tree at a discount store or at a garage or charity bazaar. Two excellent catalog sources for storage and household accessories are Walter Drake & Sons, Drake Building, Colorado Springs, CO 80940; and Joan Cook, 3200 S.E. 14 Avenue, Fort Lauderdale, FL 33316. Write for a free catalog.

7
Chic Feet

The *Chic on a Shoestring* shoe credo can be summed up like this: First, build a wardrobe of classic, understated dressy and casual shoes and boots. Second, indulge yourself (if you're an admitted shoe freak like your authors) and treat yourself to high-fashion styles and bold or offbeat colors (purchased at bargain prices, of course).

Now, look in your own closet and take inventory of the shoes that form the core, so to speak, of your footwear wardrobe. Take another look at the wardrobe chart you filled out on page 52. Do you have all the pairs of classic pumps, Chanel-style slingbacks, boots and flats in the neutral shades you need for work? Are you like most of us, always hunting for the perfect pair of bone pumps or brown boots, for instance? Is your casual and sports shoe collection adequate? The minimum requirement is several pairs of well-proportioned classic styles in your light and dark neutrals in order to get the most out of your entire wardrobe.

Proportion

Shoes should be selected and worn with a careful eye on proportion, both in terms of the shoe to the wearer and to the overall outfit balance. The major fashion faux pas is not paying attention to a balanced proportion between the shoe and the outfit or wearer.

The same goes for appropriateness of the style of the shoe to the rest of the look. For example, a day dress worn to the office looks better with a pair of pumps than with open-toed strappy sandals or, worse yet, casual canvas shoes with thick crepe soles. A sophisticated wool or silk suit looks best with pumps, too, not a pair of shoes that are too low or casual or a pair of drop-dead 4-inch spike heels. It's especially important to finish office and business looks with the appropriate shoes. A conservative dress or suit coupled with a clunky pair of wooden-soled high heels or open-toed strappy sandals sends a mixed message. At the other end of the spectrum, dressy, frilly, sexy, feminine evening ensembles are best complemented by similarly styled strappy sandals or metallic pumps. Likewise, casual and leisure wear calls for suitably styled boots and shoes.

Color

As for color, we've mentioned the importance of owning classic basic footwear in your light and dark neutrals. You'll want a pair or two in your accent color or colors, too. Red is a favorite of many women as a wardrobe accent tone, and red shoes can be just the punch an outfit needs. The same goes for blue or pink and many other colors, depending on

62 • *Chic on a Shoestring*

As a rule, longer skirts look best when worn with medium-heeled pumps. The low-heeled ankle strap cuts the leg line in half and makes the body look proportionately bottom-heavy.

your taste. After you've fleshed out the basic colors in your shoe wardrobe, add a pair in a second bright or bold color. Or stretch your dressy looks with a pair of metallic or sparkly evening shoes.

Style

Classic styles in solid tones with few or no details are the best bets for the working core of your shoe wardrobe. Spend more money on these pumps and boots and make them your investment purchases. Until you've got this portion of your shopping done, stay away from exaggerated styling, prints, unusual color combinations and impractically high heels. All these shoes are by nature limited in the number of times they can be worn. Timeless styles to look for:

- Plain pumps with $1\frac{1}{2}''$–$2\frac{1}{2}''$ heels in neutral shades; also accent tones such as red or blue.
- Solid-tone slingback pumps with a closed toe, 2" or so heels.
- Chanel-style pumps in any neutral tone combination.
- Boots with heels up to 2" tall. Higher heels look sexy but throw the balance of the body off and are difficult to walk in.
- Spectator pumps with medium heel height in classic black patent and white or other combinations such as tan and white, brown and bone, etc.

When selecting pumps, look for a medium-width heel. Anything too skinny or too heavy and thick

Timeless shoe styles to look for when organizing a shoe wardrobe include (left to right): slingback pump, three-inch heel, penny loafer, ballet flat, medium-heeled boot and ankle-strap pump.

will date quickly. At the risk of overstating the importance of heel height for everyday and work wear, do stay away from *high* heels. Three- and four-inch heels throw the body's balance off to the extent that they're uncomfortable and difficult to walk in. How many times have you seen some well-dressed woman in drop-dead high heels struggling along an airport corridor with her bags or trying to hobble across the street before the light turns red? To quote a sage male friend of ours: "Women will never be liberated until they liberate their feet."

As for casual shoes, the ubiquitous tennis or running shoes go with almost any sports or casual outfit, are quite comfortable and good for your feet and, best of all, are readily available at low prices. Casual-style boots can be riding, cowboy, hiking or weatherproof. Low-heeled or flat casual shoes in canvas or leather, walking shoes, deck shoes, moccasins and espadrilles and flattering (not clunky) oxfords are all good options for the casual side of your footwear collection. With flats, as with any shoe, proportion to the rest of the outfit is important.

Flats look fine with jeans and slacks and usually complement knee-length skirts. Mid-calf-length skirts combined with flats make legs look short. Short and tall women often feel they can't wear flats. This isn't true; it's the proportion to the outfit that's important. Tuxedo pumps, ballet slippers and other kinds of flats are good options.

As we discuss in Chapter 12, a pair of black patent strappy sandals will see you through almost any dressy evening occasion, especially if you don't want to invest in a pair of strictly formal heels.

Quality Is Chic

Naturally you'll want to buy the best possible quality in materials and construction for the "investment" shoes and boots you wear frequently and expect to last for several years. Your own eye is the best judge here. Check to see if the shoe has leather uppers and soles. These are more expensive than man-made materials, but leather uppers are more comfortable because the leather "breathes." You shouldn't necessarily shy away from synthetic soles, since they usually last longer than leather and require less upkeep.

Check for smooth, even stitching and neat, trim unions where uppers meet soles and heels. Run your fingers along the insides of shoes and boots to make sure there are no rough, unfinished seams or joints to cause calluses or blisters.

General Price Category Guidelines and Best Buys

- $100 and up. All-leather shoes and boots, both European made and American designer and private label. You'll find the very latest fashions often in avant-garde styles and color combinations. Classic boots are probably the best buy in this category because the investment in quality and comfort will pay off in years of wear.
- Medium price range: $50–$100. Expect to find leather uppers, leather or man-made soles. Look for good-quality workmanship amid a wide selection of classic and traditional pumps in this price range. In this category, casual boot styles are best buys, also mid-height ($1\frac{1}{2}''$–$2\frac{1}{2}''$) heels.
- Lower-priced footwear: under $50. Well-made casual and sports shoes of leather, suede, canvas, mesh and vinyl are recommended. Also sandals, moccasins, espadrilles plus evening and dressy shoes worn infrequently are good buys under $50. Pumps with synthetic uppers and soles are available in this price range but are not a wise purchase if they will be worn often. Bend the sole to check flexibility and check arch support for wearing comfort.

Shoe Tips

- Allow your shoes time to breathe and rest between wearings. Don't wear the same pair two days in a row and, if possible, change into another pair of shoes in the evening.
- Shop for shoes in the afternoon, when feet are slightly larger, to avoid too snug a fit.
- Break in walking shoes by wearing them around

the house for at least a day or two before putting them to the test: walking to work or sightseeing by foot in Europe.
- Your shoe size may change by up to a full size in width or length between the ages of twenty and thirty. Have both feet measured when you shop for shoes.
- Find a brand of shoes or boots made from a "last" (particular shape and length of shoe instep) that fits your foot well and stick with it. Befriend a salesperson at your favorite store and get advance notice when your brand goes on sale, or call to check on new shipments.
- A well-fit shoe or boot has about $\frac{1}{2}''$ to spare in length beyond the toes. Beware of sales pitches about leather stretching to fit your foot or how a shoe repairman can stretch an instep. Only very minor alterations can be made. *If the shoe doesn't fit, don't buy it.*

Shopping for Shoes

As you're trying on footwear, ask yourself the following questions:
- How often will I wear these shoes? What's the cost per wear?
- What will they go with?
- How important is the latest fashion or fad to me? (Designer and "fashion" shoes command top dollar.)
- Are they comfortable? Walk around for several minutes in both shoes.
- Do they look good? Are they flattering? Look in a full length mirror to check the shoe's proportion to you. Ankle straps on tall, willowy legs look great but tend to cut shorter legs and heavier calves in half. Long, slender styles and lengthwise stripes or details do wonders for petite feet but make long, large feet look like small boats.

Where to Buy Chic Shoes
- Retail stores. Watch for special purchases and end-of-season sales.
- Discount shoe stores. True lifesavers, especially if you love shoes. Look for nationwide chains and check your newspaper and Yellow Pages for discount stores. Ask your friends and co-workers for their favorite discount outlets. In addition to their regular, less-than-retail stock, most discounters also have permanent sale racks or bargain tables. Shop these frequently since they have a high turnover and feature new merchandise often.
- Resale and consignment stores. Shoes can be the very best buys among the "gently worn" merchandise selection. Many women quickly recycle footwear that doesn't quite fit or just doesn't work in their wardrobes. Some of the best shoes in our wardrobes have come from resale stores: Saks Fifth Avenue spectator pumps for $16, black peau de soie slippers for $10, gorgeous purple (!) lizard and calfskin pumps for $7.50.
- Antique and vintage stores. If you're a shoe "gourmet" and like to collect classic or even offbeat footwear from past fashion eras, you'll enjoy the hunt at these stores. We've found several pairs

Fashionable Italian shoe-boots for hiking in the concrete jungle. The original retail price was $195; Leigh picked these up for a mere $60 at an outlet for a chic Rodeo Drive boutique.

of beautiful pumps in excellent condition for only $15–$25 at antique stores.
- Mail order. Catalogs make fashionable shoes available to everyone. To decrease the likelihood of having to mail back a pair that doesn't fit, send a tracing of both feet with your order. Casual shoes that lace or have adjustable straps, sandals and slings are probably your best bet. (See Chapter 23 for recommendations of companies with catalogs for special, hard-to-fit sizes.)
- Grocery and drugstores. Casual summer sandals and beach shoes are affordable and fun when purchased in a nonshoe store. We bought molded plastic sandals in a grocery store for $4 and then saw the same shoe for $17 in Bloomingdale's summer catalog.

8
Chic Accoutrements

Creative Essentials

As clothing becomes more and more expensive, accessories become more valuable. Accessories are the *Chic on a Shoestring* way to stretch your wardrobe and keep it fashionable. Combining and recombining shoes, hats, gloves, scarves, belts and jewelry with even a small wardrobe of dresses and separates can create countless looks and outfits.

Besides inexpensively stretching a wardrobe, accessories really complete or "finish" an outfit. A simple suit and blouse becomes a distinctive ensemble with a pair of good leather pumps, a pin on the jacket lapel or a string of pearls, coordinating earrings and perhaps a pair of gloves or a hat. Many women simply drop the ball when it comes to using accessories. There is no need to fumble when the addition of just one piece of jewelry can transform "clothes" into "fashion." To start, experiment with an accessory you feel comfortable with—do you like rings, pins, scarves or bracelets? Put on a scarf, a necklace or a bracelet in front of your full length mirror before you go off to work in the morning or out for the evening and study the effect. Much like punctuation in a sentence helps us understand the writer's emphasis and intent, accessories punctuate an outfit and say to the viewer: "I know what I'm wearing and I mean it." Doesn't this extra accessory help your look? Take the time and enjoy the fun and satisfaction of exploring your own style this way.

Another advantage of accessories is their timelessness. Most accessory pieces, especially quality, classic items, don't go out of style but remain hardworking fashion components for years. Designers know the value of accessories and have jumped on the bandwagon with everything from shoes and hosiery to hats and briefcases.

Whether you choose designer-label accoutrements or not, pay special attention to proportion when selecting accessories. Each of your accessories needs to complement you—your body and frame. Check the proportion of a hat, a pair of shoes, a handbag or whatever in front of a full length mirror. Merely looking at a potential pair of earrings in a jewelry countertop mirror or a pair of boots in a shoe department floor mirror won't give you the whole picture. Your eyes won't tell you whether or not the accessory "fits" you until you try it on—just like clothing. Check for the balance of the accessory with your height and build. Does it overpower you or is it so small it's unnoticeable? Where does the accent piece fall on your body? Is this an area you want to call attention to?

Accessories play an important role in our wardrobes because they allow us to take chances with a color or a pattern at low cost. A $75 dress that doesn't fit after it's washed winds up a costly mistake. Two dollars spent on a bright bangle or $3.50 on a paisley print scarf, on the other hand, won't break anyone's clothing budget and might just rescue that so-so dress. Accessories are an inexpensive means to have fun with your clothes, your wardrobe, your own sense of style. Think of yourself as a connoisseur of accessories and begin to collect them wherever and whenever you see them.

Caveat: even though we advocate using accessories to polish your look and express your personal style, we realize that as with many things in life, accessories can be overdone. We've all seen women who look like a walking jewelry box. Trust your own eye to tell you when you've got just the right mix of pieces for your outfit that creates the desired effect. If in doubt, remember designer Coco Chanel's famous maxim: "Get dressed and then take off one piece of jewelry."

A Wardrobe of Accessories
Belts

For starters, choose belts in light and dark neutral colors that fit into your wardrobe. One-inch-wide good-quality leather belts are a good beginning point, but look at your own figure and proportion and experiment with different widths—a wide leather sash, an ultrathin metallic snake belt, an elastic cinch, for instance. To emphasize your waist, try a bright or light color. Pick up a neutral or accent color in a dress and experiment with belts you have hanging in your closet. We have found elastic belts especially useful, comfortable and versatile since they go well over many different fabrics and can change a silhouette in a jiffy. Another style you might consider is a shaped belt. One that dips to a V in front can be especially flattering to the waistline.

Fashion your own belts quickly and inexpensively out of:
- Men's ties. Wrap around your waist or hips, twist several together or braid and tie them obi-fashion.
- Hardware materials. Colored plastic extension cords, lightweight chain, insulated wire.
- Drapery tiebacks or gold or silver satin cords for fancy rope belts. Available in drapery departments of Sears, etc.
- Cord, twine, ribbon from a notions department. Especially good if you need a belt in a color combination not easily found. Simply knot together satin cord, soutache braid, gold braid or whatever appeals to your eye. Can also be used as a necklace.

You really can't have too many good belts of all kinds in your wardrobe. Look for them wherever you shop.

Creative scarf and belt treatments distinguish a look and put a lot of variety into your wardrobe for very little cash.

Where to buy belts:
- boys' departments and girls' departments
- sales
- thrift shops
- resale stores
- bargain basements
- discount chains
- hardware stores
- notions counters

Scarves

Once again, it's hard to have too many. The variety of sizes, colors, prints, weaves, fabrics, textures and styles makes scarves endlessly fun to collect and wear imaginatively. They can range from small squares and rectangles (including antique handkerchiefs) for pockets and neckwear to large squares and rectangles all the way to shawls (which are really very large scarves). Scarves are the most versatile of all accessories since they can change shape and function with a quick twist or relocation. A scarf can be a sash, a belt or a necklace, for instance. Scarves can be considered as items of clothing, too, and worn as swimsuits, sarongs, wraps and skirts.

You'll need scarves in both solids and prints. Solids will pick up tones in prints or add the right accent color to an outfit or frame the face in a flattering shade. Prints are especially good worn with suits; they soften the monochromatic, serious look and add visual interest to an otherwise solid color mass.

Scarf suggestions:

- Small silk squares to put into a vest pocket or around the neck. Cotton bandannas to tie around the neck.
- Long cotton or gauze rectangles to wrap the head or tie around the waist or hips. Nonslippery fabrics work best and stay in place.
- Antique lace or embroidered handkerchiefs add a feminine touch in a suit pocket or pinned to a lapel.
- Shawls. Even 54-inch-square bridge cloths can be transformed into shawls. Simply fold in half on the diagonal. You might think about dyeing or hand painting an antique cloth.
- Fabric remnants. Put a quick hem on a fabric of any shape or size and, presto, you have a custom-made scarf, sash or shawl.
- Try putting a rectangular shawl over your shoulder and then put a belt over the shawl to hold it in place—very French-looking. A solid-color belt over a print shawl or vice versa is a nicely balanced combination.

Ways to use scarves (scarf tricks):

- belt or sash at waist or hips
- halter bra
- head wrap
- necklace
- ascot
- bandanna
- dress
- shawl
- sunsuit

Where to buy:

- bargain basements
- sales
- discount chains and dime stores
- resale and antique stores
- charity bazaars

Handbags

These are the bane of every woman's wardrobe because of the difficulty in finding *one* bag that meets your practical needs, is fashionable and flattering and of high quality so it will last through several seasons. We all ask a lot of our bags: traveling to and from the office and on errands, serving as makeup kits and even as miniature closets at times. Most of us don't like to change bags or live in more than one at a time. With all of this in mind, here are our suggestions for handbags to purchase.

In choosing a bag, consider color, material, your lifestyle (what is the best overall style and size for your needs) and quality of construction. Pick a neutral color complementary to most of your wardrobe. Generally a lighter tone works in summer, darker in winter.

The common mistakes in selecting and wearing a bag: incorrect proportion, overstuffing that in turn ruins the bag's lines, fussy prints in fabric bags worn with outfits of conflicting prints or colors. Wearing the wrong shoes and/or bag is the easiest way to blow an outfit. Getting these two accessories right takes a little thought, not a lot of money. Look at yourself in a full length mirror and check the proportion.

Make sure that you have basic, solid-color bags that will go with most of the outfits in your wardrobe. The fewer details on the bag, the more you can use it with other accessories and the less it will tend to go out of style.

You might start with two light neutrals (white, ivory, cream, beige, taupe, grey, khaki or camel) and two dark neutrals (black, navy, dark brown, wine, aubergine or mahogany). Choose one large bag for day, one smaller one, perhaps a clutch, for evening. Black patent is an all-season bag if black is part of your day or dress wardrobe. Working women need a good leather valise or an attaché in a primary neutral. Look for styles that combine the uses of a purse and a briefcase with small compartments as well as large ones for papers.

Where to buy handbags:
- end-of-season sales
- manufacturers' outlets
- department store special purchase sales
- designer discount stores
- thrift shops—for inexpensive evening bags
- resale stores—for classics
- budget stores—for canvas and ripstop nylon (parachute cloth) bags
- mail order catalogs

Jewelry

It's probably best to wear honest jewelry, the best you can afford, rather than a lot of imitation pieces. Real bamboo and genuine plastic are preferable to fake gold and faux gems. The common mistakes with jewelry occur at opposite ends of the spectrum, wearing either too much or too little. We all know women who leave the house clanking from lots and lots of chains and bracelets and fingers dripping with oversized rings of all descriptions. The reverse is not taking the time or effort to finish an outfit by adding a bracelet or pin.

Jewelry can be used effectively to draw attention

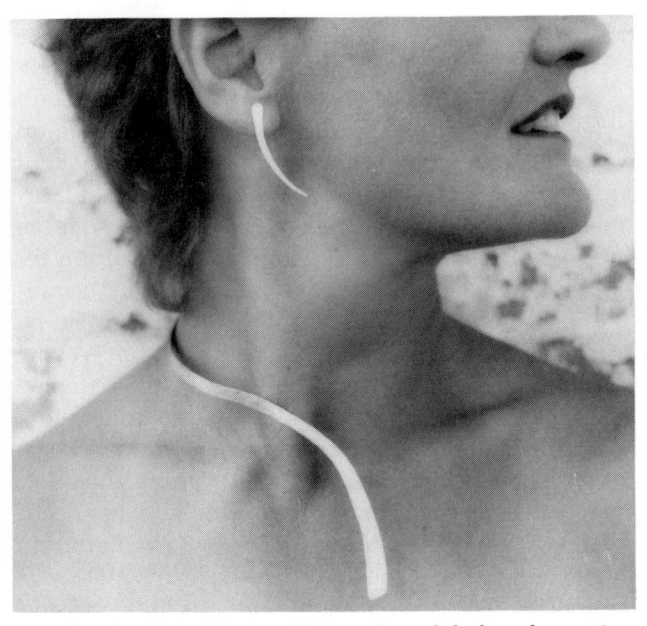

Jewelry designer Megan Diamond models her dramatic yet affordable sterling jewelry.

to your own best features. Chokers and earrings highlight the face; rings and bracelets set off lovely, graceful hands; pins and necklaces show off a pretty, long neck. Experiment with different jewelry combinations to achieve the effect you want. Try some different colors, too. Most of us have favorite types of jewelry. We're "bracelet people" or we're very fond of earrings. Begin by experimenting with your favorites.

Choose the precious metal pieces (gold or silver) that best flatter your skin tones. Gold works best for blondes and women with warm skin tones, silver for cooler skin tones. Platinum, a light, bright silverish metal, and pewter, a darker steel grey, complement cool skins.

One of the best ways to express your personal style inexpensively is through collecting your favorite jewelry pieces. Look for them wherever you shop and before long you'll have lots of interesting things to choose from. We have a friend whose pin repertoire is second to none, with brooches and pins acquired at prices ranging from five cents to five hundred dollars. All express her unique personal style.

When you're reading fashion magazines, note how jewelry is used in the fashion layouts and ads. Are big plastic bangles shown with the new styles? Try the looks shown that might work well for you and experiment with your own jewelry to stretch your jewelry wardrobe.

Learn to use jewelry accessory pieces in several ways. Some multiple use accessories:

- Button earrings—try them as shoe trim or cuff links; also clipped to a choker of velvet ribbon or lace.
- Pearl necklace—wrap around your wrist and make into a bracelet, or use as a rope belt.
- Pins—try them in a variety of locations such as at the bow of a sash or on a ribbon headband.
- Wear a pretty, sparkly pin on the neckline of the *back* of a sexy, back-baring evening dress.

Where to buy jewelry:

- thrift shops—especially for "fashion repeats" such as pearls, circle pins and rhinestones
- antique stores—great for celluloid bracelets and pins
- wholesale jewelry outlets and catalogs
- discount chain stores
- bargain basements

Invest in classic pieces that don't go out of style; spend your "mad money" on bright colors and bold shapes you might not otherwise wear.

Hosiery

Hosiery of all types has evolved from being simply utilitarian to serving as an integral element of fashion. Many designers are now marketing their own lines of signature hosiery. The best fashion advice for hosiery is to match it to your shoe and skirt or pants for a long, sleek line. The unity of color has a slenderizing effect. A good neutral hose is the tone closest to your own skin tone or one darker. Avoid the inexpensive suntan or cinnamon shades that give legs an unnatural reddish color.

Where to buy hose:

- discount catalogs
- grocery stores and drugstores
- chain stores such as Sears and JC Penney
- department store basements
- specialty and department store sales
- wholesale hosiery outlets

For everyday wear it's a waste of money to buy expensive hose. They are usually so delicate, they just don't stand up to the rigors of ten-, twelve- and fourteen-hour days. Save your legwear budget for special supersheer evening hose or a color you can't find at the kinds of stores just listed. Support hose wear longer and are now as sheer as most daytime hosiery.

Hats and Gloves

In winter climates gloves and hats are a necessity. A good pair of leather gloves is required for dress and for driving, plus a knit or casual pair. Hats, caps, tams, earmuffs and wool turbans are also used for warmth. Hats can be a fashion signature, too. Designers include them in every couture and ready-to-wear collection.

Where to buy hats and gloves:

- thrift shops
- antique clothing stores—among the best sources for hats and gloves, which were important in fashion of decades past
- resale and consignment shops
- chains—Penney, Ward and Sears—for mufflers, gloves, hats, tams
- woolen outlets
- leather outlets

Hats and gloves are being worn again to finish off an outfit and add a note of feminine drama.

9
Menswear to Your-wear

Incorporating a few items of masculine apparel into your own wardrobe can be a terrific way to manifest a unique personal style and save money, too. There's something truly alluring and downright sexy about a woman in a man's button-down shirt, trench coat or oversized sweater. The loose fit and traditional male silhouette and tailoring can emphasize femininity by contradicting or challenging our preconceived ideas about "male" and "female" attire.

Our image of strong, sexy women wearing men's clothes as their own or incorporating man-tailoring into their wardrobes dates from Hollywood movies of the twenties through forties. Who can forget Marlene Dietrich in her tuxedo or Katharine Hepburn in her gabardine slacks? More recently we have seen Diane Keaton popularize thrift-shop shopping for men's clothes with her Annie Hall look. Julie Andrews created a fashion sensation and revived the tuxedo look for women with her sexy, androgynous look in *Victor/Victoria*.

Designers of women's clothing often incorporate menswear silhouettes, tailoring details and fabrics into their collections with predictable regularity because women respond to the classic styling and no-nonsense image. With more women working and competing for executive positions, we can count on a continuing menswear influence in women's clothing. The trick now is to learn how to make the look unique (we don't want to fall into the male grey flannel suit syndrome) and stay within a *Chic* budget. Here are ways to expand your wardrobe inexpensively with men's and boys' clothing.

Shop Smart in the Boys' Department
Petite women have discovered a shopping secret. They have been mining boys' departments for clothes that fit and are less expensive than similar women's clothing. You don't have to be petite to save a bundle on select wardrobe pieces from the boys' department. Staples such as jeans, polo-style shirts and jogging shorts are found in all of our wardrobes. Buy boys' sizes and save.

Boys' clothing is usually traditional in styling and therefore good for a woman who prefers classics in her closet. A designer-brand blazer in a boys' size will cost 20 to 40 percent less than a similar woman's blazer. Labels ranging from Wrangler and Levi's to Ralph Lauren and Pierre Cardin are marketed for the entire family, so you'll be able to find all your favorites. Use this shopping modus operandi in chain stores (JC Penney, Sears, etc.), department and specialty stores (Saks Fifth Avenue), athletic clothing

Women can shop smart and save money in the boys' departments. This mother-son team shows the fashion possibilities in their interpretation of nearly identical outfits.

stores and even well-known men's stores such as Brooks Brothers. Once you learn which sizes and styles are appropriate, you can take advantage of sales and good values in catalogs and discount stores.

Shirts, sweaters, belts, ties, sweat suits and casual wear such as T-shirts, rugby shirts and shorts make good *Chic* purchases. More hot tips:

- Boys' blazers. Designer labels such as Ralph Lauren run $50 to $60 less in the boys' department for the same (or better) quality of fabric and workmanship than those found in the women's department. Boys' blazers look best on small- and medium-busted women.
- Pants and jeans. Boys' sizes fit best on slim-hipped or junior-size women. For those of us who need to create a waist after getting the correct hip measurement, take two darts in the back waistband. Ask stores if they offer free or low-cost alterations. Ralph Lauren pants are cut fuller through the leg and will work better on most women, or look for a boys' pleat-front trouser.
- Name brands. Look for your favorites, such as a Burberry's raincoat or Sperry Top-Siders, as a point of size and price comparison as you begin to shop the boys' department.
- Men's clothing. Don't despair if you can't fit into boys' sizes. Experiment with men's small or medium, even large if you like a roomy fit.

Equivalent Size Chart

Shirts

Women's	Boys'
4	14
6	16
8	18
10	20
12	22 (cadet or student size)

Pants and Jeans

6	26 or 27
8	27 or 28
10	29 or 30

Shoes run one and a half sizes smaller in boys' sizes.

6½	5

In addition to shopping in the boys' department for new clothes, you can also "borrow" items from

Menswear to Your-Wear • 75

your son's or brother's closet. If he protests, offer to bankroll an afternoon at his favorite video arcade.

Out of His Closet—What to Borrow from a Man
Now for the fun part—raid your man's closet for gems you can call your own (at least once in a while). Since it costs you nothing to shop on the other side of the closet (unless he, too, likes video games), anything goes here. Use your imagination to stretch your wardrobe and your self-image.

There's more to this *Chic* fashion adventure than just throwing on a man's shirt, vest and trousers. Synthesizing men's pieces into your own look takes a good measure of self-confidence, a dash of imagination and a pinch of panache. A touch of fashion whimsy and a sense of humor don't hurt, either. One of the best rules for wearing men's clothing is to pair a masculine item with something frankly feminine or sexy. This prevents you from looking like you're trying to ape men in their attire and allows you to assert your own feminine sense of style. Unusual nonmasculine color combinations (a man's pink oxford cloth shirt worn with your tight lavender jeans, for example) make your look distinctive. Accessories are another way to transform male garments into a feminine, pulled-together look. Bracelets, pins, earrings and high-heeled shoes are just a few of the fashion tools we women can put to use.

Menswear Tips

- Tuck a big shirt into a skirt or pants or knot one at the waist. Belt an oversized shirt low on the hips or use a long scarf to fanny wrap a big shirt over slim jeans or a straight leather skirt. Wear a lacy camisole, teddy or leotard under his shirt—open, of course—to reveal the feminine detail. Convert his big shirt into a tunic or a nightshirt.
- Knot a man's T-shirt at the waist or midriff, or belt or sash it at the hips. Wear your man's T-shirt as a tunic or nightshirt, as a miniskirt over tights or as a swimsuit or leotard cover-up.

This man's double-breasted wool overcoat cost $10 at a thrift store and only needed the addition of a set of shoulder pads to deliver several hundred dollars' worth of fashion savvy. The long-sleeved man's rayon shirt worn here as a cardigan cost an unbelievable 15¢ at a church bazaar and merely needed to be dry-cleaned.

- Overcoats with raglan sleeves accommodate feminine shoulders more easily than those with set-in sleeves. However, a pair of shoulder pads will generally fill out the shoulder dimension to balance the coat proportion. Skip the $400 man-tailored overcoats offered each year and go straight to your man's closet or to your local thrift shop and pick up a wool reefer for under $10.
- Hats have returned to fashion, but before investing $40 to $80 in a classic fedora, ask the men you know if they have any unused hats hidden away.
- Put shoulder pads in men's shirts or sweaters for an inexpensive Kamali look, or add an extra pair to a jacket or coat to improve the fit.
- Oversized sweaters and sweater vests are great worn as a top layer over jumpsuits or anything with shoulder pads. Wear a man's sweater loose for lounging or pulled low over the derriere with tight jeans and heels for sex appeal.
- Suit vests add a whimsical touch of color and pattern when worn as a top layer over an oversized shirt augmented with shoulder pads. Belt the waist or wrap the fanny to define the female shape beneath the layers, add a tie and a jaunty hat and you're set.
- The tuxedo look comes and goes out of fashion favor but is always a reliable evening ensemble. Instead of buying some designer's expensive interpretation off the rack, create your own with a tuxedo shirt purchased or rented from a formal attire shop and a boy's or small man's tuxedo or dark-colored suit. Create a waist on the man's pants by cinching with the cummerbund. Break up the suit to get more looks and experiment with various evening tops—angora or beaded sweaters, camisoles and leotards are good bets.
- When wearing men's clothing, it's important to define the female form underneath (otherwise you'll just look sloppy and careless). Create a waist where none exists by belting or cinching men's trousers over or slightly beneath the belt loops. You'll get an interesting high-waisted, zoot-suit look.
- Ties of all kinds belong on both sides of the closet, so get more mileage for your money and borrow his. Wide, colorful ties also make fun belts and sashes.
- Men's accessories such as hats, belts, cuff links and handkerchiefs take on new importance when worn by a woman.

Where to Buy

If you don't have ready access to a closetful of masculine apparel, you may want to purchase a piece or two for your own wardrobe. In addition to shopping discount stores and retail store sales, check your phone book for resale or consignment shops in your area. Find out if they carry men's apparel. We also recommend:

- Thrift shops, church bazaars and garage sales. These are veritable gold mines for quality men's clothing in good condition. Look for blazers, sweaters, scarves and ties. Overcoats and trench coats retail for several hundred dollars but can usually be found here for $10 or less. The key is fabric—avoid polyester and double knits and select garments made from cotton, wool, rayon and silk.
- Antique and vintage clothing stores are also treasure troves for classic and campy men's garments from decades past. You can often dress in the latest menswear-inspired fashion look by picking up an older (and frequently more interesting) version for a fraction of the comparable retail cost. Look for rayon challis, cotton or silk bowling and Hawaiian print shirts, classic Pendleton wool shirts and shirt jackets, white dinner jackets (dye them for fun), coats, vests and jackets. Silk and satin robes and smoking jackets, cotton nightshirts and flannel two-piece pajama sets are terrific finds.
- Military gear frequently surfaces as a fashion trend. Buy the real thing for a fraction of the cost

at a surplus store or peruse the antique clothing stores for World War II bomber jackets. Shop surplus stores for practical and rugged gear such as rain ponchos, pea coats, khaki slacks, shirts, jumpsuits and shorts, down vests and boots. Don't forget, women's military gear is now also sold at surplus stores.

Men's clothing spells smart shopping and sharp dressing the *Chic on a Shoestring* way.

SECTION III
Stretch Your Chic Wardrobe (And Thereby Your Dollars)

10
Transseasonal Chic

Transseasonal dressing may be a new concept to some of you, but rest assured you'll be hearing more about it. The transseasonal (or spanning the seasons) concept of clothing can also be defined as *seasonless* dressing. Transseasonal clothes know no particular season and can thus be worn all year round. They don't have to be retired to the back of the closet at the end of one season and dug out and sent to the cleaners at the start of the next. These clothes give you a lot of bang for your buck and can be the backbone of your wardrobe. As you might well imagine, transseasonal wardrobe pieces work particularly well for travel, too.

The cost of this type of dressing is kept to a minimum, since it's based on a few pieces purchased at the best possible prices. Since each piece is worn many times in several different ways throughout the year, the cost per wearing

$$\left(\frac{\text{purchase price}}{\text{number of times worn}} = \frac{\text{cost per wearing}}{\text{or CPW}}\right)$$

is low. For instance, a $50 silk blouse worn twenty times has a CPW of only $2.50. As you can see, even a more costly item ends up with a low CPW when it's worn frequently.

More and more top American and European designers are including transseasonal pieces in their collections. They realize that women increasingly demand versatile clothes of quality that can be worn around the calendar and, for those who travel, around the globe. (More specific designer recommendations on transseasonal dressing appear a little later in this chapter.) As we discuss this means of dressing, you can be thinking of the pieces in your own wardrobe that already qualify as transseasonal and discover particular items you might like to shop for.

We should note that our definition of transseasonal dressing encompasses about nine months of the year for most parts of the country. The cold and snowy winter months and hot and humid weeks of the summer naturally dictate apparel appropriate for those extremes. For those of us in the South and Southwest, the transseasonal concept stretches over all twelve months.

The Three Principles of Seasonless Dressing
There are three principles of seasonless dressing: silhouette or style, color and, most important, fabric (weight and fiber content). For the most part this means classic shapes and styles in neutral colors with a few bright tones, and light- to medium-weight fabrics in natural fibers.

Silhouette

Classics with a certain sense of style work best here; simple shapes that stand the test of time. Anything with an exaggerated style will be out of date before you know it. The layering abilities of a garment are central to the transseasonal idea. In warmer months or temperate climates, items are worn alone, in one layer. As fall and winter approach, these same pieces are layered for warmth. Suggestions for transseasonal shapes:

- wrap skirts and dresses
- tunics
- jumpers
- chemises
- T-shirts and T-shirt dresses
- classic straight-leg pants
- sleeveless tops
- vests
- shirtwaist dresses
- blazers
- cardigan jackets

Color

Neutrals of all hues are the key to seasonless dressing. You can build the transseasonal component of your wardrobe around your own light and dark neutrals. In the wintertime you can wear more of the darker shade with some of your favorite light neutral, and when the weather turns to spring and summer, you can shift the emphasis to mostly light with some touches of dark and brighter accents. Don't forget your accent colors. Tones such as red and primary blue really know no particular time of year and are now seen during all twelve months.

This isn't to say there are any hard-and-fast rules about color; only that you'll probably find neutrals more versatile and, therefore, get more use out of them than a wardrobe of a lot of prints or mostly brights. We do see a gradual shift by designers to the use of more of the entire color palette year round. Color has been liberated. For example, several seasons ago pink was the important accent color for fall, and all sorts of olive and loden green tones showed up in summer clothes.

Fabrics

Fabrics—their weight and fiber content—ultimately determine whether a garment is seasonless. Choose natural fibers. We recommend silk, cotton and perhaps linen, if you can live with the wrinkles. Rayon, a man-made fabric from natural fibers, is a good candidate, as are blends that have a high natural/low synthetic fiber balance, for example, 85 percent cotton to 15 percent polyester.

Specific fabrics to look for:

- Silk. Almost any weave; medium weights are usually best: silk crepe de chine, silk jersey, silk broadcloth, raw silk.
- Cotton. Again, almost anything goes made of cotton: poplin, lightweight twill, gabardine, corduroy, cotton jersey and knit.
- Wool. Lightweight wool crepe, gabardine, worsted and flannel, wool jersey.
- Lightweight denim, preferably all or mostly cotton.
- Velour.
- Knits. Light to medium weight.

Transseasonal Pieces

To combine all three parts of transseasonal dressing, here are some suggestions for garments you probably already have in your closet. Now you can look at them in a seasonless context and come up with more ways to wear them.

- Lightweight wool crepe suit, blazer or classic tailored slacks. If you need only one suit in your wardrobe, make it one in wool crepe. An A-line skirt in wool crepe is a good bet, too.
- Cotton, rayon or wool challis dress, shirtwaist dress, or jumper.
- T-shirts and T-shirt dresses in cotton knit and silk jersey.
- Cotton broadcloth or oxford cloth shirts.

- Silk blouses and tops.
- Light- to medium-weight cotton, silk or cotton/silk blend sweaters and cardigans. Look for silk/nylon blends, too.
- Floor-length silk crepe skirt. Year-round evening wear.
- Silk camisoles.
- Knit two-piece suit, perhaps in a Chanel style.
- Rayon shirts, especially vintage 1940s men's styles.
- Denim skirts, jeans, jackets, jumpsuits.
- Cotton and lightweight wool sweaters and cardigans.
- Cotton knit pullovers and turtlenecks.
- Silk crepe blouse in your light neutral and silk or lightweight wool crepe slacks in your dark neutral.
- Almost anything in lightweight cashmere knit: sweaters of all kinds, sweater dresses, shawls, sweater coats.
- Cotton broadcloth or poplin jumpsuits.
- Silk dresses: one- and two-piece.
- Vests, woven and knit.

Action wear (leotards and tights) also fits into the transseasonal mode. Leotards can be worn as the tops of outfits or as swimsuits, or they can be worn under other layers to add warmth. See the Cheap Jock Chic chapter for more details.

Tips from Designers

Several well-known designers have been incorporating seasonless dressing into their designs and collections for several years now. We thought you might appreciate a summary of some of the best designers and their thoughts on the subject.

Geoffrey Beene: "At this point, I'd say a woman should aim for at least half her wardrobe in seasonless clothes. These should include a weightless raincoat, a cardigan in silk that can be worn as a blouse or a jacket; skirts in knits or silks; sweaters in cotton, silk or rayon; and a series of pants in chino, fine corduroy and silk. As far as fabrics, wool jersey is seasonless for skirts and pants but not for tops."

Transseasonal wardrobe pieces include (left to right): a floor-length silk crepe skirt and silk knit sweater, a lightweight wool crepe suit with A-line skirt and cardigan jacket and a denim jumpsuit.

London designer Jean Muir: "Seasonless dressing has been my philosophy for years. Some colors are seasonless—navy, black or beige for a cold climate; white or beige for a warm one. Also a good red. I think the best seasonless fabrics are matte jersey, wool crepe, light suedes and any fine jerseys—plain, crinkled or glittered. Separates are the most versatile because you can interchange them: a matte jersey blouse can be worn with a skirt or with trousers. That's just the beginning of what you can do with seasonless pieces."

Paris designer Sonia Rykiel, so famous for her knits: "I have used the same fabrics, the same weight, the same quality, for twenty years. I always see jersey, crepe knits, lurex and terry velour as the basics of seasonless dressing. I believe so strongly in seasonless dressing that I feel a woman's wardrobe, today, should be a hundred percent in this spirit. You change your basic pieces by using distinctive accessories in a fantastic way. For instance, a dramatic bathing suit under a cardigan . . . a *paillette* ribbon worn diagonally from shoulder to waistline as a decoration . . . an extraordinary necklace—it's great to be a bit crazy."

Zoran: "I feel a woman could build a seasonless wardrobe by sticking to cashmere, crepe de chine or charmeuse and gabardine or flannel. Even her choice of colors could enhance this seasonless approach. For instance, I build my collections around pure white, ivory, a grey palette ranging from silver to pewter and charcoal, plus two strong brights that I see for any season—red and purple. Seasonless dressing is what I call 'Jet Pack'—you take six or seven pieces in cashmere, crepe or flannel in black or white and you're ready to travel all over the world, summer and winter."

Donna Karan of Anne Klein: "I see seasonless dressing based on fabrics and colors. For instance, there are certain fabrics, such as wool crepe or crepe de chine, that you can wear day and night. Leathers and suedes are year-round materials. I personally wear suede pants even in summer. Suede breathes, so it's comfortable regardless of the temperature. Other fabrics that I see as year-round basics include silk tweeds, cashmere, a new fine flannel, and all types of wool or cotton sweaters. A woman should keep about thirty percent of her wardrobe in seasonless fabrics. Besides black and white, I see navy and ivory in flannel as good season-spanning basics. Other years, I played up gabardine, but I think a fine flannel is richer, softer, and lighter. If I had to choose three pieces for versatile year round dressing, they would be a fabulous pair of pants, a cashmere sweater dress, and a cardigan jacket, each in black, navy or ivory."

Seasonless Shopping
Where do you find all these seasonless wonders? First of all, in your own closet. Now you are able to view your own clothes with the added perspective of transseasonal dressing. You might even list your clothes that fit into this category; you may be surprised at how many things you already have that work this way. Add the items you need to your wardrobe shopping list.

We've mentioned designers and their clothes. In addition to finding designer labels at discount stores, shop the well-advertised department and specialty store sales. If you're a credit card customer, you'll receive advance notices by mail. Mail order shopping is another option, especially from better stores and those companies specializing in natural fibers. (See Chapter 23.)

These transseasonal pieces, because they are of natural fabrics, may well cost more than their synthetic counterparts. The investment is well worth it, though, since these garments can be worn all year round. Better stores and even designer departments will probably be your best bet for quality buys on silk and wool garments. You'll be able to balance your wardrobe budget with less expensive cotton and rayon and fine blends at discount stores.

11
Travel Chic-ly

A successful travel wardrobe is the essence of being *Chic on a Shoestring*. The ideal is to travel light with a choice, finely tuned wardrobe that will enable you to be well dressed and comfortable wherever you go. Time and money savings are also factored into the *Chic* travel wardrobe.

Wardrobe Guidelines
Color, fabric and coordinating separates that mix and match and can be layered make up the principles of a travel wardrobe that works anywhere, anytime, no matter what your personal style.

Select two main colors for your trip, say your light and dark neutrals. You can then add one or two of your accent colors. Solid tones really work best for travel; however, if your wardrobe includes a lot of prints, select those that work with your neutrals. This way you gain a lot of options in mixing and matching with the advantage of taking very few pieces. Sample color combinations:
- Black, white and red.
- Navy, pearl grey and peach.
- Burgundy, tan and rose or gold as an accent.
- Black and white (Simple, elegant, always in fashion and dramatic enough for evening.)
- Black and khaki with red or bronze for accent.
- Red, white and blue or navy. (These nautical tones are especially good for summer travel.)
- Black with any color for cold climates; white with any color for warm weather.

Traveling in comfort and style necessitates choosing clothes made of natural fibers for breathability—warmth in the winter, cool comfort in summer heat and humidity. Blends of mostly natural and a small percentage of synthetic fibers reduce wrinkling. Examples are cotton/polyester, cotton/lycra spandex, silk/polyester, linen/rayon, wool/polyester, wool/acrylic, cotton/nylon and silk/nylon.

The three major natural fibers—cotton, silk and wool—travel well. Linen, on the other hand, isn't a good choice unless your lady-in-waiting–cum–laundress happens to be traveling with you. Knits are excellent travelers since they don't wrinkle. A cotton-blend knit dress or suit will take the trip better than cotton poplin or broadcloth. Another good travel fabric is cotton gauze—the wrinkles are built in! Wool and silk crepes are also smart selections, since crepe wrinkles less than almost any other fabric. If you have to include a suit, make it one fashioned from crepe. Raw silk, which is heavier than other silk weaves, works well in an area where day and evening temperatures vary a great deal, such as in a desert climate.

Many of the same principles that apply to transseasonal dressing are also applicable to your travel wardrobe. This is especially true of the layering concept. Wear a single layer during warmer daytime hours or during spring and summer. Add another layer as evening temperatures cool, or add layers for winter travel. Always keep your bulkiest layer on the outside.

Your travel wardrobe will include some of the following pieces. Note especially the double-duty nature of some of the clothes, such as leotards and a maillot swimsuit.

- Suit. Two-piece skirt or pantsuit. Crepe is a good fabric choice; also gabardine or knit.
- Dress. Two-piece for versatility.
- Separates. Blouse, top, jacket, skirt, sweater. Make sure these go with the suit and/or dress.
- Maillot. A one-piece solid-color swimsuit that doubles as a top with a skirt or pants or can be worn with the suit under the jacket.
- Sarong or big (50" × 50") square scarf in silk or cashmere. Works as a skirt and beach cover-up and as an evening wrap.
- Terry robe. Also doubles as a cover-up at beach or poolside.
- Jumpsuits. The ease of one-piece dressing. The look can be altered by adding an underlayer such as a turtleneck or leotard.
- Leotards. They work as swimwear, for exercising on the road, as tops with shorts, slacks or skirts or as a "second skin" layer for warmth under other clothes.
- Silk underwear. Doubles as an extra layer for warmth and as pajamas. Silk camisoles work well as dressy evening wear.
- Sweat suit. A "dress sweat" in velour can be worn for your morning jog and for leisure or lounging.

Your one coat must go with everything, so select a simple style in your light or dark neutral. A raincoat with a zip-out lining can go almost anywhere, even in the dead of winter. A Qiana raincoat can double as a coatdress.

When it comes to packing accessories, consider color, comfort and suitability for evening. Shoes, bags, jewelry and perhaps a hat and gloves can be your accent pieces. Since most of us walk more during vacations or travel than we do at home, comfortable walking shoes are essential. The same is true for boots—it's best to stick with lower heels so your feet can go the distance. Wear your boots on the plane and take a pair of walking shoes so you can switch off. Shoes present a challenge to even the most seasoned traveler. Designer Irene Tsu can travel for two weeks out of one suitcase but admits she overpacks shoes.

The tips we discuss in the chapter *Chic from A.M. to P.M.* are apropos to meeting evening wardrobe needs during your trip. One dressy, frilly or sheer blouse can transform a suit or pair of pants into an evening look. Add your coat or the blanket wrap, colored or metallic accessories and a pair of sandals or tuxedo pumps and you're set for a night on the out-of-town.

A Chic Travel Wardrobe

Living the *Chic on a Shoestring* creed, Annette set out for a three-day trip to San Francisco with the following items:
- black unstructured cotton-blend jacket
- khaki cotton knit top and matching skirt
- khaki-and-white-striped cotton terry jacket
- black-and-khaki jungle print blouse
- black cotton/lycra skirt
- black, khaki, rust and off-white print dress
- black, khaki and gold-with-brass accessories
- black shoes (two pair) and shoulder bag

Pieces mix and match to create day and evening looks. The combinations worked so well she has used the formula as the basis for longer and shorter trips.

Travel Planning

It's wise to gather some information on your destination before you begin to pack. Check the newspaper for weather data on the area you plan to visit. What are the predicted daytime and evening temperatures, and what's the likely precipitation at this time of year? If this is your first trip to a particular city or locale, talk to someone who has been there to find out the general dress code of the crowd you'll be doing business with or visiting. Certain cities such as San Francisco, Chicago, New York and Washington, D.C., are by nature dressier than Los Angeles or Phoenix. New York is a city for somber colors, Los Angeles a city for brights. A friend relates the error of traveling to Greece with a wardrobe of black clothes only to discover that black is a color for older women and widows in that country.

- Tip: When visiting a foreign country for the first time, it's a good idea to call the nearest consulate office and ask about local customs and climate.

Several days before your departure, start a running list of items you want to pack as they come to mind. This diffuses much of the worry about forgetting something important and helps prevent overpacking. When you return home, note which clothes you wore a lot and which you didn't take out of the suitcase. A travel wardrobe inventory will simplify packing. Remember which clothes you didn't have but wished you did. You can consult this list before your next shopping spree.

First and foremost, travel clothes should be comfortable. Pack items you wear frequently and feel confident about. Don't be afraid to wear an outfit more than once or for an entire day. The time you save can be used for business or leisure activities. Look over your trip itinerary and project the number of changes you'll need to pack. If you're on a business trip, will you be meeting with different clients each day (in which case you can wear the same outfit) or will you be with one group the entire time? Will you be entertaining clients at dinner and the theater each evening, or will you be doing business at the tennis club?

The secret of a successful and versatile travel wardrobe is limiting your color palette (here we've chosen khaki, black and beige) so that pieces can be mixed, matched and layered to meet all needs.

Packing

After you've assessed your trip (this gets easier with practice), you're ready to assemble the garments and accessories for packing. Lay everything out on the bed or hang garments on a portable rack or coat tree in the bedroom. Look at each piece and visualize the outfits you'll create. Remember the cardinal rule of travel wardrobes: Every piece you take has to work to create at least three outfits. If a wild print blouse only works with one pair of pants and not with your suit or skirt, leave it home. Coordinate your accessories now, too, and don't forget to lay out the necessary underwear, hosiery and sleepwear.

Separate everything you want to pack into four piles:
- heavy items like shoes, boots, an iron or hair dryer
- crushable items that don't wrinkle, such as T-shirts, lingerie and socks
- your "wrinkleables," like skirts, pants, blouses, dresses and jackets
- small or fragile items, including jewelry, belts, an alarm clock and portable hot rollers

Place the heavy items at the bottom of your bag. Roll the crushables and stuff them in and around other things such as shoes and boots. The wrinkle-prone garments are folded carefully in tissue paper or in clear plastic bags (from the dry cleaner) and placed on top. Small and delicate items are fit into suitcase compartments or packed inside travel pouches. If you're using molded or structured luggage, you might consider packing your clothes on hangers. This speeds the unpacking process and ensures that you'll have hangers wherever you go (hotels never have pants or skirt hangers). Hangers add a bit of extra weight, so use lightweight plastic ones.

Take the least baggage possible. One suitcase or one carry-on and one hanging garment bag should suffice for most travel. The chief complaint about travel is having to carry heavy bags miles through airport terminals and wait for hours at baggage claim areas. Theft and loss of luggage are also growing problems. Travel light and carry as much on the plane with you as is allowed.

The new soft luggage pieces have become popular because of their light weight and expandability and the fact that most of them are designed to fit under airline seats. Sets come with matching hanging garment bags that double as suitcases. We both travel with soft luggage we ordered from Crate and Barrel in Chicago. We also invested in a collapsible luggage carrier (the sturdy aluminum kind you see flight attendants and pilots pulling behind them at airports) and have never had a strained back or sore shoulder since.

Packing Tips:
- Take along a clothes steamer such as Wrinkles Away rather than a travel iron.
- Pack your prescriptions, glasses and/or contact lenses in your handbag or carry-on bag in case you and your luggage are separated.
- Organize items such as hosiery, undies and jewelry in plastic bags for easy unpacking and efficiency.
- Pack extra clear plastic bags or Ziploc bags for dirty laundry and wet bathing suits.
- Take along a clear plastic raincoat folded into its purse-size packet for emergency rain protection.
- Pack a little potpourri or air freshener if you have room. A favorite scent will make you feel at home in a stuffy hotel room, and many hotels have the windows sealed shut.
- Keep a toiletry kit with small, travel-size portions of all your creams and lotions (plus toothbrush, toothpaste, etc.) packed and ready to go at all times. When you return from a trip, refill the bottles immediately so it's ready to go the next time.
- Put together a clothes care kit for travel that includes: spot remover pads, detergent or soap flakes, safety pins, clear plastic tape for emergency hem repairs, an inflatable hanger or two for instant laundering (clothes hang on these to dry) and a small sewing kit.
- Stick a pair of warm socks into the top of your carry-on bag, attaché case or handbag on cross-country or overseas flights. Slip out of your shoes or boots and into your warm socks for comfort or wear the slippers provided on most overseas flights.
- Cut down on wrinkles by folding clothes in tissue paper or clear plastic bags from the dry cleaners.

If clothes are wrinkled when you arrive, hang them in a hot, steamy bathroom and most wrinkles will disappear as you shower.
- Wear your heaviest, bulkiest items on the plane so that you've got as much room in your baggage as possible.
- Take a big, square challis, silk or cashmere scarf or blanket wrap to wear over your shoulders in the plane if it's chilly and use it in the evening as a dressy wrap.
- Travel with a large handbag and stash your medications, eyewear, books, magazines, camera, etc., inside. The large size also comes in handy as a tote during shopping sprees and sightseeing.

Travel Advice from Top Designers
When it comes to a basic travel wardrobe, top women designers agree on the versatility of color-coordinated separates.

Liz Claiborne: "For color, I stick to khaki, loden or black. Then I'll add one bright-colored sweater." Her travel wardrobe consists of two skirts and shirts, a pair of soft jersey pants and a silk blouse for day or evening.

Linda Allard, a designer for Ellen Tracy, usually edits her separates down to two pairs of gabardine trousers, an unconstructed blazer, a velveteen jacket, a silk paisley skirt and a group of colorful silk blouses.

Carole Little, designer for Saint Tropez West, says she always travels on a plane in a white silk blouse, a black printed peasant skirt and a pair of dressy shoes or sandals. She packs a black silk top, a pair of black trousers and a black cardigan sweater. She advises, "Black doesn't show wrinkles or spots." Ms. Little also includes one pair of walking shoes and a raincoat, plus a bright chiffon scarf large enough to wear as a shawl and a couple of colorful bangle bracelets.

Donna Karan of Anne Klein says she, too, usually packs and travels in black. She adds, "Even when traveling, I'm not interested in looking basic. I take extreme shapes, like jodhpurs." She doesn't wear shirts while traveling but prefers instead sweaters for tops—cotton in summer, cashmere in winter. She wears one outfit from day through evening. She travels with ballet slippers and a dressy pair of shoes. She takes scarves, usually red or wine-colored, for accent. And, she finishes, "I take one dynamite bracelet to wear all the time."

12
Chic from A.M. to P.M.

Our busy schedules take us directly from day activities into evening appointments and social engagements with nary a moment to catch our breath, let alone time to go home and change. Working women are especially sensitive to the wardrobe decisions involved in segueing directly from a late-afternoon meeting in the office to cocktails, dinner (with friends or business associates) or the theater or movies. The challenge in these eighteen-hour days is to make the day-to-evening transition easily and inexpensively.

Generally speaking, we're concerned with changing the conservative, tailored, low-key looks appropriate for day into the more glamorous, feminine, sexy looks we like to wear at night. The exception would of course be for evening business functions such as dinner with clients, at which work attire is expected. For the most part, however, after hours time belongs to us. It's literally and metaphorically a time to let your hair down and express a unique personal style that is usually camouflaged at the office. It's not only appropriate to trade in your tailored blouse for a silky camisole when the "school's out" buzzer sounds, but it's a subtle indication of your mood change. It will give you and those around you a psychological lift that says, "Day is done, fun's begun."

There are three easy ways the day-to-evening transition can be achieved:

1. Change one or possibly two garments to create an evening look from a daytime tog.
2. Select at 8 A.M. clothes that can survive and adapt to an eighteen-hour day.
3. Switch or add accessories to inject sparkle and drama into your daytime look and transform it into nighttime allure.

You can select one idea from this trio of methods, or you can combine techniques to come up with the nighttime look most appropriate for you. Another element you'll have to take into consideration is a suitable wrap for evening temperatures and sudden weather changes. Let's look at each option separately.

A Simple Metamorphosis
When you select a garment to take with you at the beginning of your day that you can change into in the evening, you need to consider not only its dressiness factor but also its portability. A terrific black velvet cape might make just the perfect 6 P.M. wardrobe transformation of day wear into evening wear, but how are you going to carry it on the subway or squeeze it into your carpool?

One of the single best ways to change your look totally is to switch into a less structured jacket or cardigan sweater. A tailored suit becomes a softer,

The easy shift from a blouse to a camisole—which can be worn under the blouse all day and then brought out from hiding—transforms this suit into an evening ensemble.

more feminine ensemble when you take off the suit jacket and slip into a satin bolero jacket or a soft cashmere or angora sweater, perhaps with metallic threads woven into the design. Layering a dressy jacket or sweater over a work dress quickly creates an evening outfit from any workday ensemble. Choose your dressy accent piece in a basic color like black, cream or white or one of your favorite light or dark neutrals such as wine or camel, so that it can be worn with several pieces in your wardrobe to justify the cost.

When you're going through your closet to earmark the likely candidates for the day-into-evening outfit change, consider the following points:

- Color. Evening colors are often solids, especially black. Jewel tones such as ruby, sapphire, emerald and amethyst say nighttime, as does the bold drama of black and white. Try a white jacket over your black dress or vice versa for timeless sophistication.
- Texture. Think elegant, luxurious and downright sexy when you're considering your evening fabrics. Lace, satin, brocade, taffeta, velvet, silk and crepe all work, as do soft materials like angora, maribou and fur.
- Metallics. There's a reason we were all brought up on the notion that gold, silver, copper and glittery rhinestones are best worn at night. What seems trashy and overdone in daylight has a sparkle and allure after dark. The glitter principle applies to clothing as well as to accessories. Almost any kind of jacket, shawl or sweater in a metallic tone or one that has metallic threads woven into it qualifies as evening wear.

Another option is to change one part of your wardrobe and thus alter the entire look. For example, switch from a conservative oxford cloth blouse or crewneck sweater for day into a softer, more romantic version of either for night. The light blue cotton shirt you wore to work with your navy suit becomes a frilly white organdy blouse with ruffles. The navy wool crewneck sweater becomes red angora. Another easy and effective sleight of hand (or wardrobe) is to wear a sexy silk or lace camisole under your blouse during the day and then simply remove the top layer for evening.

Around-the-Clock Clothes

An alternative to changing clothes at the end of the day is to choose garments that work as well in the evening as they do during the day or require only minor modifications for nighttime. Some examples:

- If you're wearing a pantsuit or skirt suit, remove the blouse or sweater under your suit jacket. With the jacket buttoned and skin or the top of a lacy camisole showing, you'll look sexy and mysterious.
- Unbutton another button or two at the neck of your dress or blouse to show a little cleavage. We can get away with more bareness in the evening.
- Knit dresses, sweater dresses, suits and jacket dresses are a sure bet for extralong days because they don't wrinkle. They are authoritative enough for the office or the PTA meeting but not too rigid for evening wear. They are also ideal for travel if your day includes an air or land commute.
- Other fabrics that work well for day into evening are crepe (especially silk and lightweight wool crepe) and almost anything in silk.

The Added Difference

The most practical advice for day into evening dressing is to change your accessories. Accessories (scarves, earrings, bracelets, pins, necklaces, hosiery, shoes and bags) are easy to carry and they frankly offer a lot of impact in terms of outright glamour for very little effort. A sparkly pin added to a lapel or a pair of gold strappy sandals in place of low-heeled black patent pumps can metamorphose an entire outfit.

Some specific suggestions on changing accessories:
- Shoes are the most important change. Not only

This bicolor Adolfo knit dress—purchased at a charity bazaar for only $50—will go unwrinkled through an extra-long day and is sexy enough to be worn in the evening.

will your outfit be altered to evening with different footwear, your tired feet will welcome the shift to another heel height. Needless to say, comfort is important in your evening shoes, too. Nobody can exude an air of evening sociability or drop-dead glamour if her feet are screaming, "Take me home!" If you don't own a pair of true dress shoes such as a sandal or high-heeled pump in gold, silver or black peau de soie, invest in a pair of black patent leather strappy sandals. The shininess of the patent, the bareness of the style, plus the versatility and year-round wearability of black patent make this style a *Chic on a Shoestring* investment. You'll be well shod for any evening fete.

- Change your hose to a pair with sheen and shimmer or to a patterned style such as dots or diamonds. Lacy or seamed hose are sexy for evening. You can also change from a nude or natural-tone hose to a shade that matches your skirt or pants and shoes. Coordinating a wine skirt with wine hose and shoes is not only pulled together and elegant but also slenderizing. A contrasting shade of hosiery or a pair of patterned socks can add color and drama to an otherwise simple outfit. Consider red tights and coordinating jewelry worn with cobalt blue, black or purple for evening impact.
- Any sparkly or bold jewelry works well in the evening. See what a pair of drop earrings or a string of pearls can do to jazz up your conservative office attire.
- Glittery or dramatic belts can likewise transform a suit or dress into an evening ensemble. Experiment a bit at home and then pack the necessary belt for your afterhours changeover in your briefcase or purse. Any metallic belt is usually a good bet, as is a sash or cummerbund, especially one in an evening fabric like satin or taffeta. If you're used to wearing belts only at the waist, experiment with a fanny wrap for evening.
- An oblong chiffon or metallic weave scarf tied in a bow at the neck of a dress or suit softens a

Chic from A.M. to P.M. • 95

A simple change of accessories can metamorphose your office attire into an evening ensemble. Here, we've exchanged earrings, bracelet, bag and shoes and added the pearls, hat and gloves for evening.

day look. A velvet, lace or satin ribbon tied as a choker with an antique pin or earring as ornament is also an inexpensive evening accessory.
- Change to a beaded evening bag or a clutch in velvet, satin or brocade. A small evening bag can be carried to work in your handbag, briefcase or tote until needed.
- Finish off your ensemble with a cocktail hat and a pair of sheer gloves. A cloche hat is easy to carry and can disguise a wilted hairdo at the end of a long day.

As you've probably figured out by now, you can use suggestions from any of these categories or combine them to suit your needs and personal style. A *Chic on a Shoestring* day-into-evening change might look something like this: At the end of a full day at the office, Ms. Chic switches from her navy blue wool gabardine blazer jacket (that matches the slim-cut A-line skirt) to a deep-V'd red angora sweater with a peplum waist (she has removed her blouse). She steps out of her low-heeled navy pumps into a pair of red medium- to high-heeled sandals or sling-back pumps and takes a red beaded evening clutch (purchased at a thrift shop but in great condition) out of her daytime handbag. Her wrap is either the blazer jacket layered over the sweater or a woven wool shawl in black or white.

Day-into-Evening Tips

- Once you've selected pieces from your wardrobe that make easy day-into-evening transitions, hang your choice out the night before so you don't have to make complicated wardrobe decisions before your first cup of coffee.
- If it's not convenient to take your evening change of clothes and/or accessories to work with you, why not keep a sort of evening emergency kit at the office? A dressy jacket or sweater, an evening bag and some jewelry might just save the day (or in this case the evening) when you get an eleventh-hour invitation to dinner or a business cocktail party. This will also alleviate those shopping mistakes that often result from making lunch-hour purchases under pressure.
- Protect your good dressy clothes with an emergency clear vinyl raincoat, the kind you find packaged in purse-size packets in department or five-and-dime stores. Keep one at work and one in your car or bag for sudden rain protection. Look for one with a hood and you won't have to fuss with an umbrella.
- Other good evening wraps include a shawl or large (50" × 50") blanket wrap in a knit, cashmere or silk. The wrap can be worn layered over a coat for extra warmth or draped casually over your shoulders for light protection.
- Dress up your day coat for evening with a decorative pin, brooch or corsage (a single white gardenia is lovely and aromatic).
- A black polished-cotton raincoat in a classic, non-trench style can easily be dramatic enough for afterhours wear.
- Qiana raincoats come in many pretty solid colors and can be worn for evening or travel.
- Store evening wraps at work to avoid hauling them back and forth.
- Remember to freshen your makeup with your own favorite nighttime touches such as darker lipstick and a bit more eyeshadow.
- Wear your prettiest lingerie to work. You'll feel more dressed up—even if no one else sees it. Intimate apparel such as silk and lace camisoles can double as blouses in the evening. It's perfectly permissible to let a suggestion of lace show underneath a suit jacket for a sexy yet sophisticated look.

13
Cheap Jock Chic

Survival Dressing for the 1980s
Jock *Chic* is *Chic on a Shoestring* survival dressing for the 1980s and beyond. It's a low-cost, practical, packable and versatile answer to the question, "What can I wear today that will take me from the office to my exercise studio and out to dinner?" The boom in action wear, body wear and dance wear has been the major fashion news of the 1980s. Thanks to the fitness craze, a leotard industry reeling from the demise of disco in the late 1970s has been rejuvenated. All of us can benefit from the design and fabric innovations in body wear.

Designers such as Oscar de la Renta, Norma Kamali and Adolfo either design in fabrics traditionally associated with active sportswear (Kamali) or have crossed over from haute couture and are making swimwear and sweat suits for the fashionably active woman. The result is some of the most creative and wearable fashion to come down the pike since Chanel took women out of corsets.

Leotards, tights, sweat suits, jogging shoes and ballet shoes should be considered wardrobe essentials whether or not you work out or dance. Why? Because they are comfortable, affordable and can be worn many times over. Even at prices averaging $30, a leotard is a *Chic* investment because of its versatility. Dancers have used their leotards and tights as the basis of their wardrobes for years. Take their lead and experiment with skirts or pants over leotards (as an alternative to a shirt), or layer a blouse or sweater over a leotard and tights for an extra layer of warmth. There is no extra bulk to add the illusion of pounds or inches. Even better, the "second skin" comfort and support of body wear can be a body shaper and give you extra support without the stranglehold of an old Playtex. Choose leotards with cotton in the fiber content for extra breathability.

Besides their use at the Y, gym, health club or track, the action wear pieces you already own (such as sweat suits, jogging suits, running shorts, T-shirts and shorts-and-tops outfits) can be pressed into double duty to stretch your wardrobe. The same is true for the old outdoor sports standbys such as down vests and sailing and boating gear like windbreakers and deck shoes.

**How to Get Double Duty
from Your Active Wear and Sports Gear**
- Leotards (sleeveless, spaghetti strap, short- and long-sleeved styles) and maillot swimsuits work as tops with jeans, shorts, casual slacks and skirts. Wear leotards alone or layer them under jumpsuits, blouses, sweaters or jackets for an added note of color and/or warmth. Silver or gold leo-

98 • *Chic on a Shoestring*

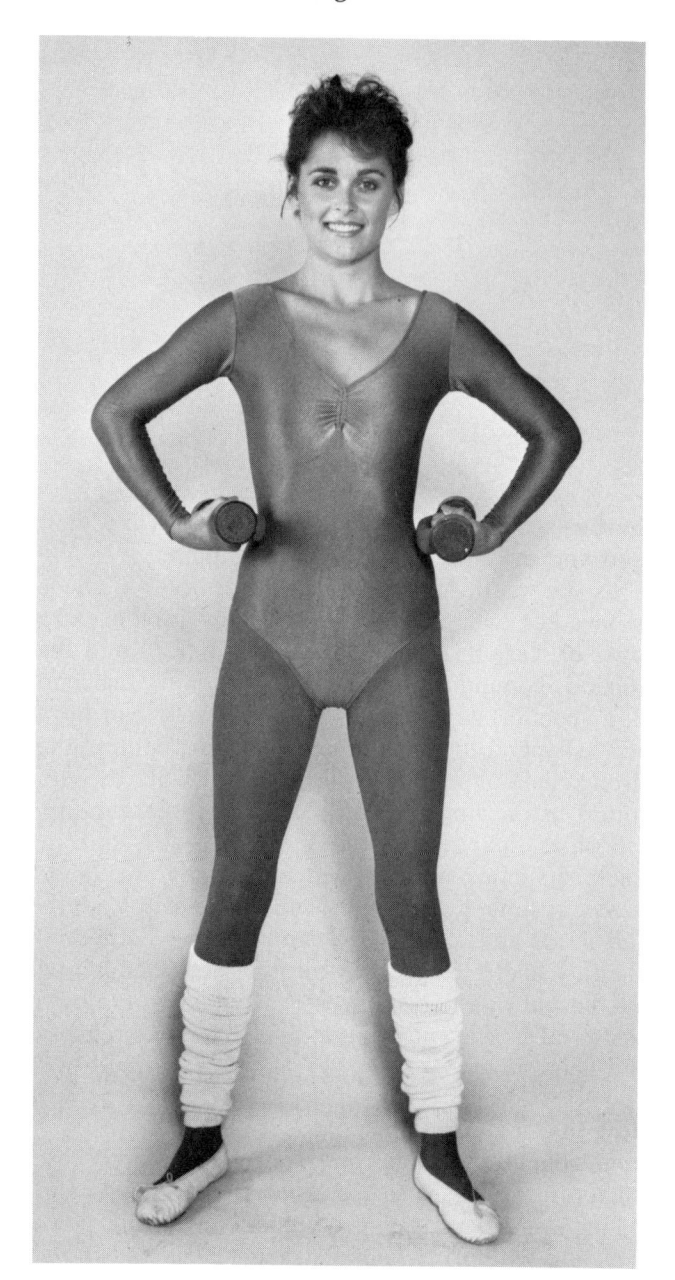

The same bright-toned leotard and tights you wear for working out can also be worn under a simple knit dress for a dash of color and a layer of warmth.

One sweat-jumpsuit can assume many personalities, depending on the accessories and attitude of the wearer.

tards and tights or body wear in shimmery, satiny fabrics can double as dressy evening wear.
- Tights can be worn under pants, skirts, shorts or minidresses. Wear them for warmth (as you did when you were a child walking to school on cold mornings) or for color emphasis to accent or unify an outfit.
- Sweat suits and jogging outfits adapt to day or casual evening wear with a change of accessories. Velour warm-up suits are even accepted as proper attire at chi-chi dining establishments these days. Don't wear your track shoes; instead, try a pair of high-heeled sandals and wear bold, dramatic jewelry.
- Shorts-and-tops sets can be worn year round over leotards and tights in the gym or for jogging around the park. They'll make you feel more comfortable as you work off those extra inches. Bold color combinations will perk up your spirits.
- Knee socks and anklets in bright colors and patterns are an inexpensive way to jazz up your tired and worn jogging shoes or deck shoes.
- Wear a down vest under a raincoat for extra warmth if your coat isn't already lined.
- Hang your sports clothes separately in their respective closet areas and not together as outfits. This way you'll see how the pieces work as separates and find ways to combine them with other items in your wardrobe.
- Silk or lightweight cotton long underwear is a super insulator worn next to the body and can also be worn alone as pajamas or lounging attire. With energy prices going up and office temps going down, your salvation might be new, old-fashioned long johns. There's nothing more practical yet sensuous than the living, breathing feeling of silk next to your body. It's a natural insulator; it will be cool in summer and warm in winter.

Above all, wear your sweats proudly. Nothing imparts style to an outfit—even the most basic sweatshirt—like *attitude*. Think *Chic* and you are *Chic*.

Where to Buy Your Jock Chic Cheaply

- Sportswear manufacturers' outlets. Look in the Yellow Pages under apparel manufacturers and call to see when and where they have sales open to the public.
- Discount chains such as Target, Marshalls, Pic-A-Dilly, K mart and many others are carrying active wear at affordable prices. Check construction and fiber content closely to avoid buying cheaply made merchandise (it won't be a bargain if it falls apart). Choose garments made from at least 50% cotton.
- Sale catalogs or sale items from sports catalogs. We've made good buys from the Sportpages sale catalog, plus selected purchases from L.L. Bean, Early Winters, Hudson's and Lands' End.
- Surplus stores stock unisex sweat suits in grey and navy plus other useful and inexpensive items such as rain slickers, wool socks and caps, cotton T-shirts and much more.
- Chain stores such as Sears, JC Penney, Montgomery Ward and Aldens manufacture and sell their own brands of sweat suits, sportswear, active wear and underwear. Watch for sales and, again, check fiber content and construction.

14
Chic Cover-ups

We believe a woman needs a wardrobe of coats. An extravagance, you say? Well, consider this: Outerwear is the first impression people get when they look at you, and the statement you make can enhance or destroy your image. Remember your high school prom, when you spent your entire year's baby-sitting money on that drop-dead gown you *had* to have and then froze to death all night because you couldn't *bear* to wear your old navy pea coat over it? Since coats and wraps are a major wardrobe expense, we offer suggestions on how you can build an optimal, low-cost outerwear wardrobe that will take you anywhere. We will show you how to shop for the most versatile, practical, yet stylish purchases in various lengths, weights and styles.

The Three Basics
In planning your coat wardrobe, first determine your needs. A coat wardrobe—whether of one or one hundred pieces—must meet all your needs and match your lifestyle with the proper garment. One of the best ways to do this is to think in terms of the basics required in a four-season climate:

- An everyday coat that can pass gracefully from day into evening; one of simple design and subtle color. An example: a classic princess-style dress-length coat made of 100 percent wool in your dark neutral.
- A coat or jacket for winter leisure activities. This will be a heavyweight or insulated garment that provides extra warmth for cold, snowy days. A three-quarter-length down jacket is an example.
- A classic trench coat with removable lining that can be worn year round.

Figure Considerations
Take your figure into consideration when shopping for outerwear. Coats are one of the single most important components of a wardrobe because they visually dominate an outfit. The quality, color, fabric, style and shape create a lasting impression. The shape, cut and drape of a coat determine its appropriateness on a particular figure type. The following figure considerations will help you select the best cut in a coat.

- Shoulders: if your shoulders are narrow or sloping, choose a coat with padded shoulders or set-in sleeves to give the coat a strong T to balance the length and bulk. If you are broad shouldered, a raglan sleeve or a style without defined shoulder seams will work.
- Waists: long-waisted figures can wear coats with wide belts. If you are short waisted, choose a coat

Three basic coats to have in your closet include (left to right): a classic trenchcoat with removable lining, a princess style dress-length coat and a three-quarter-length coat or jacket for winter leisure activities.

with no waist or a style that gives the illusion of lowering the waist. If you have a thick middle, avoid coats with waists or belts of any kind. A dark color is slenderizing and a good choice for women with thick waists or full hips.
- Bustlines: bodice details or gathers emphasize a full bust and should be avoided. A small-busted figure can wear most coat styles.
- Necks: high collars and long-haired furs are most flattering on long-necked women. If you have a short neck, choose a flat collar that can be turned up on windy days.
- Hips: if your hips are wide, balance your proportion with extended shoulders. Avoid belts or styles with gathered waists unless you are small hipped. Try, as we did, removing the belt from a coat to see if this improves the line on you.
- Hemlines: choose a coat at least an inch longer than your skirt and dress hemlines.

A Laundry List of Coat Styles

We have included a roster of the wide variety of coats and jackets popular today. The list goes from most versatile to most optional. To maximize your purchase, choose a solid-color coat or one with subtle color contrasts and minimal detail.
- Full length trench coat or balmacaan with zip-out lining. Trenches can be in your light or dark neutral, pearl grey or charcoal, for example, rather than the standard London tan.
- Sweater coat. With or without a belt.
- Leather or suede bomber jacket and/or a blazer with zip-out lining.
- Navy pea jacket.
- Wool full length coat, medium weight, flat weave; also in cashmere. The cut could be princess style, wrap, A-line or narrow reefer.
- Down vest.
- Cashmere, wool or velvet cape, shawl or stole. Long or short, these are dramatic enough for evening wear and are casual and packable enough for travel. Also, a poncho-style wrap is a practical and inexpensive addition.
- Fanny-covering wool or wool-blend topper. Choose a dressy version of the traditional car coat that can double as a suit coat for slacks and skirts.
- Qiana full length raincoat. Great for travel because they are lightweight and crushable. The sheen of the fabric makes this a dressier-looking coat than a trench. You might want to experiment with buying this coat in a favorite bright color as an accent piece and antidote to rainy-day gloom.
- Roomy A-line poplin calf-length coat with real or fake fur lining and a hood or large shawl collar.
- Down coat. Guaranteed to make you look and feel like a polar bear but ultrawarm and lightweight.

The A-line or princess style, or a narrow tube shape with broad shoulders, are generally the most flattering.
- Clear plastic raincoat purchased from a drugstore or five-and-dime. Pick one up and carry it in your purse or briefcase for cheap and *Chic* foul-weather gear.
- Fur. Warmth, luxury and lasting value are the chief advantages of furs. One of the most expensive and opulent purchases in our wardrobes. *Chic* readers are advised to keep their eyes open for fur buys at resale or consignment shops. If you invest in a fur, choose a coat or jacket style you need and would wear a lot so you get the maximum enjoyment and use for your money.

Shopping for a Coat

January end-of-season sales at specialty and department stores offer the best opportunity for consistently good deals on outerwear. Classics are the best buys when shopping end-of-season sales; be wary of trendy silhouettes or colors that will look dated next year. If you're a hard-to-fit size, make well-planned purchases in August or September, when the coat and jacket selection is at its peak.

Prowl the discount stores in your area and call to find out when coats start arriving. Remember, discount stores also have good sales. You're in luck if a local coat manufacturer has an outlet store or holds semiannual sales in your area. Check the Yellow Pages in your phone book under clothing manufacturers/coats and give them a call. We bought a Bill Blass full length down coat at the down manufacturer's outlet store in LaCrosse, Wisconsin, for only $165 (the coat was retailing for over $300). The moral is, you don't have to live in a major metropolitan area to shop discount.

A shabby coat over an expensive silk dress is a fashion faux pas. Our *Chic on a Shoestring* creed is: Buy the best you can afford, even if it means sleuthing out a bargain. We can't overemphasize the importance of quality fabric, fit and cut in a coat purchase. These are garments you'll have in your closet for *years,* so this is not the time or place in your shopping to compromise your standards or succumb to an impulse buy.

Coat "Collecting"—Building a Coat Wardrobe

Once we were converted to the wisdom (and necessity) of owning a coat wardrobe in order to be well dressed, your authors set about building one—albeit most inexpensively and, most certainly, with a sense of humor. The following tips will augment the advice given in the first part of this chapter to select quality classic coats in flattering styles, in colors that best harmonize with your wardrobe.

The first rule is: keep your eye out for coat bargains of every kind whenever and wherever you're discount shopping. Off-price stores, manufacturers' outlets, charity sales, church bazaars, rummage and garage sales, resale and consignment shops, thrift stores of every persuasion and antique or vintage clothing stores all make for great hunting grounds for coats, jackets and furs. The low—oftentimes ridiculously so—prices make the purchase of several coats well within your budget. Keep in mind that you may find your best buys on winter coats in the heat of summer, so be prepared to seize a bargain when you see it. Set a portion of your wardrobe budget aside for outerwear purchases.

A Chic Coat Wardrobe—Examples from Our Closets

- linen jacket with calico print lining—$.50 from a Red Cross Thrift Store in Rosarito, Mexico
- silver-tipped fox stole for only $20! (in excellent condition) from a resale store with a Canadian clientele
- Pauline Trigère princess-style full length wool coat in cream and soft yellow—$10 from a resale store
- 1940s-style full length muskrat coat, complete with de rigueur Joan Crawford shoulders—$150 from a resale store
- red-white-and-black wool coat in a high-fashion style designed by Louis Feraud—$15 from a thrift store

- full length black cashmere dress coat—$10 from a resale store
- green suede jacket designed by Emanuel Ungaro—$20 from a sale rack in a discount store
- man's double-breasted black-and-white houndstooth-check overcoat—$5 from a church bazaar
- classic trench coat with zip-out lining—$45 from a discount store

Think of yourself as a connoisseur of coats and jackets who is always on the lookout for bargain-priced gems to add to her collection. This is a terrific way to have fun with your wardrobe and take a chance or two on a style or color you might not otherwise try. If your closet starts to groan under the weight of these new acquisitions, add a hall tree or an expandable rack over one door.

In the photo opposite, the fabulous coat buys from our own closets include (left to right): a black cashmere cape with silk lining purchased for $8.00 from a thrift store; a Bill Blass down coat purchased for $165 from the down manufacturer's outlet store and a full-length muskrat coat purchased for $150 from a resale store.

15
Maternity Chic

How to Save Money on a Maternity Wardrobe
Since your wardrobe needs during pregnancy are temporary, you'll especially need to follow the *Chic on a Shoestring* credo of filling your clothing needs at the lowest possible prices. What you won't want to do, of course, is spend a lot of money or commit serious retail for special maternity-only garments—the cost per wearing will just be too high. You do need a miniwardrobe of color-coordinated, stylish pieces that are also flexible in size so you can integrate them into your postpartum wardrobe and beyond. You probably already have several pieces that will work just fine now that you're "in a family way."

While you don't want to waste money on clothes during this time, you do particularly need to pay attention to them. Pregnant women need the emotional lift of clothes and of looking feminine and pretty while their bellies grow and their bodies change shape. Notice we said *feminine,* not *cutesy* or *stickysweet.* The last thing you need now are the Peter Pan collars and juvenile design details and trims that are appropriate for eleven-year olds, not for adult, pregnant women. You don't have to apologize, in terms of style, for being pregnant. Princess Diana's elegant and fashionable—and even drop-dead sexy—maternity wardrobe was a good inspiration.

Maternity Wardrobe Tips

- Jumpers work well for dual-season pregnancies. You can wear blouses, shirts and sweaters under them during cool weather and wear them sans top when the temperature climbs.
- Blouses don't have to be maternity-style for wear under jumpers or sleeveless tops. Simply unbutton your regular blouses or shirts over your tummy.
- Skirts and pants with elastic waists are good for the first few months of pregnancy and again after delivery.
- Borrow freely from your man's closet; his bigger shirts, sweaters and even bib overalls will work just dandy.
- Sweats, drawstring pants and sweatshirts are perfect while you're expecting. They're ultracomfortable, easy to take care of and, best of all, inexpensive. How about two or three sets in different colors? Borrow your husband's sweats, too.
- As for maternity outerwear, capes and shawls work better than standard coats and jackets.
- Look for the flattering A-line silhouettes in dresses and jumpers. Tent dresses are a good example.
- Make sure the hems of tops and dresses are $\frac{1}{2}''$–$1\frac{1}{2}''$ longer in the front. You can temporarily hem

106 • Chic on a Shoestring

The versatile, season-spanning jumper—one answer to a Chic on a Shoestring *maternity wardrobe.*

up the back or let down the front and then correct it for postpartum wear.
- Treat yourself to some new item of clothing or an accessory during the last month or so. You'll need the lift.
- Buy cotton bras with good support at discount or on sale, since your bra size will increase (usually dramatically) while you're expecting and nursing and then return to normal.
- Support hose will probably feel especially good while you're expecting. Buy queen-size rather than special maternity hosiery; it's cheaper. Stay away from knee-highs since they cut off circulation.
- For dressy or formal evenings, nothing beats black; your dark neutrals will also work. Dress up pieces from your regular wardrobe with sparkly or dramatic accessories. Don't buy an evening maternity dress or outfit.
- Comfort is of special concern during pregnancy, particularly in lingerie. Look for 100 percent cotton bras, slips, underpants (bikini styles are more comfortable than briefs) and sleepwear.
- Wraparound skirts and drawstring pants and skirts give needed size flexibility and are readily available at discount.
- A roomy white cotton antique nightshirt can easily make the shift from nighttime to daytime—these make great dresses. Wear a long, colorful scarf tied loosely in front for fun.
- Wear sweats or an extralarge leotard for exercising. A large Speedo-brand swimsuit gives extra support for swimming and for comfort under other clothes.

This Laise Adzer ethnic-influenced cotton gauze tent dress served our model well during her pregnancy. (She bought the same dress in three colors!)

Where to Shop

As more and more women, especially those in their mid- to late-thirties and early forties, are having babies, we increasingly see maternity wear available at discount prices. Fortunately, there's a wide range of less-than-retail shopping options for maternity-only clothing in addition to the regular garments we've already mentioned that do double duty during pregnancy. Look for:

- Maternity clothing manufacturers' outlets. Check your local discount shopping guidebook or the Yellow Pages under clothing manufacturers. Find out when these manufacturers and stores hold sales.
- Maternity and infant wear resale shops. If ever there was an idea whose time has come, this is it! Ask friends for their favorite stores, consult your handy discount shopping guidebook and check the telephone directory under "Used Clothing." You can also recycle your own maternity wardrobe here.
- Keep an eye out for advertisements of sales at department store maternity departments and retail maternity wear boutiques. Shop sales at nationwide chains such as Motherhood Maternity and Lady Madonna. These specialized stores have fashion shows and publish helpful newsletters, so put yourself on your local store's mailing list.
- Discount stores, chains such as Sears and JC Penney and even dime stores are your one-stop shopping center for all-cotton underwear, big T-shirts, sweat suits and hosiery. Grocery stores and drugstores are also good for inexpensive hosiery.

Special Clothing Needs for Postpartum and Nursing

While you're busy taking care of the newest family member and working to get your figure back into shape, you'll also want to take a little bit of time for yourself and your return to a normal wardrobe. Emphasize your more slender areas and draw attention away from your waistline.

Wardrobe Tips:

- Belt longer tops and dresses below the waist or at the hip.
- Take in the side seams of your full or maternity dresses and tops.
- Wash-and-wear fabrics such as 80/20 cotton/poly blends are essential with a newborn.
- If you're breast-feeding, look for blouses and shirts that open in the front easily and have plenty of room in the bustline. Stay away from tops with frilly or ruffly details or horizontal stripes at the bustline.
- Check out the Mamamade catalog for specially designed nursing apparel. Send $1.00 to Mamamade Nursing Fashions, 110 Idlewild Lane, Media, PA 19063.

Maternity Wear Advice from an Expert, Designer Elke Lesso

For some *Chic on a Shoestring* advice on how to dress better for less during what can be a taxing time for clothes budgets, we talked to Los Angeles–based designer Elke Lesso. She produces an innovative line of dresses and sportswear under the label Zoe, operates boutiques featuring her designs on West Hollywood's fashion-forward Melrose Avenue and in Beverly Hills and also creates custom designs. Elke is the proud mother of an infant son, and she shares with us here her own tips and insights on maternity wear.

CHIC: Tell us a little about your own maternity wardrobe.

E.L.: I worked the entire time I was expecting my son, of course. Because of my pregnancy, I shifted toward designing more functional clothes throughout my Zoe line. When I was pregnant I didn't want to wear any other designer's maternity clothes, so I came up with my own ideas for myself.

I didn't want to feel restricted anywhere because I move around a lot when I work. For instance, I designed pants and leggings that didn't stop at the waist but went up to a point just under the bustline.

The waist is your biggest part and you don't want restriction or tightness there. My specially designed pants and leggings were really comfortable and didn't fall down.

I don't specialize in maternity clothes. These were just a couple of things I needed, so I put them into my line and sold them in my store.

CHIC: What other special things did you create during your pregnancy?

E.L.: There are certain cuts that work really well, such as the low or dropped waist. I like this line better, and it's more fashionable than the empire line. The empire looks so much like a typical maternity look. But a lot of women do like it because it shows right away that they're pregnant.

A lot of my designs with the dropped waist camouflaged the fact that I was pregnant a little longer. Personally, I just didn't want to take the time to discuss my pregnancy with the forty different people I run into every day. Of course, in the ninth month, you could tell I was pregnant, but even in the sixth and seventh months, most people's attention wasn't drawn to the fact that I was pregnant. It wasn't so obvious.

The dresses I designed were blouson to the hip, and the fullness in the front came either from the neck area or shoulder pleats. The fullness sort of hid the belly for a while. As for smocks, well, I'm not so fond of them myself. They're so sort of apron-like. I prefer the fullness in the front.

CHIC: Did you find yourself wearing dresses a lot or did you also wear pants some of the time?

E.L.: Mostly leggings with minidresses. It depends on which season you're pregnant and where you live.

CHIC: Where can women find these leggings? Would queen-size tights also work?

E.L.: Yes, I think they would work. You might have to put on a slightly tighter elastic since you would pull the tights up over your stomach to just below the bustline.

CHIC: Did you discover anything new about your own style while you were pregnant?

Fashion designer Elke Lesso.

E.L.: Some other women designers have used different, even older fuller styles during their pregnancies; they didn't design specific maternity wear, either. They didn't work around the stomach like I did, draping it, bringing the fullness back in at the hipline. I found for myself I really liked this semicamouflaged look.

CHIC: What's your best advice to pregnant women, especially those who don't have access to your store or Zoe line, on how to avoid sinking a lot of money into a special maternity-only wardrobe they may never wear again?

E.L.: Again, the dropped waist is a very good line for pregnant women, especially a variation of this look that has fullness in front. Many of the clothes I make now and also clothes from other designers could be worn by pregnant women.

CHIC: There do seem to be more and more fashions available now that also work during pregnancy.

E.L.: Yes, except for a professional or business woman who really needs a suit. Then you really have to get a specialized maternity suit. But for casual, fun clothes, I don't think any woman has to buy maternity clothes. When you're buying clothes, just check for a lot of fullness in the front.

CHIC: If you liked jeans or slacks, you'd have to invest in a pair of maternity bottoms, right?

E.L.: Preference for a particular type of clothing and style during pregnancy also depends on a woman's age. A woman around forty may not want as many play clothes as a younger woman and may need, for instance, more dressy, more fashionable things.

And there's a variation among women and how much they want to show off that they're pregnant. This is why some women like to wear those tentlike T-shirts with the word *Baby* printed on them and an arrow pointing down to their stomachs.

CHIC: What advice would you give to pregnant women about the changing proportions of their bodies at this time?

E.L.: They can draw attention to their faces or their hands and wrists or another slender area. Highlighting the legs and ankles may not work since edema or swelling from water retention is a problem for some women.

Proportion also depends on how a woman gains during this time. Some women gain weight in several places, such as their legs and behinds, while other women gain primarily in their bellies and remain relatively slender everywhere else.

CHIC: What about ethnic-styled fashions as maternity wear?

E.L.: The popular loose cotton gauze tops and dresses and drawstring pants are great. I think they look very clean, designwise, and they're 100 percent cotton, which is very comfortable when you're pregnant. Indian styles are good since they have a lot of pleats at the front yokeline. Kimonos are not good since they have no gatherings or fullness in the front.

CHIC: Where do you recommend pregnant women shop?

E.L.: Shop in boutiques, since they have more fashionable clothes that can be worn for maternity and afterward. Watch fashion magazines and newspaper ads for appropriate styles. Skimps or balloony shorter dresses that come back in at the bottom at mid-thigh or a little lower are good.

If a woman is working and is really pressed for time, she may have to do some of her shopping in maternity stores.

CHIC: Any more tips you'd like to add?

E.L.: Jackets don't work very well at all. They end at the hips and cut off the silhouette at a strange point. This is especially noticeable if the jacket is another color. Blazers are really odd pieces of clothing when it comes to pregnancy. Longer, oversized sweaters are better. The long, uninterrupted line works best.

Flat shoes are important. If you're used to wearing high heels like I am, you could do this in the evening, not during the day at work. It depends on how your legs look. It's important to look and feel feminine.

I was wearing a lot of makeup at the time. It's important to continue to do this.

CHIC: Any other tips?

E.L.: With color you can do a lot. For instance, match all the items you buy. If you get four or five matching pieces, you can make lots of different outfits. This is better than buying one thing at a time. You match colors in your normal wardrobe, and it's especially important during pregnancy. You might even need just four pieces.

What those pieces are depends on you. Some women may like tights or leggings, for instance. I'm a fashion designer and I wear what I want to. I'm secure in my style and I don't worry what others may think of me.

Most women aren't that secure about their style.

Especially during pregnancy you might not be as secure about yourself. So some women need certain maternity wear. If you're a little more secure, you can try some of the things we've been talking about.

In my boutique on Melrose Avenue, women try things on and ask me, "How do I look?" Well, I ask them, "How do you *feel?*" I mean, if they don't know how *they* feel in clothes, can I tell them how they feel or if something is right for them? If women would feel more secure in their clothes, they would look better in them.

The mother-to-be in the photograph on page 106 is now a mother with a two-year-old daughter. She gets Chic on a Shoestring *value from the same dress she wore during her pregnancy.*

CHIC: What about postpartum wear?
E.L.: It depends on whether or not you breast-feed. You want to have clothes that are easy to open at the top. Look for openings at the shoulder or neck.

How soon you get back into shape and into your regular wardrobe depends on whether or not you exercise. You need flexible clothes after the baby is born—the same clothes you wore during your pregnancy—so you're not buying clothes every month or so as you lose a little more weight and get your figure back.

SECTION IV
Smarter Than Fashion

16
Basically Chic

Ask yourself this question: "Which clothes in my wardrobe am I constantly wearing out and replacing?" These are your wardrobe *basics* or *classics*. Neither of your authors has a duck in her den or a Fair Isle in her closet, yet we wear many classic or basic pieces that become our signature look. In this chapter we will discuss classic silhouettes and why they have become staples in so many women's wardrobes. We will also try to expand the concept of classics beyond the realm of the shirtwaist dress and penny loafer.

This said, we'll look into our own wardrobes for the basics we couldn't live without. Leigh lives in leotards, jumpsuits, ballet slippers and Norma Kamali sweat suits and separates. She has a weakness for oversized sweaters, vests and shirts (men's or man-tailored) worn with shoulder pads and tucked into tight jeans and couldn't live without her Puma wrestling shoes and red high heels.

Annette has an extensive collection of unstructured jackets, adores her Hepburn-style softly tailored gabardine pants and has a heart seizure when she thinks of trying to replace a black, softly flared skirt with an eight-inch flounce she bought for two dollars at a manufacturer's sale. She, too, loves sweaters, especially turtlenecks. Other basics are camp shirts, moccasins, low-heeled pumps, big T-

Your personal wardrobe basics are the clothes you live in, love, wear out and immediately rush out to replace. Your authors, Leigh (left) and Annette (right), believe in comfortable classics.

shirts, sweatshirts and Mexican wedding dresses for wear at home.

Not exactly "classic" wardrobes, are they? But think again. Both of us wear sweat suits, and that's about as classic an American fashion as you can get. We like flat shoes except for special occasions and don't have an extensive evening wear collection because our social lives are more casual. What we've discovered is most important in our wardrobes of basics is *comfort*. Whether it's a pair of pants or a pair of shoes, we have to feel good wearing an item of clothing, otherwise it gets shoved to the back of the closet (or better yet, recycled to someone else's).

Simplicity and ease of care are also important qualities our wardrobe basics have in common. Simple lines that flatter our figures and don't go out of style overnight and simple, flattering colors that complement each other mean the clothes will be worn frequently and with confidence. If one of these key ingredients is missing, the recipe just won't jell. For example, Leigh's gorgeous, electric blue silk slacks were purchased as a wardrobe basic but remain on the hanger because they wrinkle so badly that she can't get into her car and drive to a meeting without looking rumpled.

We're talking about fashion *identity* and the basic wardrobe pieces that form the foundation and fill the majority of your clothing needs.

Identity is the fashion challenge of the eighties. Designer Giorgio Armani

Your fashion identity is defined by four major factors:

- Your work. Do you work in the home, in a factory or in an office?
- Your family. Do you have young children, teenagers or none at all?
- Your environment. Do you live in an urban or a rural area, in a cold climate or hot?
- Your age. Are you young enough to be tempted by every fad that comes along, or have you stopped experimenting?

Basics reflect our lifestyle and our personal style. Because of all these (and more) factors, basic wardrobes vary from person to person and over time. What remains constant are the ingredients that go into making a garment a classic. Beauty, timelessness and intrinsic value are the keys to a classic wardrobe. Whether you're eighteen, single and haunt thrift stores and avant-garde boutiques; or thirty-six, married, with an infant on your hip and a toddler by the hand and shop JC Penney; or fifty-four, president of a corporation, an international traveler with credit cards who shops by mail while you jet from city to city; you're going to find your wardrobe basics have these characteristics in common:

- comfort
- simplicity of line; no fussy or busy details
- flattering silhouette
- easy care
- dependable
- versatile
- durable construction
- natural fibers (wool, cotton, cashmere, silk, leather, angora, etc) or natural/synthetic blends
- complementary colors: your own light and dark neutrals plus a few pieces in your accent color or colors

The basic pieces in your wardrobe, whichever kinds of tops, bottoms, dresses, wraps, footwear and accessories you choose, form the backbone or foundation of your wardrobe.

The most fashionable women will always be the ones who know themselves. Designer Vera Maxwell

Why do certain clothes become classics while other styles are here today, gone tonight in the endless fashion parade? The answer is that *we*, the consumers, decide which clothes become classics, not the designers. The clothes that recur year after year, season after season are the clothes we love to wear. These are clothes the majority of American women look good and feel good wearing. The 1980s buzzwords for these kinds of clothes are "investment dressing." Women are returning to value as a key factor.

What the customers are saying to the stores is, "We don't want any more cheap thrills." They are saying, "We want great clothes that will last several seasons and can be added to." Sara Lister, vice-president and fashion merchandising director for Marshall Field & Company

Certain designs and silhouettes have been proved over time, and women insist on buying them again

Classic styles to suit every age and lifestyle include a tunic dress and vest, two-piece dress, pantsuit and sweater, bermuda shorts set and spaghetti strap cocktail dress. These garments are constructed from either cotton or linen, fabrics that are as timeless as the designs.

and again. A silk shirt worn with pleat-front trousers made fashion news in 1934 and still looks terrific today.

There's nothing more effective than simplicity.
Designer Ronaldus Shamask

Let's face it, most of us aren't bold or extroverted enough to be on the cutting edge of fashion. We want the security and confidence that comes from fitting in via our clothes and not calling an undue amount of attention to ourselves with our wardrobe. Also, we want clothes to last because we can't afford to turn over our closets four times a year.

Investment dressing has become important among cost- and clothes-conscious consumers. To be *Chic on a Shoestring*, it's important to understand the concept of timeless fashion and incorporate into your wardrobe a certain percentage of classic pieces that will take you from season to season and not become outdated or passé before you've gotten your money's worth from them.

Before getting into our recommendations of classic wardrobe-stretching pieces to add to your wardrobe, we've asked professor and author Mary Kefgen (also interviewed in the Color Is Chic chapter) to define what is meant by good design or "timeless *Chic.*"

**An Interview on Timeless Chic
with Professor Mary Kefgen**
CHIC: What is good design, and which silhouettes endure?
M.K.: Design that endures is classic. For example, a blazer, a tailored shirt or a pair of pumps is classic. The Chanel suit is the apex of good design. I was looking through a history book of the Rose Bowl recently with my students, and you can pick out certain looks that endure—what we could call the classic American silhouette. The cardigan sweater is another example. These clothes don't veer away from the body too radically. They shape the body and the points of articulation. The waists are at the waists instead of dropped, the shoulders are at the shoulders. Pieces like the shirtwaist dress or the blazer jacket continue to be worn for that reason. The lapels may get a little wider or more narrow, but generally the styles stay the same. Classic shoe styles besides the pump would be the sandal and the loafer.

On an opposite note, ethnic dressing also doesn't go out of fashion. Dresses that are patterned after kimonos, Grecian sheaths or caftans are everlasting. I made several dresses six years ago and still wear them today and don't feel out of fashion because they have their own style. They're usually costly to make but a lot of fun, so it's good that they endure.

The ethnic look is entirely different from the classic American silhouette in that it veers *away* from the body to accommodate weight changes such as pregnancy and body shifts due to aging. There's fullness incorporated into the design. These silhouettes are tried and true by various cultures—they've lived with them, worked with them, been married and buried in them, so they *function.*
CHIC: Do uniforms qualify as classic apparel?
M.K.: Wearing a uniform is sometimes an antiuniform statement. Mostly uniforms are worn because they're inexpensive, and then the looks become "fashion," but it's not a lasting fashion.
CHIC: When does a design become fashion?
M.K.: Fashion is a phenomenon that has to be accepted. A designer can try to put women in long skirts or short skirts, but unless people are ready for it, they'll reject something that's foisted upon them. A successful designer or merchant is someone who can interpret what people want. I love to watch this part of fashion—the gradual change that occurs throughout history.
CHIC: What influences do you see on fashion now and in the future?
M.K.: As far as fashion is concerned, I'm not a great observer. Fashion as such really bores me. I don't dress fashionably; I'm not *in* fashion. My emphasis is on good design. Fashion is here today, gone tomor-

The timeless caftan made fashionably current in a modern interpretation.

row. Good design is lasting, eternal. I don't spend a lot of time looking through fashion magazines even though I get them all. I *do* look through for interesting design ideas that you or I could use. In fashion now I see design influences from the 1950s as a strong factor. Many of my students are wearing this look, so I encourage them to shop the thrift stores and look for the real thing at a fraction of the cost.

Layered dressing—adding to and taking off layers of clothing for warmth and coolness—is being reintroduced after a flirtation with this idea in the seventies. It's catching on a bit more this time around.

CHIC: What is the future of fashion?

M.K.: The future is hard to predict. Rudy Gernreich certainly explored the idea and brought fashions closer to the body. Years ago Saks Fifth Avenue asked several designers to create something that would be worn fifty to a hundred years hence. Most of them had a sort of Buck Rogers space look, but I was impressed with a Bonnie Cashin design that was remarkable. It was layered and started with a body stocking. To that you could add a skirt, a cape, a top, a tunic—whatever you needed. We see some of this now with leotards. My students wear leotards under skirts, jeans, and then layer a blouse or sweater for warmth.

We also see a trend toward simpler designs in luxurious fabrics. This has come about partly because labor is so high that it becomes prohibitively expensive to create complicated garments. The simple shapes of Zoran's cashmere separates, for example, also have a somewhat oriental or ethnic flavor. The French couture relies on both—gorgeous lines and fabrics with exquisite detailing—but it's very costly to create. When they pare those designs for the ready-to-wear market, they eliminate all kinds of seaming and intricacies of design.

CHIC: What is the most important element of design?

M.K.: When I ask my students why they choose to wear something, they generally answer, "Comfort." Comfort is the reason the jean is a classic and will continue to be worn. There's comfort in wearing the fabric, and comfort in knowing you'll be accepted almost anywhere you go.

CHIC: What is your advice to *Chic* readers about timeless fashion?

M.K.: Don't follow fashion slavishly and expect to develop a lasting personal style—if it doesn't fit your lifestyle, don't wear it. Think of the individual—and timeless—look created by Joan Crawford. It's common among young people to want to look alike, but it's a symbol of maturity to be able to step out on your own. It takes guts, maturity and showmanship to do this.

Basic Classics

Describe a woman as a classic beauty or someone who dresses with classic elegance, and what comes to mind? We picture a naturally beautiful, self-assured woman with carefully applied makeup enhancing her clear complexion, a no-nonsense hairstyle, wearing expertly fitted, understated clothing in natural fibers. In short, a classic woman knows confidently that she, not this year's fad, is what's important when people meet her. Classically styled clothing is also safe, by nature conservative; it doesn't take chances or make a unique or new statement. A shirtwaist dress is a safe haven in the sartorial storm of miniskirts and granny dresses.

Another way of looking at classics is to call them the time-tested middle ground that always exists in the fashion world to give the new and extreme a framework in which to exist. The danger in buying and wearing classics is that they can be boring and not say enough about you as a unique individual. The secret to wearing classics successfully is to distinguish them as your own by combining colors uniquely, adding distinctive accessories and paying close attention to proper fit and quality fabric and construction. Because these clothes will be worn for several years, you want to buy the best quality possible without spending extra for a status label that turns you into a walking billboard.

Classics, the Fashion Perennials

Classic clothes have strong menswear influences and thus are popular choices among working women fitting into (and moving up in) corporate America. Although we don't believe women should be trapped in three-piece uniforms any more than their male counterparts, we do realize that coordinated suits for work are the most authoritative and economical way for women to dress.

The following is a partial list of classic garments and accessories that you might have in your wardrobe or consider adding.

- **Blouses and Shirts**

    oxford-cloth, button-down collar
    silk, cotton and rayon bowling, camp or man-tailored shirts
    plaid flannel shirt
    cotton blouses with Peter Pan, shawl, stand-up or notched collars

- **Suits and Separates**

    navy wool blazer with gold buttons
    boxy or fitted jacket
    wool tweed or cotton twill blazer
    dirndl, A-line, slim, softly flared or pleated skirt
    pantsuit with straight-leg trousers

- **Slacks and Pants**

    straight-leg, tailored, pleated trousers
    corduroy slacks
    chinos or khakis
    jeans
    jodhpurs

- **Dresses**

    A-line
    shirtwaist
    chemise or sheath
    princess
    tunic

- **Coats and Jackets**

    mid-calf trench, reefer or double-breasted style
    camel-color Chesterfield
    plaid-wool-lined trench
    mid-thigh navy wool pea coat
    leather blouson
    goose-down vest
    Pendleton wool plaid jacket
    collarless sweater coat

- **Shoes and Boots**

    leather pumps with mid-height heels ("walking pumps")
    penny loafers
    T-strap shoes
    Chanel-style slingback heels
    deck shoes
    deerskin moccasins
    cowboy boots
    low-heeled riding boots
    running shoes

- **Evening Wear**

    Grecian-style one-shoulder sheath
    "little black dress"
    satin A-line gown with spaghetti straps and bias-cut skirt
    silk shirt or blouse and full skirt

This classic, black-and-white polka-dot shirtwaist is as fashionable today as it was in the 1940s when it was introduced.

120 • Chic on a Shoestring

- **Sweaters**

    cable-stitched turtlenecks
    V-necks, crew necks and cardigans
    Irish wool fisherman sweaters
    handmade sweaters

- **Accessories**

    string of pearls
    gold, silver, diamond or pearl stud earrings
    shawl or wool poncho
    1½-inch-wide leather belt (also, snakeskin belt)
    French beret
    Ray-Ban sunglasses
    cotton and wool socks and knee socks
    leather envelope briefcase
    clean-lined quartz watch
    bar pin
    antique cameo

- **Sports Gear**

    sweat suits
    silk, wool or cotton long underwear
    city shorts
    tank suit or leotard
    safari suit

Basic Secrets

The secret to a satisfying basic or classic wardrobe is adding distinctive touches either with color or accessories, or by combining pieces in unexpected ways. As we discussed in the Wardrobe chapter, a *Chic* closet need not be jammed full of clothes, but every piece should be understood and worn in as many ways as possible to get the most return on your investment.

Designer Pauline Trigère's famous story exemplifies this: "A young man comes up to Trigère in a restaurant and introduces himself as the son of a valued Trigère customer. Trigère asks how her client is and learns she has recently died and was buried in her favorite Trigère dress. Trigère expresses condolences and then, after the young man has left, says to her companion, 'You see, in a Trigère, you can go anywhere.'"

A good guideline when breaking rules and stepping out from the sartorial crowd is the two-thirds rule. Think of your basic outfit as three units, say suit, blouse and pumps. Imagine a navy wool gabardine suit and navy shoes to match, worn with a bright red silk bow-tied blouse or cashmere sweater instead of a white oxford-cloth shirt. Just the one-third touch of the unexpected livens the entire outfit and makes a statement that you are unique and confident enough to personalize it. The two-thirds rule allows you to stretch and experiment with your wardrobe while still remaining well within the safe code of classics. Remember, basics need not be boring.

Here are some tips on how to add pizzazz inexpensively to a wardrobe of basics. Chances are, you've already got a gold mine of basic pieces in your closet that with a little imagination can be jazzed up to add sparkle to your spirits without tarnishing your paycheck. Check the Wardrobe and Accoutrements chapters for added *Chic on a Shoestring* tips.

- Brights with brights. Wear red and blue, for example, or turquoise with orange and then add a neutral like black, white or tan. Don't be afraid to wear more than one bright color at a time.
- Unexpected color combinations. Team pink or peach with khaki.
- Wear a sweater instead of a blouse with a skirt or suit, or try a cotton rugby shirt or polo shirt.
- Red is a versatile accent color with classics. Choose a skin-flattering shade and watch heads turn in your direction.
- Belts can be worn over sweaters and at the hip for variety. Experiment with inexpensive web belts in bright colors to liven up a pair of khaki slacks or blue jeans.
- Tuck a sweatshirt into a pair of walking shorts and wear it like a sweater. Turn it inside out for variety and texture, and think about adding an inexpensive colored sweatshirt to your wardrobe.

Declare your fashion independence with a dash of the unexpected, such as wearing a man's short-sleeved shirt with your two-piece suit.

- Create a suit look with a blouse, skirt and cardigan sweater instead of a jacket.
- Soften necklines of your basic blouses with scarves and ribbons tied softly.
- Instead of a necklace, try a bright-colored or hand-painted tie as an accessory. Stay away from too serious, mannish ties with suits unless you want to look masculine.
- Wear a sporty bowling or camp shirt with a tailored skirt.
- Colored shoes and/or socks can brighten your spirits and your ensemble.
- Belt a suit jacket and create a trim peplum look. Turn up the collar on a blazer jacket and wear a high-ruffle-collared blouse underneath for a feminine yet businesslike suit look.
- Belt a tunic-length sweater over a straight skirt (maybe the suit skirt you used in the previous tip) instead of wearing a jacket.
- Wear a tweed suit jacket over last year's sweater dress belted for polish as a new, softer suit look.
- Belt a vertically folded lambswool, flannel or cashmere rectangle worn front to back over one shoulder to update last year's jacket.
- Combine textures for an eye-catching look, e.g., wool tweed jacket and leather pants or cotton bouclé sweater and silk blouse.
- Mix prints in the same or in a complementary color family, e.g., black and white polka dots with red and black stripes, or brown and beige houndstooth with brown, blue and beige check. This technique is tricky to use, so give yourself a careful squint in the mirror before venturing forth.
- Basics can accommodate strong accessories and textures. Remember, the simpler the outfit, the more you can individualize it with accessories.

Best Buys on Basics
The key to saving money on your basic wardrobe purchases is keeping a running list of items you need to flesh out your outfits and remembering always to be on the hunt. The best buys on sweaters, for

example, will be at the end of the winter season or even in the heat of summer, before shoppers are in the mood to buy. If you're a sweater freak, you'll be able to save a bundle by purchasing yours off-season and off-price. The simple secret is to learn your wardrobe needs and likes inside out, so when you're out shopping and see something you like at a sale price, you'll know instantly that you're making the right decision to buy. We write this after just returning from a summer sale at a local discount store. Besides the summer merchandise, we found super savings on close-out sweaters from the previous winter. By choosing classic styles in basic colors that won't look dated next fall, we were able to buy better quality merchandise than we might otherwise be able to afford. These clothes will look better and wear better than clothes made to sell cheaply, and no one will know we didn't pay top dollar for them.

Where to buy is as important as *how* to buy your basic or classic wardrobe pieces. Most important, buy quality-made garments, because they're going to be on your back frequently and you want them to reflect your good taste and style.

Consult the chapter on shopping retail for where-to-shop details and a year-long calendar of special sales. The chapters on discount shopping and catalog shopping also discuss the best buys in each category.

To a certain extent, buying classics can be compared to buying tissues. You know you're going to need and use and eventually use up your tissues, and you know that certain items in your wardrobe get worn and eventually worn out more quickly than others. Just as you'd buy an extra box of tissues on sale to keep in the hall closet so you won't be caught sniffling, you shouldn't hesitate to replace or replenish your wardrobe basics before they're completely worn out.

Fashion should be classic basically with enough innovation to give variety. Designer Edith Head

More and more I believe in well-made, basic clothes with no "fashion" that last many years without transformation—exactly like a blue jean. Classic seems to be an old-fashioned word, but I think the contrary. Designer Yves St. Laurent

Fads, Trends and Classics

Laver's Law of Change: *A dress is indecent ten years before its time, daring a year before its time, chic at its time and dowdy two years after.* British Fashion Expert James Laver

The key to dressing *Chic on a Shoestring* is to know the difference between fads, trends and classics (or basics) and how much money to spend on each. A fad is a short-lived fashion "item." It could be a trendy color that becomes the rage for one season, or it could be a certain style or look that is usually exaggerated or costumey and will look dated very quickly. Remember baggy jeans or platform shoes? The *Chic* advice on fads is to indulge only if you truly look good in the color or style, and then spend as little as possible on it so you won't feel guilty when you don't feel like wearing it again next year.

Trends are slower, more general fashion changes that stick around for two years or more. Sometimes a fad can catch on with enough people to become a trend and start to affect fashion across the board. An example of a trend is the continuing popularity of dance and exercise wear. The close-to-the-body silhouette, stretch fabrics and active-wear comfort are popular ingredients in dance wear that are now being incorporated into other forms of dress.

Classics, as we have already discussed, are garments that have been proved over time to be popular with a large percentage of the clothes-buying public. We think of them as conservative, understated silhouettes that have well integrated form and function.

Fuchsia spandex jeans and jacket are examples of a fad purchase; a denim skirt would be considered a trend item because it has caught on and remained popular over several seasons; and the dirndl skirt and vest are wardrobe classics that could be considered an investment purchase.

If clothes don't make it on the streets, they're just eccentricities.   Designer Coco Chanel

Spot Trends Early

In fashion real news is rare. In the twentieth century we can point to only a handful of dramatic fashion shifts. Coco Chanel's pure and simple "little suit" revolutionized women's clothing and attitudes about their bodies in the early 1900s. Dior's "New Look" in 1947 emphasized women's curves again with small waists and full, long skirts. Courrèges introduced an architectural attitude toward clothing in 1963, and then, of course, we had Carnaby Street and the Youthquakers from England. Counterculture chic took over in the 1970s, with lots of denim and granny dresses. And now what? We seem to be surfing the fashion waves waiting to catch the next big one.

"Couture is the laboratory of fashion," Hubert Givenchy has said, and to this we might add, "So is the street." At the affluent end of the spectrum, couture designers cater to women with insatiable appetites and unlimited budgets for clothing. Designers are able to experiment freely and let their imaginations loose on the female form as the artist's canvas. On the street level, the young and young at heart respond to their personal needs and the current Zeitgeist to create outfits that express how they feel about themselves and the world. It's interesting to note that despite the disparity of dollars, the two aren't usually too far apart. On one level you see ripped and torn black T-shirts and black jeans, and on another you find black backless gowns with latticework sleeves. The statement is similar even though the interpretation is different.

By keeping your eyes open to magazines, newspapers, television and movies, you can stay in touch with the global fashion village. Fashion is simply an extension of life and lifestyle and thus continually evolving. Even if you don't blow with the wind, it's nice to know which direction it's coming from. Remember, too, that truly unique and stylish people would rather have respect and approval. They are aware of the styles around them but able to go their fashion route alone if they have to, because setting a style is more important than following one. A unique individual is never in or out of style; she has a style of her own.

Fashion is what you adopt when you don't know who you are.   Quentin Crisp, sartorially eccentric British author

The Flow of Fashion—
Interview with Fashion Editor Genevieve Buck

Fashion, we complain, changes too rapidly and doesn't reflect what real women want and need to wear. The real women we know don't wear leather minis or three-piece butter suede suits to the office

124 • Chic on a Shoestring

or PTA meetings or operate on unlimited clothing budgets. What we have to realize is that in fashion, as in anything else, there's something for everyone, and the challenge is to find where you feel most comfortable stylistically and financially.

We asked Genevieve Buck, fashion editor of the Chicago *Tribune,* for some *Chic* tips on how to outsmart fashion trends and get the most value for our clothing dollar.

CHIC: How do you outsmart fashion?
G.B.: Start to look at fashion photos in magazines, newspapers and catalogs and separate the flamboyance from the clothes. Learn to see the *fashion message*—color, silhouette, fabric, feeling, attitude and structure. Remember, fashion photography is art photography. Makeup, lighting, hair and accessories are all intended to make an artistic statement.

Look at the clothes as clothes, not at the model or her hat or hairstyle or exaggerated makeup. In your mind's eye, remove the trimming and look at the tree.

CHIC: How do you begin to analyze what you see photographed?
G.B.: Try to look at *pieces.* Look at the whole first to get an overall visual impression; notice the silhouette and attitude. Then isolate pieces. Is the skirt full or tight; long or short? Are the jackets boxy and long or short and fitted? Notice the use (or lack) of layers, the choice of colors and the texture of the fabrics. Learn from photographs how to put pieces together and you'll be able to save money and dress better.

CHIC: What is your wardrobe shopping advice to *Chic* readers?
G.B.: Pieces are the key now in buying. *Key* pieces, *investment* pieces and *accent* pieces all stretch your wardrobe and maximize the use of your dollars.

CHIC: Timing is so important in fashion. How can we detect when a trend is coming in, and when does a fad become a trend?
G.B.: Start to adapt to trends when you first notice a change; that way you'll get more mileage out of your purchases. Don't put off tapering your bell-bottoms until just before wide pants return—it would be better not to bother at all.

You can be in at the beginning, middle or end of a trend, but what really counts is having the sense of personal style to make almost every purchase work all the time. Some things will transition in and out, but a good purchase will be wearable for years, with your personality marked on it.

Also, some pieces are classic and shouldn't be changed, ever. For example, the Chanel suit is so intrinsically right—the fabric, scale and look—that it will always be in fashion. A more current example is a Ralph Lauren prairie skirt. Never, ever shorten

Genevieve Buck, fashion editor of the Chicago Tribune.

a Ralph Lauren skirt, come hell, high water or miniskirts.

CHIC: Where can we learn more about fashion trends?

G.B.: From magazines, store windows and catalogs. You don't have to wait a year now between seeing a fashion introduced in Europe start to influence styles here and be copied at all levels—even Sears and Penney. There's less lag time in fashion now than ever before, and any woman on any budget can stay current with a little thought and planning.

CHIC: Should we buy every trend that comes along?

G.B.: My advice is, if you love it, get it. You may have to be a stronger person to stick with it, but this way you'll start to discover and develop personal style through which all trends, fads and fashions can be filtered. Your own look will emerge and imprint everything you purchase and wear.

CHIC: Since clothing is so expensive, what is your advice on investment dressing?

G.B.: Investment dressing has expanded in concept to include items that are more fashionable, not just the wardrobe warhorses like a three-piece wool gabardine suit or cashmere crewneck. An investment purchase might be a pair of suede jeans, a gold bracelet or a mink coat, depending on your lifestyle and personal style. Think of all your purchases as having multiple uses. That's the best way to get the most return on your investment. This philosophy, plus creatively using accessories to stretch your wardrobe, will enable you to dress *Chic on a Shoestring*.

17
Quality: More Value for your Chic Dollar

Just what do we mean by the term *quality?* Quality is admittedly a somewhat elusive concept; it means different things to different people. Yet each of us wants quality, especially in our clothing and accessories. We want *value* for our money in properly made garments that will serve us well over time. Another way to put this: we don't mind *spending* money, but we sure don't want to *waste* it.

Stanley Marcus, co-founder of the well known Neiman-Marcus specialty stores, sums up the concept of quality this way:

You should buy the best you can afford, not the poorest of what you can't. From the best quality you will get the most satisfaction, the longest wear and the enjoyment of knowing it is the best without having to apologize for it.

Actually, the realities of being on a budget—in particular, a clothing budget—can be viewed in a positive light. Being forced to watch our pennies has heightened our awareness of quality, of finding the best values for the least money. As a result, we're moving gradually toward a more European way of shopping. European women have always made fewer, more careful purchases than we conspicuous consumption-minded Americans. A European woman might buy one really good quality outfit per year (rather than, as do many Americans, spending the same amount or more on several, less expensive outfits). She adds this chic new purchase to her closet filled with other quality garments, and thus always dresses fashionably and well. In a sense, this European woman *collects* rather than buys clothes.

Some of us on this side of the Atlantic are adopting this quality, not quantity credo. We women would do well, too, to take a wardrobe tip from our male friends who are more used to buying the best suit, slacks or sport jacket they can afford and having it last for years. As designer Mollie Parnis puts it, "Buying good clothes turns out to be the most economical in the long run."

You don't have to be a fashion designer or hold a graduate degree in homemaking to be able to judge quality for yourself. In these days of fewer discretionary dollars and more things to spend our money on, we have to arm ourselves with a little bit of nuts-and-bolts information on what to look for in a garment in order to size up its quality before we make a purchase. We'll go through each of the three aspects of quality step by step.

Quality Components

Naturally we all want garments and accessories that are well made, so that they'll stand up to frequent wear over a period of time. To check for quality of construction, you need to check an item thoroughly inside and out. It's especially important to do this when you realize that a manufacturer's first priority is to make the outside of the garment attractive to you, so that it will catch your eye as it hangs on the rack or on display and so that it will look good when you try it on. But the other, equally important half of the story is inside the garment, and that's where your inspection comes in. Here's a laundry list of pertinent things to look for:

Construction

- Generous hems and seam allowances.
- Quality zippers, buttons or snaps.
- Seam allowances and raw edges overcast to prevent raveling. Stay away from garments with insides that resemble a nest of loose, straggly threads.
- Smooth, flat seams, darts, tucks, pleats. Beware of puckering.
- Neatly stitched buttonholes without loose threads. Likewise, buttons securely stitched on. Extra buttons and a hank of thread are a sure sign of a quality garment.
- Sweaters with full-fashioned sleeves and cuffs and collars that are knitted on are more durable than those with sleeves, collars and cuffs sewn on.
- Matched plaids or stripes. Be extra certain you check this front and back from a distance in a three-way mirror. Nothing is a bigger tipoff to low quality than the jagged lines of mismatched patterns.
- Collars or lapels that lie flat and smooth. No bubbling, rippling or buckling.
- Do the fabric weight and weave match the type of garment? Gabardine makes a good blazer; a loose, open weave doesn't.

A sign of quality is patterns that match at the seams, as in the garment on the right.

- Check shoes and boots on the outside for smooth, even stitching and neat joinings of uppers to soles and heels. All-leather shoes are nice but more expensive than those with leather uppers and man-made soles. Synthetic soles often last longer than soles made of leather.
- Bend the shoe to make sure it's flexible enough for lots of comfortable wear.
- Check the insides of shoes and boots by running your fingers along seams, joinings and soles. Beware of any rough or bumpy areas; they'll cause blisters and generally make your feet miserable.
- All these construction checks should be made on accessories, too, such as handbags, scarves, hats and gloves.

What about linings? Actually not every garment needs lining in order to be of good quality or to wear well; it does help in some garments, though. Wool skirts and slacks usually require lining in the back to prevent sagging or sitting out the seat. While full lining isn't necessary in wool slacks, it is more comfortable, since the wool won't scratch or rub your legs. Knits, especially skirts and dresses, also need lining in the seat; jackets may or may not have lining. In general, looser or more open weaves will need lining, while more tightly woven fabrics will not. Cotton and linen don't usually require lining, while wool usually does. You'll often see expensive or designer garments, including cotton or linen, lined. A nice touch, but not absolutely essential for wear and durability.

Occasionally price can be a reliable overall indication of quality. This is especially true in fine, hand-tailored suits for men and women. Obviously the more hand labor involved, the higher the price. The hand stitching is necessary to properly shape the back of the collar and to give the lapel the proper roll. Shoulder areas and tops of sleeves are also properly formed and shaped with fine hand stitches joining the interfacing to the fabric. There are still a few things in this world that require hand labor that no machine can duplicate; the hand work in fine wool suits, coats and jackets is one of the best apparel examples of this.

One more comment about construction before moving on to the next area: Just because a garment has a top designer's label in it and a matching top-level price tag doesn't guarantee correspondingly high quality. Many ready-to-wear garments from designers are manufactured by licensees. Designers don't inspect these garments for quality of construction, and thus you will often find a pricey garment that looks spiffy on the outside but is a maze of loose threads and raw seams on the inside. Beware, consumer. Also, most small specialty shops and boutiques look through goods before they're put out on display. Big stores and chains usually don't, so you'll often find garments and accessories with fairly obvious flaws right out there on display. This is another good reason for making a thorough inspection before purchase.

The consumer on the left is inspecting the construction on the inside of a pair of slacks, the other consumer is checking for care properties with the "scrunch" test.

Fabric

Besides looking a garment over thoroughly inside and out, your inspection work should also include reading the fiber content and care label of every garment you're considering. This label or labels will tell you a lot about the quality of a fabric, how best to take care of it and what kind of wear you can expect from it.

Generally speaking, natural fibers (wool, cotton, silk and linen) are superior to synthetics (polyester, nylon and acrylic, for instance). Other natural fibers that are not seen quite so often are cashmere, alpaca, vicuña, mohair and angora. And of course there are all the natural furs. Acrylics and Orlons are most often spun and woven to imitate these natural yarns and furs. The naturals look better and last longer, for the most part, but also usually cost more and require more care. Here's another case of price equaling quality, roughly speaking. Top European, American and Japanese designers use natural fabrics for their beauty and luxury.

On the other hand, most of us do prefer some natural/synthetic blend fabrics in our wardrobes for ease of care. What synthetics don't always have in looks or durability, they make up for in wash-and-wear and drip-dryability. With good-quality blends—usually 65 percent or above natural to 35 percent synthetic—ironing can be almost eliminated. However, some synthetics and finishes such as permanent press may actually hold stains more steadfastly than natural fabrics. Consult the Tender Loving Care chapter for specific stain removal information.

While all-natural fabrics are generally good, there is some variation in the quality of all-cotton or all-silk fabrics. Let your eyes and fingers (by checking the "hand" or feel) tell you if a fabric will give you the wear you require and if it's appropriate for the garment. A hardworking suit blouse, for instance, needs to be made of good quality, solidly woven silk, while a silk evening top that will be worn a few times a year doesn't have to be of quite the same level of quality.

Fabric nomenclature can be confusing. Fabric names are derived from the fiber itself (cashmere), the type of weave (oxford cloth or crepe) or even the finish put on the fabric (chintz, for instance). We'll give you a brief primer on commonly used fabrics. For more detailed information, consult the Recommended Reading section at the end of the book.

Cotton. Probably the most popular and widely used fiber of all, cotton weights and types range from heavy, "bulletproof" denim and canvas to medium-weight broadcloth and oxford to sheer lawns and batistes. Cotton is absorbent and therefore cool in the summer. It's usually lowest in cost of all the natural fibers. It launders well, but you'll probably have to spend some time ironing it.

Wool. Sheep donate their long, warm hairs every spring so that we can all enjoy the wide range of wool garments available. Mother Nature has made this a very resilient and thus durable fiber that can be made into a vast array of fabrics from heavier gabardines and felt to flannel and crepe and even sheer wool gauze. Wool is warm and is usually dry cleaned; some sweaters can be washed in cool water. Never, ever dry wool near heat or in the dryer unless you want the garment to turn into a mere shadow of its former self.

Silk. The "queen of fibers" has been around since the Chinese developed silkworm culture about five thousand years ago. This luxurious, lustrous fabric is strong and absorbent, although not quite as absorbent as cotton. Silk is usually the most high priced of all fibers. Check the care label of a silk garment for dry cleaning or washing instructions. Like wool, silk is loomed into a broad range of fabric weights and types. You'll find silk broadcloth and crepe, silk satin, taffeta and chiffon, to name a few. Silk dyes very well and is a favorite fabric for evening and dressy apparel.

Linen. A heavier weight, stiffer fabric that is made from the flax plant, linen is a very durable fabric. Its natural body lends itself well to structured garments such as jackets, suits and coatdresses. It is, however, the most wrinkle-prone of all fabrics. We've seen linen garments with care labels that state "Guaranteed to Wrinkle." Nothing beats linen for a clean, starched, crisp look, but it certainly requires a lot of care, namely ironing.

Synthetics

There are a number of popular man-made fabrics that have been on the market for about forty years. These synthetics are sometimes referred to by their generic names (polyester or nylon) or by their brand names (Dacron or Antron) and sometimes by both (Acrilan acrylic). We'll run through the major properties of each.

Acrylic. Lightweight and easy to care for, this bulky yarn is often used with wool or as a wool substitute in sweaters and knits. Sweat suits are also made of acrylic. Acrilan, Creslan and Orlon are trade names for acrylics.

Polyester. The most popular man-made fabric, probably due to its ease of care, polyester also retains a press or crease well, wet or dry. Common brand names for polyester are Dacron, Fortrel and Kodel.

Nylon. One of the oldest man-made fibers, nylon is characterized by durability, light weight and elasticity. It's often woven into shiny or lustrous fabrics. Antron is the most commonly used nylon for garments.

Acetate. This low-cost synthetic is often used in linings and for dressy, crisp fabrics such as taffeta, due to its natural body and drapability. Most acetates cannot be washed and are heat and light sensitive. Arnel, a triacetate, does wash well and can be ironed without fear of scorching or melting.

Rayon. This popular fabric is an interesting hybrid of natural cellulose fibers that have been treated via man-made processes to create one of the most versatile of all fabrics. This, combined with its low cost, accounts for the fact that it is the granddaddy of all synthetic fibers. You'll find rayon loomed into almost every weight and type of weave and combined with almost all other kinds of fibers.

Follow care instructions on garments carefully, since some rayon fabrics shrink when washed or are quite heat sensitive. Antique and vintage clothing stores are full of lovely old rayon Hawaiian and regular men's shirts and women's blouses, rayon taffeta dresses and other older garments made from high-quality early-generation rayon.

Spandex. This lightweight fiber with superior stretchability and holding power was developed to pick up where rubber left off in elastics and other stretchy garments such as underwear. Today Lycra spandex can also be found in many leotards and swimsuits.

While synthetics are low cost and easy to take care of, they share a few other common characteristics that should be noted. For the most part, they pill and snag easily. Run your own pill test when shopping by rubbing the fabric vigorously between your thumb and fingers. If little beginnings of pills form, beware. Also, most man-made fabrics are not nearly as absorbent as natural fibers and can, therefore, be hot and sticky in summer and cold and clammy in winter. Some have a tendency to grey over time, especially nylon, and most are heat sensitive, which means they should be washed and ironed at low temperatures. Wrinkles can be set into these garments in the dryer, so it's a good idea to tumble dry for ten or fifteen minutes and then hang them up to complete drying. Check a fabric's tendency to wrinkle by using the "scrunch" test: Grab a handful of fabric and wad it up in your fist. If gentle wrinkles have formed, you'll have to do a bit of ironing.

As for accessories, most of us prefer leather for bags, boots and shoes because it wears better and is easy to take care of. Other materials such as canvas, rope, straw or wicker are fun for shoes and bags that will not be worn frequently, since they won't be as durable and are hard—if not impossible—to clean.

Decoding Care Labels

Here's a handy reference to give you more inside information on what certain terms listed on garment labels mean.

Colorfast dyes won't run or fade noticeably during garment's lifetime.

Crease-resistant fabric won't wrinkle much during wearing and what wrinkles do develop will hang out overnight. Usually needs little ironing after laundering. (Same as wrinkle-resistant.)

Drip-dry if fabric is hung up sopping wet to dry—

Reprinted by permission of *Woman's Day* Magazine. Copyright © 1968 by CBS Publications, The Consumer Publishing Division of CBS, Inc.

not wrung out or tumble-dried—it can be worn with little or no ironing.

Permanent-press garment needs absolutely no ironing after machine washing and tumble drying. (Same as durable-press.)

Permanent press garment needs absolutely no ironing after machine washing and tumble drying. (Same as durable-press.)

Shrink-resistant garment will not shrink beyond a stated percentage in washing. (Same as preshrunk.)

Soil release fabric treated to release grease and oil spots during washing—an important factor in permanently pressed and some synthetic garments.

Spot- and stain-resistant fabric has been treated so that spills can be wiped or washed in hot water with ordinary soap or detergents.

Washable unless tag contains specific laundering instructions, fabric won't shrink or fade if washed in hot water with ordinary soap or detergents.

Wash-and-wear garment needs little or no ironing after normal laundering. (Same as minimum-care.)

Waterproof fabric pores are sealed so that no water can penetrate.

Water-repellent fabric sheds water so that rain tends to roll off before it can be absorbed.

Water-resistant fabric sheds water and fights its absorption, but is not completely waterproof.

Fit

Proper fit in any garment ensures you'll look terrific and makes the clothes appear more expensive. Even the best fabric and finest construction won't spell quality for you if the clothes don't fit well. Here's a fit checklist to help you make sure you're getting your money's worth.

- When trying a garment on, move around in it; bend your knees and move your arms to make sure it's comfortable. Comfort is an essential component of fit. Close your eyes. Is every part of you comfortable, or does the garment in question bind anywhere?
- Check for enough ease in the shoulders, across the back, through the bustline and hips and at the waist. These areas should just be comfortable, with no binding or bagging.
- Pockets, zippers and openings should lie flat, not gap.
- The shoulder line of garments with regular, set-in sleeves should extend out a little ($\frac{1}{4}''-\frac{1}{2}''$) beyond your natural shoulder line.

Careful inspection in a store's three-way mirror is the best way to check the look and fit of a proposed purchase coming and going.

- Pants probably present the greatest challenge when it comes to getting a good fit. Besides waist and hip areas, note the "rise" or length from hipline to waistline. Sit down in pants while you're trying them on to make sure the rise matches you, along with the crotch length. This should be comfortable without binding. Check for any pulling across the upper back of the pants or "smile" lines (pulling in the front or back near the crotch).
- Give the garment a thorough once-over, front and back and sides, in a well-lighted three-way mirror.
- Now for more personal aspects of fit: Do you like the proportion on you? Does the item show off your good points while not highlighting the areas you'd just as soon not call attention to?
- Does the silhouette or the shape of the garment flatter you? How about the design lines and details?
- Do you like how you look in it? Does it feel good on and do you feel good in it?

Finally, ask yourself a few questions in summing up the overall quality of a potential purchase:

- How often will you wear the garment? Does the cost per wearing seem to make sense? Everyday, workhorse items in your wardrobe need to be of good quality so they'll stand up.
- What kinds of activities will you wear the garment to? Sports clothes for strenuous activities need to have reinforced seams, for instance.
- Can you wear the garment the way you want to? If you wear your blazer collars turned up, is the underside finished?
- Can you take care of or have minor, not major, alterations done?

One final note on quality. After all this urging to buy the very best in your price range, we must say, too, that it's okay to sacrifice quality once in a while. For a fun, fashion fad item or something you will wear or use infrequently (like an evening bag), you can get by with less than the very best in materials and workmanship. Just remember that these items won't last as long as your regular, higher quality wardrobe pieces and they may need to be repaired somewhere along the line.

Fashion designer A'lone Alakazia.

An Insider's Views on Quality:
Interview with Designer A'lone Alakazia
We talked to A'lone Alakazia, Southern California–based designer of the Alakazia line of better dresses and sportswear, about quality. A'lone's design and modeling training in Europe, combined with his experience in this country as a successful designer, have given him an insider's perspective on quality.

CHIC: What is your advice to women on how to determine whether a garment is a quality one?
A.A.: Quality has several components. I would first tell a woman to see if the garment is suited to her. A lot of women will buy things they see on other people and they have no concept how long it will last for them.

You have to look at how something is made. I would tell women to judge a garment by the inside first as opposed to the outside, because the way a garment is put together denotes the type of quality that it is: the type of seams, the type of buttonholes, the type of hem and the way a collar sits. I don't look for a woman to know all the technical terms, just to know, for instance, what kind of seams last in her garments.

There's also quality in the type of fabric that goes above and beyond the workmanship and the price point. Certain types of fabrics tend to last longer.

CHIC: What would those fabrics be?

A.A.: I find that natural fibers tend to last a little bit longer than man-made fibers. I think the blends last even longer because you have both properties going. Each fiber content of a fabric has various properties and good points and bad points. You need to go above and beyond how a fabric feels on the body. How are you going to care for it?

CHIC: Is there some sort of personal aspect to quality?

A.A.: Quality is an individual thing. It has to be the quality *you* need. When my customer or any woman is going to buy a day garment, I think she should look a little bit harder, a little bit closer at all those points and especially at workmanship. I have things for years. And they've lasted because—it wasn't the price—of the fabric and the way it was made and the way it *fit* because there is a quality to fit also.

CHIC: I see you in leather a lot. With the new tanning methods, leather is now almost a fabric. Is it one of your favorite fabrics?

A.A.: Yes, I have a lot of leather. Like a number of other designers, I wear it year round. Leather breathes. As a matter of fact, I wore it yesterday in eighty-five-degree weather. A leather garment becomes a valuable part of one's wardrobe. And it can be worn year round, really. There are summer-weight leathers that I have that are almost like cotton voile. When it's hot, leather becomes porous; it's a little like skin. When it's cold, it contracts. It still gives. Leather is very comfortable and you don't have to clean it a lot. So when you spend three hundred dollars for a pair of leather pants, you should buy a pair that doesn't show a lot of dirt. Most of my leathers are dark.

Leather, ninety percent of the time, denotes quality, but to be sure, look for double-stitched seams because leather stretches. Look for tacking (reinforced stitching) at pocket corners and pockets that lie flat.

People look at leather and say, "Oh my, those garments are very expensive." But leather should last for years. I've shopped a lot in thrift shops and there are many really good old leathers.

CHIC: Is the old leather still supple, and are the hides still in good condition?

A.A.: Yes, and you can have a leather tanned and finished again at a cleaners. I have bought leather pants that cost me twenty dollars and I bought pants that cost me five hundred dollars. They both have lasted.

One thing to keep in mind is that leather expands in *width,* not in *length.* That's why leather pants begin to look baggy around the seat and the knees.

Leather to me is an investment. That's quality.

CHIC: What other aspects of quality should we be on the lookout for?

A.A.: You have to be concerned that the lining inside a garment—any garment, leather or not—is going to react the same as the outside. Because you're going to wash or clean the garment and its lining together. Sometimes manufacturers put in the wrong lining. Maybe the outer layer stays the same but the lining draws up and the pants begin to ripple and fit funny. And, some silks are lined with polyester. The polyester won't take the water that the silk throws off when one is sweating; therefore, the silk stains.

CHIC: Do you think we're becoming more like the Europeans, more concerned about quality?

A.A.: I do think people and women especially are

becoming more concerned about quality because of the economic situation. As you know, in fashion now there are no certain lengths, there are no certain collars, there are no certain cuffs, no certain bottoms and tops. When that happens in the market, people begin to look for what works for them as opposed to seeing something in the newspaper and thinking, "I've *got* to have this." You see *everything* in the paper now.

You know, it's the price now, too. If you're looking at something for two hundred dollars, you may try it on and come back the next day. You may shop around and try to find the same feeling for less. I do that. I hate to pay retail. I think women are more concerned about quality because the price of gasoline is going up. I've asked women and they tell me they will go to where the prices are good and the quality is good, but they don't go that often.

The women of the eighties are not concerned with fashion. They just know there's something new out there. It has to work for them. It has to make them look good. Because you can throw yourself into a different, higher echelon, socially and economically, by dressing differently. And that's what the consciousness is now. "I want to look like I am somebody because everybody else is doing it." That is the fad the eighties woman is following.

CHIC: How would you say you can determine quality in design?

A.A.: The way a garment fits. No matter how extravagant the design may be, if it hangs right, if it fits right, if it falls in the right places, it's quality.

CHIC: Do you think women are getting better at putting together a total outfit or quality look?

A.A.: I would use the word *merchandising*. Women are getting better at merchandising themselves. It's a sense of "I'm merchandising myself and I'm worth it." That's why the average woman is not concerned about fashion. That's why I don't want to be known just as a fashion designer. I also want to be known as a merchandiser. Each woman has her *own* fashion. I want you to buy something of mine because it works in your wardrobe, not because it's an "item." I want you to buy an Alakazia piece because it works *for* you, not just to hang in the closet. No, I want my clothes *on the street*. I want you to wear them until you wear them out. If you just hang something in the closet, you don't give me a chance.

18

Tender Loving Care

The *Chic on a Shoestring* woman knows that with proper care techniques, the life of any garment can be extended. This is the single best way to save money on clothing. A well cared for garment not only looks better on but will give you years of additional wear. An expensive garment shabbily cared for will look cheap. The opposite is also true. In fact, inexpensive garments may require extra attention so that they can perform like thoroughbreds.

Those of you with personal laundresses can skip this chapter. For the rest of us who still throw the black socks in with the white bras and wonder why our underwear looks as grey as Omaha in the winter, read on. We'll discuss care in two sections: first, general terms and tips on dry cleaning, laundering and storing clothes; and second, proper care techniques for individual fabrics, antique garments, leathers and furs.

Dry Cleaning

Since dry cleaning services are essential to clothes care, we'll begin by explaining the various dry cleaning processes and specialties. Because of the rising costs of dry cleaning, one has to arm herself with a bit of working knowledge on the subject in order to get the most for her money. First, a definition of terms.

Dry Cleaning: the chemical cleaning of fabrics with the use of little or no water. Recommended for clothes that will shrink, lose shape or fade in water.

Invest the time and extra money in finding a top quality, reliable dry cleaner. If you're new in an area, ask friends to recommend a good cleaner or, better yet, ask the proprietor of an antique clothing store. He or she will know the best.

The three types of dry cleaning:

Bulk dry cleaners. Good for sweaters, knits and woolens that don't need pressing. Save money by waiting until you have the full pound limit and then dry clean sweaters and other garments together. Colors can be mixed. Check your Yellow Pages for the most convenient bulk dry cleaning operation.

Regular dry cleaners. Take clothes here that need to be cleaned and pressed, for example, suits, coats, slacks. Also, severely stained clothes that have to be spotted first. A special tip on stained garments: take stained garments into the cleaners as soon as possible so that you can describe the stain and so the dry cleaner can get at it when it's still somewhat fresh.

The cost of dry cleaning varies remarkably from establishment to establishment. Geographical location seems to play a big part in this variable pricing. Check prices where you live, shop or work.

Factors to consider in choosing a dry cleaner: Are the cleaning services reasonably priced, convenient, thorough and careful? Are all the stains gone? Are the collar and cuffs clean? Are garments hung on paper-covered hangers with tissue stuffed into the sleeves to retain their shape, or are several items jammed together like pancakes in one plastic bag? We have a theory that you can tell the quality of dry cleaning by the way garments are packaged when they're returned to you.

Check clothes carefully when you pick them up. If work is not satisfactory, ask that it be redone.

Custom dry cleaners. This type of establishment should be used only occasionally (because it is more costly) for valuable garments such as brightly colored fine silks, fragile antique garments and leathers and suedes that require special handling. These custom cleaners are the most difficult to find but are well worth the effort. Again, an antique-clothing-store owner will be helpful, or the owner of a fine boutique who knows how to care for expensive clothes. Another key is to find an established dry cleaning business with a track record. If the person behind the counter has been dry cleaning clothes for thirty years, chances are he or she knows how to handle your clothing with care.

Laundering

Our discussion here will center on commercial laundries and home laundering.

Basically, laundries handle the commercial washing of clothes, linens, towels, and so on that can be cleaned with water and detergent and then pressed. There is no difference these days between a Chinese laundry and a French laundry. Hand laundry is also a thing of the past. The onslaught of polyester drip-dry or no-iron shirts put many a fine laundry out of business. The few remaining are, for the most part, volume businesses, and the quality of the laundering suffers as a result. Today, with the returning popularity of natural-fiber clothing such as cotton and linen, we predict that more and more busy women will turn to laundries for care of their blouses in the way men have used laundries for years to wash, press and starch their shirts.

When you patronize a particular commercial laundry, be sure to point out and describe any stains that garments have incurred. As with dry cleaners, look for a laundry that has been in business a long time.

By the way, most dry cleaners offer their customers the convenience of handling garments for laundry. Most cleaners send laundry out rather than handling it in their plants.

Hand Washing

There's a fine line here with certain fabrics, for example, silk that can be successfully hand washed as well as dry cleaned. Every garment is required to have a fabric content and care label, but manufacturers are only required to list the preferred or safest method of cleaning. Some of your dry-clean-onlys may actually be hand washable. Test fabrics for hand washing by snipping a piece of fabric from the seam allowance and immersing it in soapy water to see if it is colorfast. The same goes for interfacings and linings.

A mild soap such as Ivory Snow is recommended for delicate fabrics such as fine cotton and silk. Woolite is recommended for woolens and cashmere.

After a fifteen- to twenty-minute soak, gently squeeze the soapsuds through the garment without scrubbing or wringing. Rinse two or three times in cool water; the final rinse should be crystal clear. Roll the garment in an absorbent towel to blot excess moisture and help the garment retain its shape. Dry sweaters, knits and heavy garments on a flat surface. In order to retain shape and reduce ironing, lightweight blouses and tops can be hung on inflatable hangers (never a wire hanger) to drip dry. For best results, press garments on the reverse side while they are slightly damp.

Machine Washing

We've all been told to separate lights from darks before loading the washing machine, but here's another tip to make your washday less frustrating and more efficient: Don't wash lint-producing fabrics such as terry cloth and velour with lint-attracting fabrics such as cotton broadcloth or polyester permanent press. Heavily soiled garments should either be prewashed or washed separately for best results. Mend clothes before washing to avoid creating gaping holes from small tears due to the washing machine's agitation. Secure loose buttons or risk losing them forever. Make sure pockets are clear of foreign objects such as fountain pens and tissues that can damage machines and soil the load. Specific stains should be pretreated according to one of the recommended guides listed at the end of this chapter.

Pour in detergent as water begins to flow and then add clothes to the machine. This enables the detergent to dissolve completely and not become trapped in folds of the fabric. If your clothes are heavily soiled or you have extremely hard water, use slightly more soap. In our experience, however, manufacturers recommend more soap than is actually needed to clean a load. If clothes feel sticky when you take them out of the wash, use less soap next time until you achieve optimal squeaky-clean results. A tablespoon or two of salt added to the wash with the detergent will prevent most colors from running. This will prevent vegetable-dyed Indian and Mexican cotton garments from running. Washing and rinsing in cool water helps prevent color fading in the wash, too.

Money may not always be well spent on expensive detergents that promise "whiter whites" and "brighter brights," or on all-fabric bleaches. Experiment with more economical, generic-brand laundry soaps. Old-fashioned liquid blueing is still the best product for putting the punch back into your whites. Chlorine bleach is not safe for fabrics such as silk, wool, spandex and some flame retardant finishes. Oxygen bleach is safe for all fabrics but won't miraculously make greyed or yellowed fabrics white again. If you're machine washing delicates, turn them inside out to prevent snags or, better yet, put them inside a fine-washables laundry bag (usually made of mesh or net and available in a notions department or by mail order).

Whichever antistatic method you use—fabric softener in the wash or softener sheet or small pouch in the dryer—is up to you. The dryer methods do seem handier, though, and may well be cheaper in the long run.

More damage is done to clothes in drying than washing, especially to clothes sentenced to life (and premature death) in commercial coin-operated laundries. The regular or normal setting on a dryer is generally hot, so for heat-sensitive or permanent-press items, use delicate or tumble dry to avoid damage. Large commercial dryers at coin-op laundries operate even hotter than home units, so dial a cooler than normal setting. Dry light and dark clothes separately; clothes can bleed in the dryer, too. Don't overdry. Clothes are not meant to be fried. We have a friend who thinks that hot temperatures kill germs and then wonders why her clothes wear out.

To avoid wrinkles, remove permanent-press garments from the dryer when they are slightly damp and then hang on rust-proof hangers immediately.

Here are more tips on laundering to help extend the life of your clothes.

- Don't cram more garments into the washer than it can handle; crowded clothes won't come clean.
- Use the shortest washing time or lowest agitation speed possible to save wear and tear during washing.
- Use cool-rinse cycle to save energy and to remove soap residue more efficiently.
- Wash clothes as needed. Perspiration and stains damage fabrics and are more difficult to remove the longer they remain in clothes.

Indispensable and inexpensive clothing care tools extend the life of your clothes.

Ironing

Even with the modern steam iron, clothes come out better and are easier to iron when they're damp. If you can't iron immediately, fold or roll slightly damp garments, put them in a plastic bag and refrigerate them (no kidding!) until you're ready to tackle the task. This keeps them damp yet prevents mildewing and allows you to wait until you have several garments to iron at once. Silks, especially, should be ironed when they are slightly damp, wrong side out, using a low to medium, dry (*not* steam) setting. Silk blends also require a cool setting to avoid scorches. A man's white handkerchief or a linen towel placed on top of the fabric will prevent scorching.

To permanently pleat or repleat a pair of pants, try this *Chic on a Shoestring* technique: First, lay a three-foot strip of aluminum foil on your ironing board, then place the pants on top. Dip a man's white handkerchief in full-strength white vinegar and wring it out. Lay the handkerchief on the area to be pleated or creased and press with a steam iron set to the fabric temperature. (A regular iron will also work for this.) You'll smell the vinegar while you're pressing, but don't worry—the odor will quickly dissipate. Naturally you'll want to test the garment with a little vinegar on a seam allowance to make sure the dye is colorfast for vinegar.

Iron fabrics with a nap or embroidery on the wrong side on top of a terrycloth towel or pad of soft fabric. Use this method for fabrics with sheen, too.

To avoid making fabrics shiny, use a press cloth. If you don't have a steam iron, dampen the press cloth to help remove wrinkles. Iron wools on the reverse side, using a press cloth.

Individual Fiber Care

Cotton. Almost all cottons can be washed in mild soap and warm water. Exceptions are imported cottons, which may not be colorfast; cotton that has not been preshrunk; or cotton fabrics that contain sizing. When in doubt, dry clean or test washability by snipping a piece of fabric from a seam allowance and dipping it in soapy water. White cottons may safely be brightened with chlorine bleach.

Silk. Depending on the quality, the weave and the dyes used, dry clean or hand wash silks. Delicate or dressy silk fabrics such as chiffon, taffeta and crepe and brightly colored silk prints should always go to the cleaners. With repeated visits to the dry cleaners, however, silk garments lose their freshness, so don't overclean.

The American Silk Mills and Loré Caulfield, designer for the luxurious silk line known as Loré Lingerie, recommend hand washing silks, particularly light-colored silk broadcloth, crepe de chine, shantung, raw silk, pongee and surah, in Ivory Snow and warm water. Check colorfastness with the snipped-fabric-from-the-seam-allowance test. If the dye doesn't run, the garment can be washed. Rinse thoroughly in cool water and gently squeeze out excess moisture by rolling in a towel. Most silks should be ironed while they are still damp. Press with a cool iron (don't use steam) on the reverse side to prevent scorching and shiny marks. Do not use bleach on silk.

Linen. Most linen garments will be labeled Dry Clean Only because this protects the original shape and crispness inherent in the fabric. However, if you have a softly structured garment such as a blouse or a pair of shorts or something of handkerchief linen, you can safely hand launder it in mild soap. Iron while damp, using a hot iron. Starch can be used if added shape is desired. We've got linen garments in our closets with care labels that state: Linen. *Guaranteed* to wrinkle. If you're not willing to do a fair amount of ironing, don't buy linen clothes.

Wool. Wool suits, coats, jackets, skirts and slacks should be dry cleaned. Because wool doesn't wrinkle easily, wool garments can also be successfully bulk dry cleaned.

If the care label says a garment is hand or machine washable, use Woolite or a laundry detergent made for fine washables. Wash and rinse in cool water and dry flat, away from direct heat, to prevent shrinking. Do not ever dry woolens in the dryer. Iron on the reverse side or use a press cloth with steam, otherwise the fabric will become shiny.

A word on taking care of sweaters: before washing, lay sweater flat on an old towel and trace the garment's outline with a pencil. After washing, block sweater to the original shape drawn on the towel. Store the towel for the next washing or wash the towel and the pencil line will come out and you're ready for the next sweater.

Cashmere. Cashmere sweaters may be hand washed in Woolite or a laundry detergent recommended for delicate fabrics. Dry flat, away from direct heat, to prevent shrinkage. Other cashmere clothing such as coats should be dry cleaned at a custom dry cleaners, if possible.

Synthetics and natural/synthetic blends. Acrylic, polyester, nylon, rayon, spandex, Lycra and blends of these fibers with natural fibers or other synthetics can for the most part be safely laundered by hand or machine. Observe the manufacturer's care label, especially when you are laundering dark colors and prints and garments such as a linenlike rayon jacket that might lose its shape in water. Rayon is the one exception to the washability guideline for synthetics. A very few rayon garments can be washed, but most should be dry cleaned to avoid shrinkage. A blend with a small percentage, say 10 or 20 percent, of rayon can be washed.

Polyester is generally the best of the synthetics and combines well with natural fibers. Its immense popularity is due to the fact that it doesn't wrinkle, is durable and is easy to take care of. Look for garments made from mostly natural fibers, such as wool or cotton, with a smaller amount of poly; a good blend is 60/40.

Acrylic knits can be dry cleaned, but they can also be permanently stretched out of shape, especially by steam heat. Check the label; some acrylic knits are clearly marked Do Not Dry Clean. Hand wash these in cool water and mild detergent and block carefully on a towel.

Preserving Antique and Vintage Clothes

Most antique garments can be safely cleaned by a dry cleaner who specializes in or has experience with vintage clothing. Obviously these clothes need the special care and cleaning procedures of experienced professional or custom dry cleaners.

Antique "whites" (Victorian cottons and antique lace) require a bit of special care. You can usually remove any yellowing by soaking in a solution of two parts warm water and one part safety bleach (such as Snowy Bleach). Rinse in cool water and lay flat to dry. For rust stains on white lace, put lemon juice and salt on the stained areas and expose to bright sunlight until the stains disappear.

Cottons from decades past can be, for the most part, safely hand washed in lukewarm water and mild detergent. It's usually safer to dry clean older garments since the dyes used in the past aren't colorfast by today's standards. If you do decide to wash a dark solid or a print, test a small piece of fabric from a seam allowance first.

Maintaining Leather and Suede

To clean suedes, brush gently with a dry rubber sponge, soft bristle brush, terry cloth or a gum eraser on lightly soiled areas, especially around neckline and cuffs. Also recommended is a suede stone cleaning bar, made by the Tandy Leather Co., which is sold in shoe repair shops. Light stains or soiled areas on leather can be touched up with a damp cloth.

If leather becomes wrinkled, use a cool iron with brown wrapping paper or a paper bag as a press cloth. Move the iron constantly and quickly. Wrinkles in lightweight leather or suedes may smooth out when hung for a brief time in a steamy shower.

Condition and waterproof leather with a silicone and lanolin conditioner or mink oil.

Prevent wrinkling and cracking of leather with a metallic finish by applying a silicone or acrylic spray fixative available at shoe or art supply stores. Metallic finishes may chip or crack easily and will then have to be reapplied or repaired professionally, so don't buy cheap or brittle metallic leather garments. Sponge off stains whenever possible.

Dry cleaning dries leather and suede hides and can slightly alter the garment's color, so it's advisable to keep leather cleaning to a minimum—once per season at the most. Have all leathers and suedes cleaned by a hide specialist. Take time to investigate how and where the cleaning will be done before risking your investment. Most regular dry cleaners send leather and suede garments to cleaners who specialize in hides. You'll probably save money and obtain better results by going directly to the leather cleaners yourself. Check the Yellow Pages and call to find the most experienced and most reasonably priced operation.

Protecting Furs

Furs do require special storage in a fur vault during the off season. Don't skip this important part of special fur care; you'll get years more wear from your fur investment. Fur vaults are specially controlled for humidity and temperature and protect the underlying hides from drying out, which in turn prevents premature shedding of the fur. Make sure your insurance covers your furs in your home and at the fur vault.

As with storage, furs should also be professionally cleaned by a furrier, not by a regular dry cleaner. The latter's chemical processes can dry and ruin furs in no time. Fur collars and cuffs should of course be removed from coats and jackets and cleaned separately by a furrier.

Check your fur periodically for rips and tears. Look particularly at shoulder and armhole seams, pockets and near snaps or buttons. Have these repaired at once before they turn into major problems.

Shake a fur out after you've worn it. Never comb or brush fur; you'll only comb the dirt or dust into the fur.

Commonsense Guidelines for Leathers and Furs
Since furs have a hide base, they share a number of characteristics with leathers and suedes and, thus, should be cared for in similar ways.

It's a good idea to wear a scarf at fur or leather garment necklines to prevent makeup or perspiration stains. Never pin jewelry on fur or leather garments and don't spray perfume or cologne on or near these coats or jackets, otherwise they may discolor. Don't carry a shoulderbag when you're wearing your fur.

After wearing, shake the garment gently and hang it in a cool, dark closet—light can cause discoloration—on a padded or shaped wooden coat hanger and protect shoulders from dust with a lightweight cotton cloth or sheet. Stuff sleeves with tissue paper to help them retain their shape. If a garment is damp, hang it in an open area away from direct heat. If it is soaked, take the garment to a fur or leather special-

These clothing care and laundry booklets (most of which are free) lighten the consumer's laundry load.

ist. Leave plenty of breathing space between garments in the closet. Never, ever store leathers, suedes or furs in plastic bags and do not use mothproofing materials on or near them; do not store in a cedar closet.

One final note on leathers and furs. As you can see from the foregoing detailed care and storage recommendations, maintenance of these garments isn't cheap and shouldn't be taken lightly. Your leather or fur jacket or coat will never give return value for the purchase price unless you also invest the proper time and money into taking care of it. All this is important to think about before you make a fur or leather garment purchase.

Stain Removal

There are several excellent free pamphlets available to consumers on stain removal.

- *The Facts of Laundry.* Send a postcard to the Maytag Co., Consumer Information Center, Newton, IA 50208.
- *Consumer Guide to Clothing Care.* Send a stamped, self-addressed envelope to the Neighborhood Cleaners Association, 116 E. 27th St., New York, NY 10016.
- *Removing Stains From Fabrics.* Send a check for $1.20 to Dept. 169H, Consumer Information Center, Pueblo, CO 81009.
- Also from Maytag, a helpful booklet entitled *Learn How to Predict Fabric Performance.* See address above.
- *Clothes Lines.* Laundry tips from Bold detergent. Write to Grey & Davis, Inc., 777 Third Ave., New York, NY 10019.
- *K2r Stain Dial* and *Spray 'n Wash Soil & Stain Guide.* Send a postcard to Consumer Relations Dept., Texize, P.O. Box 368, Greenville, SC 29602.
- *Look to the Label.* Information on national and international fiber-content and garment-care labeling laws. Write to the Cooperative Extension Service, Iowa State University, Ames, IA 50011.

Care for Shoes and Accessories

Fortunately, shoes and other accessories require a minimum of special care and storage attention.

A suede brush cleans and restores the nap to suede shoes, boots and bags. Remove stains and marks with a soft rubber eraser or one of the commercial suede cleaners available at a shoe repair shop. Keep leather accessories and footwear clean and supple with regular applications of leather balm or mink oil. Polish shoes, boots and bags regularly to keep them in tiptop shape and so you won't have to worry about doing a slapdash job as you're running out the door to work. Black patent is maintained quickly and inexpensively with a light coat of petroleum jelly: Wipe clean with a soft cloth and buff to a patent shine.

Wooden shoe trees are an essential investment for retaining the shape of good leather pumps and boots. Boot forms or even a rolled-up magazine along with wooden shoe forms will help boots retain their form. Otherwise a costly pair of boots can lose their shape and begin to look sloppy and fit poorly. The ankle area of boots is particularly susceptible to loss of shape.

Other footwear tips:

- Dry soaked shoes or boots by stuffing with paper or newspaper and keeping away from direct heat. Apply leather balm or mink oil once footwear has dried thoroughly.
- Have a shoe repair shop put heel and toe clips (plastic, not metal) on new shoes and boots. Replace worn heels and soles immediately to prevent damage to shoes and to your body. An irregularly worn heel can throw your spine and balance off.
- Driving a car can wreak havoc with the heels and backs of right shoes, the accelerator and brake shoe. Use a special heel protector or keep a spare right moccasin or slipper in the car to wear while driving.
- Winter precipitation, especially mixed with road salt, makes cold weather footwear care a chal-

lenge, to say the least. Put two coats of waterproofing spray or cream on new boots and shoes and then reapply regularly throughout the winter season.
- Scarves. Remove stains immediately. Most scarves should be dry cleaned.
- Hats should also be cleaned and reblocked by a dry cleaner who specializes in hats. Call a hat shop or the millinery department of your local specialty or department store for a recommendation of a good cleaner.
- Gloves should be cleaned by a cleaner who specializes in leather. Consider the frequency of cleaning before purchasing a pair of light-colored leather gloves.
- Handbags need the same general care and maintenance as good leather shoes. Take good leather bags to the shoe repair shop once a season for a thorough conditioning and dyeing, if necessary. Don't skip this step with good bags. A small investment each season for upkeep will add years to the life of your handbags.
- During the off season, stuff bags with tissue paper or newspaper to help them retain their shape.
- For canvas, cloth and wicker bags, clean with a damp sponge and mild soapsuds. (Don't immerse in water.) Blot dry.

Storage Tips
The careful storage of clothing like cleaning, is vital to its longevity. The closet chapter includes a number of tips on the best ways to hang or store your clothes and accessories. We offer a few more tips here:

- Old pillowcases make excellent and inexpensive hanging garment bags.
- Dr. Scholl's callus remover also works magic on sweater pills.
- Try these old-fashioned remedies for moths: dried rosemary stems and flowers (in baskets or bowls on closet shelves) or a mixture of cinnamon and clove oils (moisten cotton balls with the oils, then hang them in muslin bags away from clothing). Another moth-off: a mix of fragrant cloves and moth balls tied in cheesecloth.
- Check all clothes for dirt or stains immediately after wearing and before they go back into closets or drawers. This is especially important when you're putting clothes away for storage at the end of a season. Smaller repairs and fresh stains are easier and less costly to fix than those left to become major problems.
- Freestanding metal clothes racks are the discount armoires of the eighties. If you find yourself, like we did, with clothes mercilessly sandwiched together and spilling out of closets and drawers, buy a heavy-duty metal rack from a store fixture wholesaler or manufacturer. (Pick up a used one, if possible.) Hang a curtain or put a couple of bamboo screens in front of it, and *voilà!* You have made a new closet.
- Take an extra moment to button top buttons and straighten sleeves when hanging clothes up. A garment hung askew on the hanger will come out of the closet looking ragtag and will require the extra effort of ironing.
- Don't cram clothes together in your closet. They need to breathe, just like we humans do. It's better to weed out seldom-worn and out-of-season garments and store them separately than take up precious closet space and ruin the look of the clothes you depend upon.

SECTION V
When the Going Gets Tough, the Tough Go Shopping

19
A Chic Shopping Primer

The Zen of Shopping

Before we get into the nuts and bolts of how best to shop, we thought it might be fun and informative to take a look at various shopping styles. We are all creatures of habit, so in order to stretch ourselves and our concepts of ourselves (and to get the most for our time and money expenditures), it's helpful to know not only our strengths but also our weaknesses. We've listed the advantages and disadvantages of each shopping type to help you zero in on your unique style.

Your Shopping Style

	Pros	**Cons**
Bargain Huntress	You're bright; you're a savvy shopper. You pride yourself on finding the best at the best price. Depending on how much and how often you shop, you save a lot of money.	You spend an inordinate amount of time shopping. You may even be a bit boastful about your shopping conquests to the point of of being unable to accept a compliment without replying, "Gosh, it only cost $5 at . . ." You may have several mistakes in your closet that were just too cheap to pass up but just weren't *you* and didn't fit into your wardrobe after all.
Indecisive	For the most part, this style doesn't have many redeeming qualities. The only good thing	You're not sure what you want or need and generally find shopping an unpleasant and somewhat

	Pros	Cons
	about being indecisive may be that since it's difficult for you to make up your mind, you may not have to worry about keeping your clothing budget in check.	fearful experience. You rely on the judgment of others too much and not enough on your own. See the chapter Expressing Your Chic Self. Get out of this shopping-style category as soon as possible.
Faddist	You're hip; you're up to the minute fashionwise. Your friends look to you for fashion advice and admire your position on the stylish leading edge. You enjoy the newness and freshness of each change of fashion's whims.	You can easily get so hooked on fads that you lose sight of *you* and what's special about your own unique style. You can get sucked into a lot of looks that, although they're "in," don't really flatter you. Fashion victims fall into this category. Put your voracious clothing appetite on a diet and learn to savor clothes.
The Shy Shopper	For the most part, you find what you need efficiently at a few lower priced stores. Your ego isn't solely defined by a store or a label's status.	By staying in your comfortable shopping groove, you may be missing out on some intriguing fashion and good buys. Explore different types of stores, including the best. It doesn't cost to look; neither should you let any store intimidate you.
The Status Shopper *(the flip side of the Shy Shopper)*	You insist on the best no matter what the purchase. You pride yourself on quality and on knowing labels. You frequent the finest stores and receive personal attention and demand good service.	You're myopic in the opposite direction from your Shy Shopping cousin. Because you shop in the most pricey stores, you may be spending more than you need to. Ease away from your dependence on labels to give you fashion credibility. Learn to judge quality for yourself. This way you can branch out to different kinds of stores and trust your newly found shopping savvy when making bargain purchases.

Cautious	You most likely don't make very many shopping mistakes. You live in your wardrobe of tried-and-true pieces that you're comfortable with.	You're timid about yourself and your style and are probably keeping your fashion light hidden under a bushel basket. Screw up your courage and step out of your fashion rut. Experiment with different types of stores. Exploring costs nothing, and you'll discover new sides of you that you didn't know existed.
Impulsive	You like to shop and you know what's in the stores at any given moment. You know the shops that are best for you.	Since you don't think through your purchases, you also wind up with a number of sartorial booboos. Learn the joys of planning a shopping trip to find what you need rather than being manipulated by your moods or the enticing display windows.
Instinctive Shopper	You know what looks good on you and you're fairly successful in finding what you want and need. You know your own personal style and you're comfortable with clothes.	You rely on instinct and thus don't plan your purchases. Your wardrobe, especially basics, may have a few holes that need to be filled by concrete shopping effort.

Nobody is all one type. You'll recognize yourself among several types. Experiment with shopping styles other than your usual ones so that you can improve your shopping skills and get what you want and need.

If you hate to shop, maybe this chart will help you discover why. It's a question of technique. Are you always going to stores that don't have what you want? Do you always shop alone, hurried and tired? Try a leisurely afternoon with a friend. Do you find your blood pressure rising at the sight of high prices? Look into discount outlets in your area. Try resale stores, thrift shops or manufacturers' outlets. Do you bemoan the lack of quality in merchandise? Buy one exceptional piece and watch it bring the rest of your wardrobe up to snuff. Take a tip from each of your shopping pet peeves and adopt a shopping strategy to counteract it. You'll finally get the clothes and accessories you've been looking for and you'll have a more pleasant shopping experience.

We offer here an overview of shopping, including some timely tips on saving time, planning your shopping forays and making your shopping trip successful. This advice applies to any type of shopping, from discount outlets to department stores. In the following chapters we will discuss each particular type of shopping in detail.

152 • *Chic on a Shoestring*

The Bargain Huntress and the Indecisive Shopper.

The Faddist and the Shy Shopper.

A Chic Shopping Primer • 153

The Status and the Cautious Shopper.

The Impulsive and the Instinctive Shopper.

Planning Your Shopping Trip

Shopping actually begins at home. Watch fashion publications, newspapers (ads and women's fashion sections), catalogs—anywhere you can get fashion information and inspiration that will contribute to your overall fashion viewpoint. Note the trends, looks and accessories that you can expect to find when you hit the stores.

Then ask yourself: What do I need? What do I want? How much money can I afford to spend? Now walk back to your closet and take a look. What do you have that needs to be added to? Note mistake purchases. What are these and how did you come to make these poor buys? Is the color simply not "you"? Is the size or fit wrong? Did a sale item or low price seduce you into a purchase that hasn't been worn? Take a minute or two and think about your past shopping errors and how you can avoid them on this next shopping trip.

Check the wardrobe/shopping list that you keep handy near your closet. Take it along. Bring any items from your closet that need to be matched or snip a swatch from a seam allowance. Don't trust your memory when you're trying to match colors.

Don't forget to take along a good attitude when you go clothes hunting. Looking and feeling good, complete with makeup and your hair fixed, will help you make the best shopping decisions.

As for clothes, you'll probably want to wear comfortable walking shoes to shop, but bring along a pair of high-heeled sandals, for example, if you're looking for an evening gown. Wear clothes that are easy to get in and out of; the fewest pieces possible is advised. For comfort and convenience, one-piece dressing (T-shirt dress or jumpsuit) is best. You'll be more likely to try on clothes if it isn't an ordeal to get dressed and undressed. We especially recommend wearing leotards, particularly for discount stores and manufacturers' outlets, with their group dressing rooms.

Map your shopping route. Note the stores most likely to have what you need. Call first if you have something specific in mind. Check size and color availability.

Allow plenty of time; a rushed shopper makes mistakes. If you have only limited time, such as a lunch hour, then limit yourself to one purchase—a blouse, for example, or a pair of shoes. Don't expect to buy a complete outfit in sixty minutes.

Tips on Special Needs and Where to Fill Them

If you're petite or short:
- Shop at the beginning of each season for the best selection.
- Try the teens' department for basics.
- Likewise, the boys' department is good for jeans, shirts and blazers.
- French and Italian clothes are good bets since they are cut for smaller shapes. Look for discount stores that carry these European goods or wait for sales.
- Designer clothes usually come in sizes 2 and 4. Again, buy these at discount or resale stores or on sale.

If you're tall or long waisted:
- Check the men's department for pants. (The waist may have to be nipped in a bit.) The crotch length or rise in women's pants is usually cut longer than those in men's pants, so check the fit of the rise by bending your knees and crouching to see if a particular pair are cut long enough for you.
- Also, look for men's sweaters and shirts.
- Men's warm-ups, shorts and T-shirts are also good buys.
- Army/Navy surplus stores should be investigated, too.

If you wear a large or half size:
- Try maternity clothes. They are cut full through the middle but won't fall off the shoulders. These are especially good if you're short or stocky. Many styles now don't make you look pregnant. You may

Complete Size Comparison Chart for Clothes and Shoes

Clothing

Women's– U.S.	4	6	8	10	12	14	16
Women's– French	36	38	40	42	44	46	48
Women's– Italian	38	40	42	44	46	48	50
Boys'–U.S.	14	14	16	16-18	—	—	—
Men's– U.S.	28 pants	29 pants XS	29-30 pants 14-14½ shirt	30 pants 14½-15 shirt S 36 jacket	31-32 pants 14½-15 shirt S 37 jacket	32-33 pants S-M 15-15½ shirt 37 jacket	34 pants 15½-16 shirt M 38 or 39 jacket
Girls'– U.S.	14	14-16	—	—	—	—	—

Shoes

American	5	5½	6	6½	7	7½	8	8½	9	9½	10
French*	4½	5	5½	6	6½	7	7½	8	8½	9	9½
Italian	35½	36	36½	37	37½	38	38½	39	39½	40	40½
British	3½	4	4½	5	5½	6	6½	7	7½	8	8½

* French shoes may list a 3 before the size, for example, 35½.

have to even the hem a bit, since maternity blouses and dresses are longer in front.
- Try the men's department for tall and large fits.
- Import stores are good for caftans and one-size dresses and tunics.

Tips for the Hunt, or "Inner Shopping"
- Don't be bullied by pushy salespeople. Browse as long as necessary before asking for help.
- If you know what you want, ask for help immediately to save time.
- The more confident you are about your personal style, the less likely you'll be persuaded to buy something that's not for you.
- If you're not sure what you want or are trying out new looks and want to decide for yourself what looks good on you, shop with a friend whose judgment you trust. Remember that salespeople frequently work on commission.
- Develop a relationship with a salesperson who is helpful and knowledgeable. She can save you time, notify you of new arrivals, hold purchases and let you know when your favorite labels are about to go on sale.
- Find out how much alterations will cost before making a purchase.
- When traveling, try to set aside a little time for shopping. This is a good way to stretch your imagination. Perfect for a rainy day.
- For the most part, it's better to shop a few stores regularly (and well) rather than flit around.
- Stores have personalities, too. Find those that match yours with merchandise you like at prices you can afford.
- Be wary of the hard sell.
- Avoid impulse buying. Stick to your plan.
- If a favorite item goes on sale, buy several to save money and time. This is especially good for lingerie, hosiery and basics such as cotton turtlenecks. This is also the ideal time to pick up a favorite blouse in several colors.
- Before you try something on, ask: "Do I need this?" "Does it go with at least three things in my wardrobe?" "Does the color sync with my wardrobe colors?"
- Don't buy out of desperation or as a last resort or compromise.
- Don't buy with the idea of returning an item. What's your hesitation?
- "Do I love it?" This is the single most important question to ask yourself before making a purchase.
- Try clothes on in front of a three-way mirror; front and back views are important.
- Fit tests: sit, walk, move your arms and bend your knees in a garment. Close your eyes and move in the garment. Does it feel comfortable?
- Look at yourself in natural light. Go to a window or a doorway and check the fabric against your skin tone to make sure you like the match.
- Check care and fabric-content labels to allow for shrinkage and dry cleaning expense.
- Always try garments on. Sizes vary with manufacturers.
- If possible, don't shop with husbands, boyfriends or children. You don't need the distraction.
- Sometimes it's best to buy entire outfits including accessories. This is especially helpful if you're not as good at accessorizing as you'd like to be. Take advantage of a saleswoman or personal shopper's help if you're pressed for time.
- If you're really having trouble making up your mind about a purchase, you should probably pass on it.
- Consider the cost per wearing or CPW before you buy. A $20 silk blouse is no bargain—as a matter of fact, it's a wasted $20—if you never wear it because chartreuse doesn't work in your wardrobe. Put your money into the garments you'll wear

the most. Don't spend a fortune on a seldom-worn evening gown.
- After you bring your purchases home, try them on with things from your closet to create as many new outfits as possible.
- Shop early in the day to avoid crowds and to make your choices from the best merchandise selection. You'll also get more help from salespeople, especially during sale times.

We'd like to share one more piece of shopping advice, and this is that not all shopping has to result in buying. If you have the luxury of even a little bit of recreational shopping time, browse through stores at the beginning of a season; attend trunk fashion shows; get a feel for the choices available.

Hint: If you're browsing, go to the designer floor or department or to an expensive boutique or specialty store you might not ordinarily frequent because of price. It doesn't cost to look. Stretch your imagination and your shopping habits and even try clothes on to get the look and feel of the best being offered. This will give you a better idea of what to look for in terms of silhouette, color, proportion, and the like in less expensive lines. Most designs are copies. Almost any style can be found at several price points. Design ideas eventually filter down from the top (couture) to the bottom (ready-to-wear) in every kind of store.

20
You, Too, can be Chic at Retail

Shopping retail may seem at first glance to be the antithesis of dressing *Chic on a Shoestring*. Rest assured, though, that we have a few smart shopping tricks up our sleeves to help you save money while shopping at retail stores.

By *retail* we mean the suburban and downtown department stores, specialty stores such as Ann Taylor and specialty chains such as Saks Fifth Avenue, Bonwit Teller and Neiman-Marcus. Smaller establishments run the retail gamut from local dress shops to popular chains such as Pappagallo, I. Miller Shoes and those operated under the aegis of top European designers such as Yves St. Laurent, Courrèges and Valentino. The selection of retail stores near you depends on the size of your city and the area of the country you live in.

Pros and Cons of Retail Shopping

Let's first discuss the advantages and disadvantages of retail shopping.

Pros:

- large selection of clothing and accessories with lots of sizes, colors, styles and price ranges to choose from
- store credit cards
- delivery of phone and mail orders (what a timesaver!)
- easy returns and exchanges
- personal shopper services
- forward fashion in the designer departments
- frequent ads offer essential information on arriving merchandise and sales
- fashion shows and seminars, designer trunk showings
- seasonal and sale catalogs

Cons:

- Price. Let's face it, paying full freight at today's prices is not fun.
- Information overload. Five or six large floors of clothes and accessories can often be overwhelming. Where does one begin? This is not the optimal shopping environment for everyone.
- Lack of sales help. While some stores are strengthening their personal shopper services, most seem to be cutting back on sales personnel within each department. Unfortunately, the salespeople you do find often don't know their merchandise very well and are unable to direct you to other parts of the store that might have what you're looking for.

- Merchandise selections that are out of sync with the current season. When you're hunting for a bathing suit three days before the Fourth of July weekend, who wants to be confronted by endless racks of wool blazers, sweaters and mufflers. Most of us prefer to buy in season.

For our money, we frankly recommend using discount stores of all types for as much of your wardrobe needs as possible. Depending on the availability of off-price stores in your area, you may be able to get most everything you need at discount. But if discount retailing is a new phenomenon in your city and the number of discount stores is still small, you'll naturally continue to do most of your shopping at retail stores. We also recognize the undeniable convenience of shopping at nearby stores, either discount or retail, during your lunch hour and after work. For most of us a combination of discount and retail shopping is the best solution to our buying needs.

Shopping Tips

As with any shopping expedition, it's best to plan your retail buying trip. Even if you don't *save* money at retail stores, a bit of wardrobe and shopping planning will prevent you from *wasting* money. However, if you want to save money at retail stores, you'll have to take advantage of sales, markdowns and special purchases.

It's no secret that retail stores are hosting more and more sales all the time in order to boost business and compete with the growing number of less-than-retail apparel sources. The days of only January and July clearance sales at department stores are long gone. They've been replaced by "sale events" of every description plus "special purchases" announced weekly. The best means to deal with shopping sales? Read on.

Guerrilla Tactics for Retail Sales Shopping

- Open a charge account at your favorite stores so that you can (1) be notified in advance of all sales and of special "preferred customer" sale days held prior to the general public sale, and (2) receive the stores' special mailings and catalogs. Ordering by mail or phone saves enormous amounts of time, and, of course, time is money, especially these days.
- Shop sales the first day and as early as possible for best selection and chipper, helpful service.
- Don't succumb to impulse buys unless you really *want* and *need* the item. Does it make three outfits?
- Buy sale items from designer lines or manufacturers that are carried consistently. You can add to or create an expensive coordinated look exclusively from the sale rack or mix in an extra piece purchased on sale that will extend the wear of an outfit purchased earlier in the season at full retail.
- Buy your spring and summer wardrobe from the cruise/resort or early spring sales racks. You'll not only save money but be more fashion forward, because designers introduce summer ideas in their cruise/resort collections.
- Buy the lines on sale at retail stores that aren't sold at discount stores. It takes a bit of sleuthing in your area to discover which labels are carried where and for how much less. (Whew!) But it's worth it.
- Not all sales are announced, so be sure to ask when the next one will be and then arrive early. If the next sale is only a day or two away, ask the salesperson if you can purchase the item at the reduced price or have it held for you until the sale.
- Familiarize yourself with the regular retail prices of your favorite labels. This way you'll know if a sale price on your preferred blouse or shoe brand represents a good value.
- Consider the best first. The biggest markdowns are on the high-ticket items. Therefore, don't rule out the sales at designer boutiques or departments—you might be pleasantly surprised at what your money can buy.

- On the opposite end of the spectrum, don't forget to check the budget floor or section in a department store. You may find good values in wardrobe staples such as shirts, sweaters, blazers, pants, underwear, active wear and sleepwear.
- Don't forget department store clearance centers, parking lot or warehouse sales. After-sale merchandise from department stores and specialty store chains is moved to a central location for final markdown. In Los Angeles, for example, sale merchandise from all of the Robinson's stores winds up at their downtown headquarters.
- Check special purchase items thoroughly (inside and out) for quality of fabric, construction and fit. Based on your shopping experience, is this special item "special" enough in terms of value (price vs. quality) for you to buy it?
- The big, end-of-season, Christmas and other holiday sales such as post–Fourth of July and Washington's Birthday still represent the best reduced prices at retail stores. Rest up, pop a stress-B vitamin and arm yourself with your credit card. Good luck!
- Inspect sale merchandise most carefully. Delicate items get tossed into bins or crammed together on racks with everything else and can even get stretched out of shape or soiled.

Markdowns (regular retail goods whose prices have been reduced one or more times) are becoming more and more a part of the retail apparel scene. Many stores today live or die based on how well their markdowns sell. Markdowns are, of course, especially important on high-priced designer goods. These, fortunately, are usually the first to be reduced by 10 to 20 percent. Other departments begin marking prices down about three weeks later.

The Sales and Selection chart that follows will help you get a fix on the best times to buy.

Boutiques and smaller specialty stores are becoming more and more popular with busy, quality-conscious women who need to spend their shopping time

Our model is fashionably "Kleined," head to toe, from department sales. The $350 Anne Klein jacket was marked down to $99, the $175 wool skirt (also Anne Klein) was $55 and the Calvin Klein silk blouse was reduced to $20 from an original price of $75.

Sales and Selection Chart

	Jan.	Feb.	March	April	May	June	July	Aug.	Sept.	Oct.	Nov.	Dec.
Shirts				*		$		*	*			$
Sweaters				*		$		*	*			$
Sportswear			*	*			$	*	*	$		
Swimsuits		*	*				$	$				
Dresses			*	*	$			*				
Coats	$		$				*			$		
Suits	$			*			$		*			
Evening wear	$									*	*	$
Shoes		*	*		$	*	*			$		
Boots	$	$					*					
Hosiery			$									
Handbags		$	*					*		$		
Jewelry	$											
Lingerie	$				$			*		*		
Furs	$							$	$	*	*	

* = Best Selection
$ = Best Sales

efficiently. The cohesive, edited merchandise selections of boutiques coupled with experienced sales *help* have attracted a growing legion of satisfied customers, especially working women.

The secret of successful boutique shopping is to find one or two stores that harmonize with your style. Watch newspaper ads for the labels and looks you like and see especially the ads in your area's city or regional magazines.

Many women shop boutiques only two or three times a year, during major sales. Boutiques and specialty-store sales offer good values on all types of clothes and accessories, especially shoes, dresses and suits. Many career women do most if not all of their suits and separates buying at these sales.

Boutiques are particularly good for quality and fashion forward accessories. If you don't want to or can't afford to buy clothing here, you might want to add some punch to your wardrobe with one terrific belt or bag.

Shopping Chic Tips
from Fashion Director Patti Fox
Here are some tips on how to save money by shopping at retail stores from an interview with Patti Fox, fashion director of Saks Fifth Avenue, Beverly Hills.

CHIC: How can we as consumers get the most for our fashion dollar at retail stores?
P.F.: Rather than shop around as a nonentity, develop a friendship and a relationship with a store and a sympathetic salesperson. Become a "special person" by making yourself and your needs known. Customers may not realize it, but salespeople keep client books and will make an effort to notify a customer when new merchandise arrives or will hold something back until you have a chance to come in and try it on. It's the salesperson's job to know her customers and their personality type and what they prefer to wear. You don't have to spend a lot of money to get this attention. What you must have is an eagerness to develop an image and a wardrobe

Patti Fox, fashion director at Saks Fifth Avenue, Beverly Hills.

over time. Also, we know in advance when merchandise is going to be marked down or when there is to be a consolidation sale and merchandise will arrive from other stores. Cultivate a relationship with a salesperson so you can get optimum service—and special treatment—at sale time.
CHIC: What's the best way to get to know a store?
P.F.: Use the store's personal shopping services. Also watch the fashion calendar in your local newspaper and attend some of the special workshops and trunk shows that come through your city or town. Don't be afraid to go in, get to know the stores, the services they offer and the merchandise they carry. Shopper and store must match. You not only have to find the right store but the right personal shopper or salesperson within the store to help you. It's a

bit time consuming up front, but worth it in the long run.

CHIC: Saks has a staff of personal shoppers and an Executive Club to service busy women, but does this kind of treatment exist in other stores?

P.F.: Definitely. If stores don't have personal shopping clubs or departments, they're instigating special boutiques and specialty-stores-within-the-store concepts and boutiques for working women. Across the board, stores are trying to service the customer with special needs and limited time by developing more of a one-stop-shopping department. Many times in a big store you don't know where to go for what and that limits your creativity in coordinating a wardrobe.

CHIC: Can a young woman just getting started with her career and on a limited budget use a shopping service to build a wardrobe economically?

P.F.: Personal shopping is geared to the person's needs, no matter how much money she has to spend. If the customer isn't "fashion conscious" but has a job that requires she look a certain way, a fashion consultant is trained to give advice and make suggestions based on occupation and lifestyle. They will also help you create an image and help you discover your personal style. After working with a client over a period of months, I've found time after time that the woman feels I've saved her a lot of money. She hasn't just gone into a store and said, "Oh, this is cute, I'll buy it," or run out at the last moment to buy something for an annual party. You should already have something in your wardrobe that can handle a special occasion if you've planned your needs. You learn with help to understand your personality and buy within that framework so that all your clothes go together and you can create everything from a dressy to casual look. In the long run, even though you may be buying full price at a retail store, you wind up saving money because you know what you're buying, why and for what purpose. If you've already cultivated a special salesperson or personal shopper, you can tell her, "I know I'm going to have a couple of special occasions this year and I'll need a cocktail dress or gown so call me when one comes in you think I'll like." Then the salesperson will be on the lookout and you won't have to waste time shopping. It's a nice feeling to be prepared. Besides, I don't recommend wearing a new dress or suit for an important party or big interview. You don't need the extra pressure of new clothing. You need to feel comfortable; you need to know you look good and that usually means you've worn the item before and received compliments.

CHIC: Where do you find personal shoppers in a department store, and does the service cost extra?

P.F.: Ask at store information. Usually personal shoppers have a separate office. These people have more longevity as salespeople and are the cream of the sales crop. They are specially trained and know the entire store inventory, not just one department. Best of all, you don't have to pay extra for their expertise.

CHIC: Are "special purchases" a come-on or a real savings?

P.F.: They represent a legitimate savings. These are items that are usually private labels (or store labels) that have been contracted with the same manufacturers who turn out designer-label merchandise. The manufacturer is contracted directly by the retailer; thus the store is able to offer the goods to the consumer at a lower cost. If the store's quality level is generally high, the same quality will be enforced in their private label merchandise. This is a growing trend because retailers can offer merchandise at a better price to the consumer and at the same time have more control over the item produced.

CHIC: What's your advice on shopping sales?

P.F.: The best advice is to be fully aware already of who you are fashionwise and where you are going with your wardrobe. Otherwise a sale shopper is an impulse buyer, and that ends up costing you a lot more money than if you bought at full retail value. Don't just buy because it's on sale; buy because you need it.

CHIC: Is it safer to look for bargains at a quality store rather than shop budget stores to save money?

P.F.: Yes, because quality standards at a store with a good reputation are very important. Reputation for quality and service is even more important to maintain in today's competitive retail market. Quality and customer service are two important ways a retail store can have an edge over budget or discount stores. The sale buys can be fantastic when you combine high quality and low prices.

CHIC: A friend went shopping for a black angora sweater in January and found the stores filled with swimsuits and summer clothes. How can shoppers cope with this conundrum?

P.F.: You have to be aware of when new shipments of clothes arrive at stores for optimum selection. But here again, if you are prepared, and buying smart, you're not really buying for a season, you're buying to add to your wardrobe. You're not buying the new spring fad, but you're buying a certain piece that will work in your wardrobe. You're in control of your wardrobe, not a victim of fashion trends. If you're an astute sales shopper, it can be to your advantage that clothes are marked down just when you want to be wearing them.

CHIC: How can consumers take advantage of fashion shows offered by stores?

P.F.: When a trunk show comes through town, make a point to see it and remember that you can order anything you see presented. This is a way for a shopper to personalize her wardrobe. You can be your own fashion director and choose any piece from the line. Let's say you want a piece that the buyer in New York didn't think would sell so she didn't order it for the store's collection. You can request the store to special order it for you. Unless you see the trunk show of manufacturers' samples, you may never see the complete line.

Linking into Chain Stores

Before we leave the retail shopping chapter, we want to discuss briefly those ubiquitous chain stores located in every hamlet and city—JC Penney and Sears, Roebuck & Co. If ever there was a universal shopping experience in this country, these two giants, among the biggest apparel retailers in the world, are it. Both companies now produce about thirty different catalogs *each* per year. These general catalogs and "specialogs," coupled with thousands of retail stores in literally every part of the country, mean you're never far from either Sears or JC Penney.

What can the shopper expect in terms of fashion and quality from these stores? Well, as Jack Simpson, national fashion director of women's and children's apparel at Sears, says, "We're not high fashion. Don't look to us for the latest avant garde look." Both appeal to the "price conscious" woman who favors basic, traditional styles in easy-care synthetics and blends.

You'll find the biggest selection in standard casual wear and coordinated separates, with some more dressy and career items such as blazers and dresses. Coordinate pieces are displayed in groups in the stores, although it's much easier to hone in on them and make mix and match selections from the catalogs. Sears is especially big on career and sportswear groups, some with designer names attached.

While most fabrics are synthetics or synthetic/natural blends, each chain is adding more and more natural fiber garments (especially cotton) to their merchandise selection. National Fashion Consultant for JC Penney catalogs Lois Cohen tells us she lives in her Penney 100 percent cotton oversized sweater from several seasons back and has them in all colors. Natural fiber fans should note that these items are a little easier to find in the catalogs, since they're more clearly displayed as such.

While both stores claim to shun the high-fashion image of department stores and boutiques, they have responded to their customers' desire for designer labels in certain items, particularly more traditional and classic separates. If you're a card-carrying member of the polo shirt/plaid skirt/crewneck sweater set, you'll like the Silver Unicorn insignia at Sears

Annette's $19 fashion-forward sweats from Sears worn by model.

and the Fox and Hunt Club labels at JC Penney. These have been manufactured to be similar if not identical in quality to higher priced "preppy" attire, but they are priced 10 to 20 percent lower and are thus good values.

The Sears catalog also features a few exclusive Jack Mulqueen silk dresses plus Cheryl Tiegs casual wear and Evonne Goolagong active wear. JC Penney has enlisted Halston to add some pizzazz to its offerings.

One tip on shopping Sears and JC Penney stores: the merchandise selection and general shopping ambience vary greatly from store to store, even within the same city. The larger, newer mall locations cater to a more fashion conscious clientele than the smaller, older stores.

Our *Chic on a Shoestring* suggestions on getting the best values at these stores:

- Best buys are in hosiery and underwear. Sears and JC Penney both have justly earned excellent reputations over the years for their high-quality, moderately priced lingerie. Bras, slips and underpants, including some in all cotton, will last just as long as if not longer than similar items with higher price tags. The size and style selection is extensive; you'll find most of the latest fashion colors in hosiery. Sears' prices, by the way, seem to be just a bit higher than Penney's.
- Loungewear and sleepwear also represent good value. Once again, you'll find quality similar to higher priced goods elsewhere and thus better value here at the chains.
- Active wear and sportswear, including the trustworthy sweat suit (now offered in fashion colors) and serviceable leotards, tights and leg warmers, are also recommended purchases at these stores.
- According to Lois Cohen, the most fashion forward items at JC Penney are accessories and shoes. We would add that accessories, especially hats, belts and scarves, at both JC Penney and Sears are up to date for the most part and extremely reasonable in price. We've supplemented our hat wardrobes with shrewd purchases from both stores.
- JC Penney does offer a number of attractive shoes in its catalogs and in stores. Styles and colors are current season; materials and construction represent good value, since prices are about 10 to 20

percent less than those for like shoes in other retail stores.
- Sears' main catalogs have special small sections on clothing specially designed for the handicapped.
- The Penney catalog has one of the best fit and size ordering sections we've ever seen. Men's, women's and children's clothing and shoe measurement instructions and corresponding size charts are clearly explained to help customers get their mail order selections right the first time.

If you haven't shopped a Sears or JC Penney lately or picked up one of their catalogs, we suggest you give them a try. New departments such as bridal boutiques and petites have been added, and there's a noticeable effort being made to meet the clothing needs of all age groups. We still put our earnest money on wardrobe "underpinnings" and staples for men and women plus selected accessories and shoes. These represent the best *Chic* values at both chains.

Discount Shopping at Chains

In addition to shopping at regular retail, *Chic* bargain hunters can also pick up good buys at Sears and JC Penney outlet stores, which carry sale items, returned and discontinued goods plus clearly marked "as is" or slightly damaged merchandise. Prices range from 20 percent to over 75 percent below original retail.

Sears has more than one hundred catalog outlet stores across the country. Check your local White Pages directory for the outlet store nearest you or call a nearby Sears retail or catalog store for information on outlet store locations.

JC Penney operates twelve outlet stores plus two locations that sell "catalog returned goods" or merchandise that is slightly damaged.

JC Penney *Outlets:*
6651 Fallbrook Avenue
Canoga Park, California

1028 E. Baseline Rd.
Tempe, Arizona (Phoenix area)

250 W. North Avenue
Northpark Mall
Villa Park, Illinois (Chicago area)

10332 W. Silver Springs Drive
Milwaukee, Wisconsin

9495 W. 75th Street
Overland Park, Kansas (Kansas City area)

South Expressway & Highway 41
Forest Park, Georgia (Atlanta area)

3317 Buford Highway
Atlanta, Georgia

2434 Atlanta Road
Smyrna, Georgia (Atlanta area)

Route 270 & Interstate 75
Columbus, Ohio

8770 Colerain Avenue
Cincinnati, Ohio

Eastgate Plaza
East Alton, Illinois (St. Louis area)

700 Boston Road
Town Plaza Center
Billerica, Massachusetts (Boston area)

JC Penney *Catalog Returned Goods Stores:*
190 E. Baseline Road
Sparks, Nevada (Reno area)

5656 S. Packard Avenue
Cudahy, Wisconsin (Milwaukee area)

21
Discount Glad Rags

Well, we've finally arrived at your authors' absolute favorite pastime: discount shopping. It's been said: "When the going gets tough, the tough go shopping." Today we would qualify this by saying, "the tough go *discount* shopping."

The continuing recessionary trend combined with inflation that began in the late 1970s has fueled the explosion of discount stores all over the country. As our clothing budgets have shrunk, we consumers have become much more discriminating in our purchases. We're demanding more value for our money and we're flocking to stores that offer less-than-retail prices. We Americans are not fond of cutting back or doing without; we much prefer to keep our lifestyles current by continuing to *buy*. In decades past we bought at retail. Today we're probably buying as many items and shopping as often as we used to; we're just more careful about how much we pay. The most significant change in our buying habits has been a turn toward less-than-retail stores of every ilk. Welcome to the Discount Decade.

Now, you ask: "How do all those discount stores get their merchandise at prices below wholesale?" The answer to this question is another reason for the growth of discount stores. Discount store owners and retailers usually pay cash for merchandise, while many of the department stores and chains pay for the goods some time after they've received them. In these economic times, it's easy to understand a clothing manufacturer's need for cash. There are several other factors that account for the attractive sales tags at off-price shops. (1) Most discounters buy slightly after regular retail establishments place their orders, and thus manufacturers are eager to sell odd lots and closeouts at below regular wholesale prices to get rid of their entire inventory for a particular season. This is called off-price buying. (2) A few discounters buy their merchandise at regular wholesale prices and then take a "shorter" or lower markup than the standard "keystone" or 100 percent (or more) increase added by most retail stores. These discounters hope to make their profits in volume sales. (3) Lower overhead expenses (little or no advertising and lower rents, for instance) allow an off-price or discount retailer to pass the savings along to you, too. Although there's a technical difference between discount and off-price retailing, the terms are used interchangeably.

Discount Myths
While discount stores do operate with lower expenses, don't get the idea that they're devoid of the shopping amenities we all enjoy. Discounting is no longer the poor stepchild of the retailing business.

As discount shopping experts, we've encountered many myths and misconceptions about off-price retailing. Here is what we've learned:

- Discount stores are located in every part of the country, in large and small communities and, increasingly, throughout a given city or metropolitan area. Your shopping is no longer limited to Orchard and Delancey streets in Manhattan or the garment district in downtown Los Angeles. There are good discount stores near where you live, work and vacation.
- Almost all discount stores accept personal checks. You don't have to worry about taking along a wad of cash to these stores. Many stores take bank cards (MasterCard and VISA); a few even accept American Express.
- First-quality, current-season merchandise is the order of the day at most discount establishments. It's not true that you'll be confronted with only seconds or out-of-date goods from seasons past.
- While a few stores (like Loehmann's) retain an All Sales Final policy, most will exchange your returned purchases and some will even refund your money.
- Shopping ambience or lack thereof used to keep a lot of potential customers away from discount outlets. Who wants to shop in a big, forbidding warehouse or get undressed in a dressing room packed with forty strangers? Well, we're delighted to report that more and more less-than-retail shops resemble their straight-retail cousins in looks. Expect to find individual dressing rooms, carpeting, good lighting, piped-in music, displays—in short, everything you'd expect to find in a *real* store.
- When discounting began years ago, about the only sizes available were sample sizes of 8 and 10 sold in "sample shops." Now every shape and silhouette from petite to queen size plus half-size and maternity is available in abundance at discount.
- While new discount stores do seem to sprout like weeds after a spring rain, a good share of them have been in business for years, even several decades. Most discounters have solid reputations and pride themselves on their operations and their merchandise. Fortunately, the fly-by-night operators are few and far between.
- Labels are left in most garments sold in discount stores. Sometimes labels have been cut in half, but you'll still be able to recognize the name. If labels have been completely cut out, ask the manager to identify the manufacturer. If labels are missing entirely, this usually means the garment was manufactured for (and sometimes by) the discounter. Look at these items carefully to determine whether you are buying quality.
- The manufacturer's RN number or WPL label (sewn into the garment near the care label or printed on the union label) also identifies each garment. If you frequent a discount store (such as Loehmann's) where labels are removed, you might consider investing in the *RN and WPL Directory*, available from Textile Publishing Corp., Box 50079, Washington, D.C. (202)248-5000. Cost is $75.

Decoding Labels

Sometimes designers' and manufacturers' labels are removed from garments in discount stores. But take heart, all you bargain sleuths. Law requires that a maker's identifying number, either an RN or WPL, appear in the garment even if the label does not. Here are a few popular manufacturers' numbers.

Abe Schrader	Bal Harbour	Catalina
RN15579	RN51488	RN16578
Act I	Bill Blass	RN16580
RN36486	RN38344	Christian Dior
RN36789	Bonnie Cashin	RN03005
RN51331	WPL10113	Clovis Ruffin
Anne Fogarty	Butte Knit	RN42992
RN30669	RN31691	Cole of Cal.
RN48648	Calvin Klein	RN39378
Anne Klein	RN41327	RN39375
RN40803	RN42642	RN31562

WPL03600
WPL03574
College Town
RN42424
RN38916
Daniel Hechter
RN54042
Donnkenny
RN24903
RN31691
Echo Bay
RN43517
Evan-Picone
RN35685
WPL08582
Geoffrey Beene
RN33293
Gloria Vanderbilt
RN52130
Halston
RN46616
RN41564
RN57302
Harvé Benard
RN40679

Huk-A-Poo
RN34104
J.G.Hook
RN51898
Jantzen
RN37966
Jonathan Logan
RN34972
RN44290
Leslie Fay
RN43857
RN42711
RN16890
Lilly Pulitzer
RN39805
Lilli Ann
RN29563
RN14962
Liz Claiborne
RN52002
London Fog
RN47396
RN47398
RN47400
Marisa Christina
RN44278

Oleg Cassini
RN32203
Pendleton
RN29685
Perry Ellis
RN57272
Ralph Lauren
RN56158
Rose Marie Reid
RN19362
St. Tropez
RN55862
Ship 'N Shore
RN38494
Stanley Blacker
RN30219
RN41550
RN55639
Sue Brett
RN18220
Villager
RN17470
RN31242
Willi Smith
RN49528

Advantages and Disadvantages of Discount Shopping

Advantages:

- Year-round lower prices for quality, current season clothing and accessories. You'll be able to afford better clothes than before.
- Nationwide off-price chains and local discount outlets make discount shopping accessible to everyone now.
- Shopping amenities, including use of credit cards or personal checks, individual dressing rooms, regular business hours and return and/or exchange policies are now the rule.

- Saving $ $ $ puts the *fun* back in shopping.
- Sales at discount stores mean savings of as much as 80 percent on quality goods.

Disadvantages

- Rapid turnover of merchandise at discount stores means you should shop (or browse) frequently for the best buys.
- Incomplete sizes may be a problem, since off-price retailers buy after a manufacturer has filled regular orders. Reorders are also difficult.
- Unpredictable inventories—a discount store may carry a line one week and not the next, depending on merchandise availability.
- A few stores offer a bare-bones, no-nonsense atmosphere, and some discounters require cash for purchases and/or have an All Sales Final policy. The bargains at these operations are often, however, some of the very best available. So it's a tradeoff: low overhead for low, low prices.

Less-than-Retail Options

Just what do we mean by the term *discount?* Well, you might be surprised at the broad range of discount shopping resources available to you. These are the stores that carry new, current season merchandise.

- Designer discount stores. These shops offer high-quality apparel and accessories from top European and American designers and better French and Italian labels.
- Neighborhood discount outlets. Your basic right-around-the-corner or just-down-the-street store featuring popular brands at reduced prices.
- Discount chains. Keep your eye on these stores. The sharp merchandisers at chains like Marshalls, B.F. Shoes, J. Brannam and Pic-a-Dilly, to name a few, were savvy to the discounting boom early on and are continuing to expand to every region of the United States. Dayton Hudson Corp. may represent a trend among huge retailing conglomer-

ates by shifting its primary focus from retail department stores to large, pleasant discount emporiums in shopping malls. Its Target and Mervyn's branches are doing very well and will continue to expand. If your area doesn't have one of these stores now, it will soon. Watch your newspaper for store opening announcements.

- Specialty discount stores. These outlets pride themselves on their extensive array of one or two types of apparel. We enjoy shopping at one local discounter who specializes in coats and another in evening and formal wear. Southern California, for instance, boasts several terrific swimsuit discounters, one of which stocks 10,000 suits year round.
- Shoe and accessory discounters. An entire store devoted to your favorite shoe brands, all at half price. Too hard to believe, you say? Not so in this Decade of Discounts. Discount handbag havens are another growing sensation.
- Manufacturers' outlets. These often represent the lowest prices around, usually 50 to 80 percent below retail. Since the manufacturer is selling directly to you and bypassing all middlemen (wholesalers, jobbers and retailers), you reap the tremendous savings. First- and second-quality goods are available here. Some manufacturers don't run outlet stores but prefer to dispose of their excess goods once or several times a year at special warehouse or parking lot sales. Incredible buys can be had at these.

Before we move on we'd like to clarify one more important point about discount merchandise, and that is that it should not be confused with lower-quality, less-expensive merchandise that is manufactured to sell, with full 100 percent markup, at prices in the same range as those in discount stores. The best way to illustrate this point is to give an example for shoes sold at $40.

Low-end shoestore chain—These shoes were manufactured for or by the chain at $20 and were designed to sell for $40 at retail.

Department store shoe—This shoe probably wholesaled for about $25 and retailed for $55 and is now on sale for $40.

Discount shoe store—These shoes were probably originally made to retail for around $75 ($35 wholesale value) and are for sale here for $40.

The point is that some goods are originally manufactured to sell at lower prices than others but may wind up at the same price in different types of stores. Look for quality no matter where you shop. The single most important lesson to learn from discount shopping is that you don't have to sacrifice quality to save money. This example is also a good illustration of varying levels of quality. The $40 chain store shoes look and feel inferior to the $75 shoes selling for $40 at the discount store.

Discount Shopping Tips

All the hints and tips we outlined in the general shopping chapter go double when you're heading to a discount store or two. We'd like to reemphasize a couple of these earlier points and add a few more pertinent ones.

- Do your fashion homework; watch ads and read a fashion magazine or two. This will enable you to recognize a bargain when you see one. A good bargain hunter knows which styles are going to be popular and stays ahead of (or avoids) trends. Discount-store sale racks are gold mines for the fashion forward shopper. Clip ads and photographs of items you need or like and bring along your wardrobe shopping list every time you hit a discount outlet.
- Allow plenty of time for browsing and nosing around. Let discount shopping bring out the sleuth in you.
- Dress in a one-piece or easy-in-and-out-of clothes; wear a leotard, too.

This decidedly discount outfit was picked up for $25 at the manufacturer's sale of designer Carole Little.

- In a large store or a big manufacturer's outlet, pause a moment when you first walk in the door to get an overview of the merchandise and the store's layout. Give yourself a few minutes of walking briskly all over the store to get the lay of the land and a sense of the merchandise mix.
- Shop during off or nonpeak hours if possible.
- Ask when new shipments arrive and visit the store at that time for best selection.
- Add yourself to the store's mailing list (most discount stores have them) to be notified of sales. Remember: a sale at a discount store is a discount on a discount!
- Frequent nearby or favorite stores often, since many receive weekly or semiweekly shipments. Many discount stores unpack and display cartons of new clothes and accessories *daily*.
- Shop with an open mind. There's a discount shopper's adage: Buy it when you see it, not when you need it.
- Be adventurous on your discount shopping expeditions. Here's your chance to stretch yourself and

your wardrobe and have a good time doing it. Remember years—too many years—ago when shopping was actually fun? Well, discount has put the *fun* back into shopping.
- Is there a bit of the horse trader in you? Do you enjoy the friendly back and forthing over prices at a garage sale? Don't be afraid to barter or bargain for a lower price, especially when you're paying cash, buying a number of items or if it's a rainy or slow day. Don't go shopping in jewels or furs if you expect to barter.
- Check the exchange and refund policy before you buy. If it's All Sales Final, make sure you love the item, because after you buy, it's *yours*.
- Don't be scared by seconds or irregulars, especially if you sew or are at least handy at mending. Most imperfects are only minorly so and can be easily remedied.
- If your area doesn't have very many discount outlets yet, it may well be a good idea to take a trip once or twice a year to a nearby metropolitan area to fill your wardrobe needs at wholesale prices.

How to Spot Fashion Forgeries
Before we move on, we'd like to cover a couple of areas that pertain to discount shopping. The first is fashion forgeries, or counterfeit goods. How does one avoid being deceived by these clever fakes? Follow these guidelines:

- Become acquainted with the authentic designers' labels and emblems. Note the fine details: size, color, lettering, style and positioning on garments.
- Keep abreast of manufacturers' and designers' names.
- *Where* you shop is as important as what you buy. Be on guard at garage sales, street corner stands, flea markets, swap meets and low-end discount outlets.
- If you suspect that a garment or handbag, for instance, isn't genuine, turn it inside out and inspect it thoroughly. Look for uneven stitching and seam finishing, lots of loose threads or ragged buttonholes. Scrutinize the right side for similar details plus rivets, zippers, trims and closings. Compare what you know about your genuine Levi's jeans at home with the pair in front of you. Are they the same or do telltale differences tip you off to a possible fake? Many counterfeiters have been nabbed because their logos on buttons or snaps gave them away.
- Fabric weight can be another clue. Does the denim in a pair of "designer" jeans feel strangely lightweight? The real McCoys are usually fabricated from 12- or 14-ounce denim; copies are sometimes made of only 10-ounce goods.
- Don't be confused by the garment's place of manufacture. An Yves St. Laurent shirt made in Hong Kong rather than in France doesn't mean it's an imitation.
- Is the price ridiculously low? Do you really believe a $100 Gucci bag could sell on a street corner for $14.95?
- Report any rip-offs or suspected counterfeit merchandise to local law enforcement agencies and/or consumer protection bureaus.

When to Think of Seconds First
Buying seconds and irregulars can be one of the single best ways to save a lot of money on your clothing purchases. In order to shop successfully for these, there are a few words of advice to follow. Most garments marked *second* or *imperfect* or *irregular* (the terms are used interchangeably today) have only a minor imperfection that is usually clearly marked with a bit of tape, a chalk mark or sometimes a colored basting thread. Garment hang tags and racks where these goods are displayed are usually clearly marked, too. Check the flaw. It may be an oil mark or a soiled area that can be cleaned or washed out. If it's a seam that's come unstitched, it can be mended easily. Is there a small rip or tear in an obvious or

This all-cotton T-shirt-and-brief set, with imperceptible flaws, is a terrific value at $5.00.

more hidden area of the garment? You may be able to patch or appliqué over it so no one's the wiser. If the repair looks as if it will be too major or if you're just not the fix-it type, pass.

Once in a while you may find, especially at a manufacturer's outlet, a garment with *irregular* stamped on its label, yet your closest inspection doesn't reveal any flaws. Ask the salesperson. It may well be a perfect or first-quality garment that has been marked irregular to prevent customers from returning items to retail stores and getting the regular retail price back in cash. The Los Angeles–area Olga lingerie outlets, run by the manufacturer, found they had to start this practice after local women bought undergarments at the Olga outlet store for a discount price and then returned them to local department stores to get full retail refunds. Tsk, tsk. It seems some of us will go a bit too far to get a good deal.

How to Find Discount Stores

Since we're the co-authors of two discount clothing directories, we naturally feel it's essential to own a discount shopping guidebook for your area. This is the best way to find all the shopping information you need in one handy package. Check your local bookstores or libraries. Buy a copy for your car and keep it in the glove compartment so it's close whenever the urge to shop strikes. Better yet, buy two copies and keep one at home so you can plan your shopping trips. How about three copies: one in your car, one at home and one at your mother's or girlfriend's . . . Seriously, there are a number of terrific discount shopping directories available:

Glad Rags II—A Directory to Discount Fashions in Los Angeles and Orange Counties, by Leigh Charlton and Annette Swanberg, Chronicle Books, San Francisco, California.

Factory Outlet Shopping Guide, by Jean Bird, F.O.S.G. Publications, Oradell, New Jersey.

McQuown's Designer Markdowns, a weekly New York–area newsletter, self-published by Judith H. McQuown in New York.

New York Shopper magazine, by Carol J. Richards, New York.

L.A.'s Best Bargains, a monthly newsletter published by Geri Cook in Los Angeles.

S.O.S.: Save On Shopping, by Iris Ellis. Today Press, Jacksonville, Florida. Nationwide information.

The Underground Shopper. A guide to discount mail-order shopping by Sue Goldstein. Andrews and McMeel, Inc., Kansas City, Missouri and New York.

The Good Buy Book—one version covers the upper Midwest and another covers the Southeast.

South Bay Bargain Guide for the greater San José area by Dian Brazil. Chronicle Books, San Francisco, California.

Seattle's Super Shopper, by Priscilla Johnston and Dinah Stolter, and *Portland Super Shopper,* by Connie and Terry Hofferber. Both published by The Writing Works in Seattle, Washington.

I Never Pay Retail, by Sue Lee and Starr Phillips. D.C. Publishing, Costa Mesa, California. Covers Orange County.

This is not an exhaustive list (it just looks like it). New and updated editions of directories and newsletters come out all the time; check your local bookstore or library.

For more inside information on local discount stores:

- Watch newspaper ads. A few stores run small ads.
- Ask your friends and co-workers. Nothing beats word of mouth on bargain information.
- Call your local chamber of commerce. Chamber staff members, most of whom are women, are eager to give you help about their members, many of whom are successful discounters.
- Ask discount store managers and owners for recommendations of stores carrying other types of clothing and accessories. There's a camaraderie among discounters; they're happy to spread the word.
- Check the Yellow Pages for discount stores in the apparel, clothing and shoe store listings. Call the firms listed in the apparel and shoe manufacturing section to see if they have factory outlet stores or seasonal parking lot or warehouse sales. Ask to be put on their mailing list to be notified of special sales.

22
Secondhand Chic

Why shop for secondhand or "gently used" clothing? The answer is, quite simply, value—low, low prices for high-quality merchandise. A wide range of secondhand stores, from elegant resale boutiques at the top of the scale all the way down to funky neighborhood garage and lawn sales, is cropping up in every part of the country to meet the burgeoning demand for affordable apparel. The former "poor relations" stigma associated with used garments is evaporating as more and more bargain hunters discover the rewards and enjoyment of this unique form of discount shopping.

Secondhand stores, with their one-of-a-kind selections, make terrific bargain havens for those women who prefer to manifest their own individual sense of style by combining different pieces and designer looks rather than walk around as a fashion clone in new mass-produced clothes. Expensive styles and forward fashion looks can often be duplicated with secondhand purchases of similar cut, detail and styling. There's an old fashion adage that says there really are no new silhouettes or styles, only new ways to interpret and present them. Fashion is certainly cyclical, so use re*cycled* pieces to keep yourself in tune with the latest fashion *cycle* at a fraction of the cost. The revival of the figure-conscious 1950s looks of several seasons past is a good example of this. This trend started on the street, and then Seventh Avenue capitalized on the look with all sorts of pricey offerings; savvy individualists purchased the parts of the look they liked at much lower secondhand prices and came up with their own unique interpretations of the trend.

Quality at affordable prices is another incentive to shop secondhand sources. Vintage and antique clothing is often superior in fabric and workmanship to present-day garments manufactured to look like their predecessors. It's true that in some cases, they just don't make them like they used to. A classically tailored wool gabardine jacket lined with silk crepe from the 1940s might sell for $45 or $50 in an antique shop. A brand new jacket of comparable quality would sell for several times that amount—$100 or more—and not be as distinctive.

The types of secondhand stores we'll cover in this chapter are:

- resale and consignment stores and boutiques
- antique and vintage clothing stores
- thrift shops, charity bazaars, church rummage sales
- flea markets and swap meets

To give you some more background and information on shopping for used clothing, we'll summarize the pros and cons.

The Glories of Secondhand Shopping

- Lower prices on all your wardrobe needs, including designer and better labels. Keep your eyes open for a designer's signature detail or familiar styling on a better garment that has had the label removed.
- True "finds." These stores' one-of-a-kind selections include a myriad of unique and interesting pieces perfect for the woman who wants to experiment with or express her own personal style.
- Certain types of garments, namely furs, that might otherwise be completely out of reach pricewise, may suddenly come into the realm of possibility via secondhand shopping.
- Don't be put off by the fact that these clothes are used. They are not unhygienic. Antique and resale stores (or resale store consignees) thoroughly wash and clean garments before they are put out on display.
- Secondhand stores are useful for *buying* and *selling* clothing. The principle of "one person's castoff is another's treasure" applies to all of us. The money saved plus the fun and adventure involved will be just rewards for your efforts.
- Used clothing is ecologically sound shopping. No kidding. Think of yourself as helping the environment by recycling clothes as a buyer and seller.
- Learning the ropes of secondhand shopping will take a bit of time and effort on your part, but you'll soon get the hang of it.

But remember:

- Used clothing stores are generally not located in shopping centers and malls. You may have to do a bit of sleuthing to find them in their sometimes out of the way locations.
- Since almost everything in these stores is one of a kind, you may not be able to find what you want in your size.
- There can be a great deal of "rough" camouflaging the diamonds in used clothing stores. Be patient and keep wading through the racks—you're bound to happen on something nifty.
- Store ambience may be less than you're used to in other discount and retail stores. Low, low prices result from low overhead and correspondingly fewer shopping amenities.

Secondhand Shopping Tips

Here we list hints that will help you save time and money on any and all of your used clothing purchases. We'll pass along tips for each specific kind of store in each corresponding section.

- Again, since each item is one of a kind, shop all these stores with an open mind. Do bring along your wardrobe shopping list, though, to remind yourself of what you need. Especially at resale shops, you'll be able to find basics.
- Our usual advice to check every probable purchase inside and out goes double for used clothing. Scrutinize every square inch. If you find a stain, it's most likely in for good since garments have been cleaned or washed before they go on display. If you're a seamstress, you can probably make small repairs, but if an item requires major alterations or mending, skip it. Major alterations are never advisable on any purchase, new or "gently used." Check for worn places: collars, cuffs, openings and hems. Look for permanently soiled collars and cuffs and perspiration stains. Examine the crotch area on pants and jeans. Check zippers, snaps and buttons. Go over furs especially carefully to make sure the hide is not dried out or cracked and that there are no worn areas. Check every garment in natural light, too.
- Get to know the proprietor or store manager and

leave your name and phone number so that you can be called when special items come in.
- Put yourself on the store's mailing list to be notified of sales.
- Find out when merchandise arrives and the recommended time of each season for the best selection. Resale stores especially key their inventory to seasonal needs just as retail stores do.
- Shop your favorite recycled clothing stores often, since merchandise turns over quickly. When you see something you like and have to have, buy it. It won't be there when you come back again.
- Check several size ranges, since things that fit you may be in more than one size category. Used or antique clothing is frequently mis-sized or not sized at all.
- Most stores accept personal checks; many resale and antique shops also accept plastic money (credit cards). Be prepared with cash at garage sales and the like.
- Negotiating the sale price is accepted behavior in the used clothing business and is, of course, expected at garage sales, swap meets and flea markets. A little friendly haggling will help you get what you want at the lowest possible price.
- Wear a leotard under your easy-in-and-out-of outfit, since some stores may have no dressing rooms. If you've come prepared in your leotard, you can duck behind a rack and slip into things to make sure they fit.
- Be sure to check the exchange/return policy in advance of purchase. Many of these stores have an All Sales Final rule.
- Check the men's sections at vintage clothing stores and thrift shops. A small man's or boy's suit might work just as well as a woman's; men's shirts in good fabrics are terrific wardrobe stretchers.
- Check the fabric content and care labels; go for good quality natural fibers and blends. If the label is missing, note the "hand" or feel of the garment and ask for a second opinion from the store owner or manager. Owners of antique clothing stores are knowledgeable about fabrics and how to care for garments properly.

Now, more detail on each specific type of used clothing store.

Resale and Consignment Stores
Think of a resale store as a well-heeled friend's closet that you've just been invited to help yourself to. These stores are the "boutiques" of secondhand shopping options because of their high-quality merchandise selection (including designer and better brand name accessories and clothes) and cozy, classy boutiquelike store atmosphere. They operate by accepting a consignee's gently worn or even brand-new wardrobe items, not more than one or two seasons old, all of which have been washed and ironed or dry cleaned. The recycled raiment is then displayed and sold at prices about one-fourth to one-third of original retail value. Thus the bargains at these stores can really be terrific. We bought a $100 dress from a top California designer for a mere $28 at one of our favorite shops.

Consignment boutiques split the selling price with the consignee on a 50–50 or 60–40 basis, so everyone goes home happy. Merchandise turnover is usually rapid at these stores. Most begin marking items down after thirty days, and if something hasn't sold from the sale rack after approximately sixty days, it's returned to the consignee or donated to charity.

Consignment shops came into being several decades ago when wealthy socialites and actresses expressed a desire to recycle their expensive designer and evening wear. (After all, you can only give away so much to the maid.) Gradually, more and more women caught on to the wisdom, that is, low prices and ecological logic, of this concept, so that today there are top-notch resale shops everywhere. If your town doesn't yet have one, it will soon.

You don't have to be rich to recycle. This is a

Resale shops are terrific one-stop shopping centers for evening ensembles. This floor-length designer dress and angora sweater's resale price was $110, compared to its original retail value of $640.

perfectly good opportunity for you to recycle and profit from your own wardrobe, too. Just think of all the clothing, shoes and accessories you own and don't wear. They're too good to give away but not too precious to sell, right? Wash and dry clean your good-quality discards and take them on hangers to a local shop. (Call first for an appointment and any special instructions.) The two or three hundred dollars you get won't enable you to retire to Florida, but it will make a serious contribution to your current clothing budget.

Some resale stores, in addition to their used inventory, also carry new items, including manufacturers' closeouts and salesmen's samples.

Resale Shopping Tips

- Ask about designer items; they may be kept in a separate area.
- Become acquainted with the store owner or manager and ask to be notified when a particular item you need, such as a ranch mink jacket, comes in.
- When you're buying clothes at a consignment shop, look on the tag to see if the items are from one consignee. Ask to be notified the next time this woman brings in her clothes so you can get in early for best selection.
- Resale stores have fashion personalities just like retail stores. Find the one that suits your style and stocks your size.

Best Buys:

- Furs!
- Evening gowns and cocktail dresses.
- Shoes and boots.
- Handbags, hats, scarves and costume jewelry.
- Sweaters.
- Wardrobe basics (blouses, skirts, dresses).

Antique and Vintage Clothing Stores

Into this category we lump stores that sell clothing

Secondhand Chic • 181

One of our favorite antique apparel buys is this $40 vintage Lilli Ann wool crepe jacket in pristine condition.

from the mid-1800s to the late 1960s. Usually you'll find clothing from the 1920s on, especially the 1930s and 1940s. Antique and vintage clothing stores do a lot of the searching for you, since owners constantly scour thrift shops, rummage sales and estate sales for clothing. Vintage store proprietors also frequent used clothing wholesalers, "bale houses," salvage yards and department store liquidators. Forgotten bales and trunks of old used and even never-worn clothes can turn up in the most unlikely places—barn lofts and store attics. The cost of this service will be passed along to you, the consumer, but you will save time and find a better selection of cleaned, repaired garments. Also many vintage and antique clothing stores offer alterations at no extra charge.

A 1940s wool gabardine suit, for example, may cost $10 at a thrift store or church bazaar but may run as high as $80 at a fine vintage clothing store. Still, the value, when compared to the price of a wool gabardine suit in today's retail market, is reasonable for high-quality fabric and construction. You'll find tailoring and detail work (such as covered buttons, lined skirts, etc.) that are only found today on the most expensive designer goods.

You might be asking yourself why anyone would want to shop at these stores or wear something that is thirty-five or forty years old. Well, there are several sensible and even forward fashion reasons why the phenomenon of antique and vintage apparel is growing. As we already discussed in this chapter, "new" silhouettes and styles are merely reinterpretations of past looks. Lots of women enjoy the thrill of creating an up-to-the-minute, designer look by careful selection from vintage racks. We recently copied a $200 Ralph Lauren resort look using a $50 antique French white cotton nightshirt.

Those of you who consider yourselves fashion individualists will find the unique wardrobe items you're looking for at these shops for far less money. Maybe more than any other type of used clothing store, vintage and antique shops are just a lot of *fun* to shop in. Clothes are historic time capsules, and we can discover a lot about ourselves and our attitudes in each decade by sampling fashion.

Best Buys:
- Women's and men's wool jackets, suits and pants. Look for the Lilli Ann label in women's suit jackets from the 1940s and early 1950s. This line (still in business today) has the quality and lasting style you want in vintage clothing.
- Furs. Be sure to check carefully before buying to see that the pelt is not dried out.
- Antique jewelry. Store owners should guarantee authenticity or allow you to have the item appraised before purchase.
- Gloves, leather and cloth.
- Victorian whites: cotton and linen camisoles, slips and nightgowns.
- Hats.
- Silk and satin nightgowns, robes, dressing gowns and smoking jackets.
- Oriental kimonos.
- Beaded sweaters.
- Pendleton jackets and shirts.

One final comment—these best buys illustrate the *Chic on a Shoestring* credo: Always buy the best quality you can afford. Quality garments from decades past represent some of the best values your money can buy.

The fact that fine vintage apparel is available to all of us today is thanks to another *Chic* principle: Quality clothes deserve quality care. Your antique purchases will give you years of fashion value, just as they did for their previous owners, with loving care and maintenance.

Thrift Shops
These are operated by charities such as churches and hospitals, school auxiliaries or well-known organizations such as Goodwill Industries and the Salvation Army. For example, there are Junior League

Thrift stores yield remarkable values such as this Italian knit dress for $15.

stores in 111 cities across the country. Clothing and accessories of every size, shape and description for the entire family, plus furniture, household items and books are sold at rock-bottom prices. In addition to used items, you may also find brand-new items that have been donated by department stores and boutiques. These stores may be operated on a full-time basis as a regular business or as a special once-a-year benefit sale.

A word of caution: don't succumb to the seduction of an especially low priced item unless it really looks good on you and dovetails into your wardrobe. This advice is particularly worth remembering when shopping in thrift stores; otherwise you can wind up with half a closetful of things that you never wear but were "great buys." A bargain is *not* a good buy if you don't use it.

Another tip: take along a friend if you feel you need advice and/or restraint, since you won't find experienced sales help at these stores. Shop frequently, since new merchandise is donated continually. One of our friends hits her local thrift shops once a week during her lunch hour. This kind of shopping has become part of her regular routine as a result of the fashion finds she's discovered.

Don't forget to donate your no-longer-wanted items

to these stores. Be sure to request a receipt for tax deduction purposes.

Best Buys:

- suits and casual jackets
- shirts: bowling, men's rayon and cotton styles
- sweaters of all kinds
- slacks: tailored, pleated and military styles
- tuxedos
- boys' and men's suits
- lingerie: antique satins and rayons
- accessories: hats, belts, costume (especially rhinestone) jewelry, ties, etc.
- coats and capes (men's and women's)

Garage Sales, Church Rummage Sales, Charity Bazaars, Swap Meets and Flea Markets

You'll find both new and used clothing plus an endless array of other items at these "events." You may or may not be able to try things on privately, so it's best to attend said sales in a leotard just in case.

More tips:

- Attend early in the day for best selection, later on for better prices. As the sales day draws to a close, sellers are more apt to bargain.
- At swap meets and flea markets, be wary of counterfeit and stolen goods.
- Know regular prices. Swap meets in particular are just not the gold mines they used to be for good, low-priced deals.
- When purchasing clothing, find out about returns or exchanges. Is the seller a swap-meet regular, or is there a local contact number? Don't buy clothing gifts unless you can exchange easily, no matter how terrific the savings.
- Notices or advertisements of garage sales and church bazaars are usually listed in the classified section of your local paper. Check your church or organization bulletin and the bulletin board at your local grocery store, too. Note the addresses and hours and plot yourself a course to save time and gasoline.
- Wear comfortable shoes to all bazaars and swap meets and protective headgear and sunscreen to any outdoor events.

Best Buys:

- vintage clothes and accessories
- jackets and coats—men's and women's, new and vintage
- casual and sports shoes at swap meets, plus jewelry from independent artisans and manufacturers' overruns and end-of-season sales directly to the public
- knits: sweaters, dresses and suits of high quality, preferably designer made

23
Armchair Chic

Does the idea of taking care of your shopping needs while reclining in a hammock in the shade on a lazy Saturday afternoon appeal to you? Can you picture yourself updating your wardrobe while lounging on your living room sofa before a crackling fire in the evening as snow gently falls outside your window? If so, you're about to join the growing millions of energy-conscious and time-saving consumers who have jumped wholeheartedly on the mail-order bandwagon, checkbooks and credit cards in hand. An average catalog-shopper receives more than forty catalogs a year (sometimes it seems like your authors receive that many in a month). From this deluge consumers order more than $45 *billion* worth annually. That's a lot of business in a "slow" economy.

What's the secret? Women have always played a key role in the success of mail-order, which got its start just before the turn of the century. Isolated from stores in their rural habitats, farm women turned to the new "wishbooks" from Sears, Roebuck & Co. and Montgomery Ward for their families' work clothes. JC Penney joined the growth of these large, multi-item catalogs that quickly became "department stores between covers." Today women who work outside the home and have greater clothing and accessories needs but less time to shop for them are stimulating the current catalog boom. We've gone from a few big 1,200 page books to lots of smaller, specialty catalogs offering everything from cookware to cruises.

A primary witness to this trend is Spiegel. Known for decades as a general-purpose catalog, Spiegel has shifted its focus to appeal to upscale working women between the ages of twenty-five and forty-nine with a family income of $25,000 to $30,000. Their customer wants reliable fashion merchandise from known designers such as Liz Claiborne. The shift from *mass* market to *target* market occurred in 1976, explained Walter Killough, merchandising vice-president for fashion. He predicts a 25 percent growth in catalog sales in the next five years, as more and more women equate saving time with saving money.

The Convenience of Mail-Order Shopping

If you haven't yet tried this ultraconvenient form of buying, here are a few reasons why you might consider giving it a try.

Pros

- You save time and energy (yours and your car's) by shopping via mail. And there are no parking hassles, no surly sales help to contend with, and bad weather won't prevent you from doing your

shopping. If you're homebound or hate shopping, this is the answer to your prayers.
- Catalogs offer a broad range of merchandise at price points to fit all budgets. You'll see name brands and designers you're familiar with.
- Formerly hard-to-find and imported items are now at your fingertips.
- More information about the merchandise is given in the catalog descriptions than is known or volunteered by store salespeople—assuming, of course, you can even find a salesperson.
- Clothes are photographed on models so you can see what a garment looks like on a real person. Stores have a few mannequins on floor and window displays; otherwise you'll only see the garment on a hanger.
- There are separate sale and discount catalogs to satisfy the mail-order bargain hunter.
- Retail catalogs have sale pages and special purchases mixed in with regular priced merchandise.
- Receiving your orders in the mail or by United Parcel Service is a real lift—like giving yourself a gift. It's fun.
- Orders can be delivered to your place of business if you're not home during the day.

Cons:

Naturally there are two sides to every story, and you need to be aware of all the potential pitfalls before you fill out your first order blank.

- You can't actually see, touch or try on the merchandise before ordering; you have to rely on photos and written descriptions.
- Quality is hard to judge. Again, you have to determine quality as best you can through photos and copy plus what you know about a particular label. Note especially the fabric content descriptions.
- You can't have the item immediately.
- Returns by mail or U.P.S. are somewhat inconvenient but really no more so than returning an item to a store. Allow at least two weeks for delivery. You *do* pay return postage, though.
- Colors in photos are occasionally a little misleading. Sometimes the orange red in the photo turns out to be a bluer red when you get the item. Likewise, color descriptions are sometimes vague, and this is frankly one of our pet peeves. What color is *peony,* anyway?
- Hard-to-fit women are better off buying in stores, where clothes can be tried on.

Mail-Order Shopping Tips

Here are some hints on how to make your catalog shopping sprees successful:

- Order easier-to-fit items such as sweaters rather than something like leather pants. Read size ordering instructions carefully in the catalog or on the order blank.
- When ordering by phone (most catalog companies have toll-free numbers; "mail-order" is almost becoming a misnomer for telephone shopping), ask the operator for availability and delivery information for the items you're ordering. Most order operators have this at their fingertips in their computer terminals. Ask the operator for size and color information, too.
- When ordering shoes, send an outline of your foot to ensure proper size.
- Before ordering, check the return and refund policy. Don't order nonreturnables such as swimsuits, hosiery and underwear unless you know your size in a particular label. Sale merchandise is not always returnable, so beware.
- Familiarize yourself with retail prices so you'll know if you're getting a bargain in a discount or sale catalog. Even "retail" prices vary a bit from catalog to catalog, so shop comparatively.
- Send a check or money order through the mail, never cash. Credit cards are really the easiest to

use since refunds are handled on your card account.
- Have items delivered to your office so you or your secretary can sign for them. When you have a choice, select U.P.S. for deliveries. They make 90 percent of all mail-order deliveries in this country because they do it right.
- Keep a photocopy of your order with the catalog or circle the items, sizes, colors and quantities you ordered in the catalog. Note the date and whether you ordered by check or credit card (if so, which one). If you order by phone, note the operator's name. This way you'll have a complete record if there's a problem or if you need to return something. Likewise, hang on to canceled checks, credit card records, order blanks and packing slips.
- Use catalogs for current fashion information just as you would fashion magazines. Notice how outfits are accessorized, what colors and combinations are current, how garments are layered, etc.
- Don't pay sales tax unless you live in the same state as the catalog company or one of its branches.
- At first it's probably best to order items you're already familiar with, especially those in your favorite brands. Later, after your mail-order confidence is built up, you can branch out and take a flyer on something new or fun.
- Order early—as soon as you receive a catalog—to avoid the disappointment of finding out that the item you wanted is sold out. We've experienced this several times, but *no more*. Now we order immediately, especially from the discount beauty supply catalogs, to get what we want.
- Patronize catalog companies that are members of the Direct Mail/Marketing Association, which is like a Better Business Bureau for mail order.

What to Do if There's a Snafu

If a time period is stated, such as four to six weeks, the company *must* deliver your order to you within that period. If the goods haven't arrived by the end of that time, you can cancel and get a full refund. If no time period is indicated, the catalog firm has thirty days to ship your merchandise to you or notify you of a delay or back order. Again, after that period you're free to cancel and demand a refund even if the merchandise has been back ordered.

If your attempts to work out an order or return with the company's customer service department fail, you can turn to:

1. Your local or state consumer protection agency. Or write to:

   Director, Bureau of Consumer Protection
   Federal Trade Commission
   Washington, D.C. 20580

2. Your local postmaster, who will give the name of the appropriate postal inspector.
3. The magazine or newspaper that ran the ad for the catalog or mail order item in question. These publications are usually most helpful in assisting readers.
4. Direct Mail/Marketing Association, Inc. (DM/MA)
   6 East 43rd Street
   New York, NY 10017

For more information on shopping by mail, contact the catalog industry's association, the DM/MA for their free booklet entitled *Make Knowledge Your Partner in Mail-Order Shopping*. The federal government also has a free booklet available on your rights under federal law when ordering merchandise through the mail. Request pamphlet 623 J (free) from the:

Consumer Information Center
Department DD
Pueblo, CO 81008

Write *Free* on the envelope.

Let your fingers do the shopping.

How to Get Catalogs

There are two good ways to get yourself on catalog mailing lists (assuming you're not inundated with them already) or to request particular catalogs for special sizes or types of clothing and accessories. (1) Write to the DM/MA for their terrific booklet listing several hundred catalog companies and their addresses. Send $1 and ask for the *Great Catalogue Guide.* You can also write to the Mail Preference Society at the DM/MA, and they'll send you forms you can fill out to request the particular types of catalogs you'd like to receive. If you'd like to be removed from any mailing lists, the Preference Society will help you with this, too. (2) Check your favorite magazines, and fashion magazines in particular, for special catalog-ordering inserts. These are plentiful in the fall as companies push their big holiday catalogs. Magazines such as *Mademoiselle* and *Glamour* have a regular mail-order department in the back of each issue.

A List of Catalogs by Categories

We've listed catalogs by their types and the merchandise they offer. Unless otherwise noted, catalogs are free by writing to the address given.

General Merchandise

JC Penney
Circulation Dept.
Box 2056
Milwaukee, WI 53201 $2. Applied to first purchase

Sears, Roebuck and Co.
Sears Tower
Chicago, IL 60684 $3. Applied to first purchase

Spiegel
1061 W. 35th St.
Chicago, IL 60609 $3

Montgomery Ward
Montgomery Ward Plaza
Chicago, IL 60671 $2

Department and Specialty Stores

Bloomingdale's
115 Brand Rd.
Salem, VA 24156 $5

Neiman-Marcus
Dept. 100
P.O. Box 2968
Dallas, TX 75221 $5

Saks Fifth Avenue
Folio Collections
449 West 14th St.
New York, NY 10014 $2

I. Magnin
P.O. Box 2096
Oakland, CA 94604 $2

Sakowitz
1111 Main St.
Houston, TX 77002 $2.50

Bonwit Teller
P.O. Box 1642
Long Island City, NY 11101

Joseph Magnin
P.O. Box 7784
San Francisco, CA 94120

Bergdorf Goodman
754 Fifth Avenue
New York, NY 10019 $5

Garfinkel's
1401 F Street, N.W.
Washington, D.C. 20004

Robinson's
600 W. Seventh St.
Los Angeles, CA 90017

Lord & Taylor
424 Fifth Avenue
New York, NY 10018

190 • *Chic on a Shoestring*

Macy's New York
Herald Square—Broadway & 34th St.
New York, NY 10001

Marshall Field's
Box 1165
Chicago, IL 60690 $2

Classic and Traditional
Talbots
Hingham, MA 02043

Laura Ashley
Mail-Order Dept. 177
70 Marcus Dr.
Melville, NY 11747 $1

Brooks Brothers
346 Madison Ave.
New York, NY 10017

Carroll Reed
North Conway, NH 03860

Gorsuch Ltd.
263 E. Gore Creek Dr.
Vail, CO 81657

The Tog Shop
Lester Square
Americus, GA 31710

Lilly Pulitzer
1101 Clara Ave.
W. Palm Beach, FL 33401

Chadwick's of Boston
One Chadwick Place
Boston, MA 02072

Boutiques
Peachtree Report
4795 Fulton Industrial Blvd.
Atlanta, GA 30336

La Shack
19 The Plaza
Locust Valley, NY 11560

Brownstone Studio
1 East 43rd St.
New York, NY 10173

Willow Ridge
135 Kisco Avenue
Mt. Kisco, NY 10549

Career Guild
2500 Crawford Ave.
Evanston, IL 60201

First Editions
340 Poplar St.
Hanover, PA 17331

Fashion Forward
FBS
659 Main St.
New Rochelle, NY 10801 $1

Esprit
800 Minnesota St.
San Francisco, CA 94107 $1

Ann Taylor
3 East 57th St.
New York, NY 10022 $2

Sweet Willy
114 East 32nd St.
New York, NY 10016 $2

The Ingram Collection
214 West 39th St.
New York, NY 10018

Honeybee
2745 Philmont Ave.
Huntingdon Valley, PA 19006

Beautiful & Co.
800 Third Avenue
New York, NY 10022

Sports and Outdoor
L.L. Bean
1610 Birch St.
Freeport, ME 04033

Banana Republic
76 E. Blithedale
Mill Valley, CA 94961

Orvis
10 River Rd.
Manchester, VT 05254

Cris Craft
Algonac, MI 48001

Camp Beverly Hills
9615 Brighton Way
Beverly Hills, CA 90210   50¢

Hill's Court
Manchester, VT 05254

Eddie Bauer
Fifth and Union
Seattle, WA 98124

Austin-Hall Boot Co.
491 N. Resler, Suite B
El Paso, TX 79912

Early Winters
Dept. YI
110 Prefontaine Place South
Seattle, WA 98104

Lands' End
Lands' End Lane
Dodgeville, WI 53533

Abercrombie & Fitch
2302 Maxwell Lane
Houston, TX 77023 $2

River Junction Trade Co.
312 Main St.
P.O. Box 275
McGregor, IA 52157 $1.50

I. Buss & Co.
738 Broadway
New York, NY 10003

Western
Cutter Bill Western World
5818 LBJ Freeway
Dallas, TX 75240

Sheplers
6501 West Kellog
P.O. Box 7702
Wichita, KS 67277

Discount

Clothing:

Avon Fashions
Avon Lane
Newport News, VA 23630
(women's dresses, sportswear and lingerie)

Sousa & Lefkovits
621 South B St.
Tustin, CA 92680
(traditional)

The Company Store
Dept. B
1205 South 7th St.
La Crosse, WI 54601
(down coats, jackets, vests and comforters)

General:

Grand Finale
P.O. Box 340257
Farmers Branch, TX 75234

Cosmetics:

Beauty Buy Book
65 East South Water
Chicago, IL 60601

Beautiful Beginnings
Spencer Bldg.
Atlantic City, NJ 08411

Beautiful Visions
810 S. Hicksville Rd.
C.S. 4001
Hicksville, NY 11802

Jewelry:

The Jewelart Collection
16734 Stagg St.
Van Nuys, CA 91409

The Westerly Collection
P.O. Box 60
Cranbury, NJ 08512 $1

Adco Beauty Products
P.O. Box 10949
Chicago, IL 60610

Lingerie:

Chas. Weiss & Sons, Inc.
38 Orchard St.
New York, NY 10002

Specialty

Dance & Active Wear:

Hang Ten Sportswear
Daisy Productions
109-B Pasadena Avenue
South Pasadena, CA 91031

Danskin
1114 Avenue of the Americas
New York, NY 10036 $1.50

Taffy's
701 Beta Dr.
Cleveland, OH 44143 $3

The Finals
39 East 12th Street
New York, NY 10003

Ethnic Fashions & All-Natural-Fiber Clothing:

Garnet Hill
Franconia, NH 03580

Tantra
121 Union St.
Providence, RI 02901

Shopping International
P.O. Box 27600
Tucson, AZ 85726 $1

The Peruvian Collection
Canaan Farm
Tonganoxie, KS 66086

French Creek Sheep & Wool
Elverson, PA 19520

Royal Silk
45 E. Madison Avenue
Clifton, NJ 07011 $1

Monarch Trading Co. of New Zealand
Pier 2
Honolulu, HI 96813

Cotton Dreams
999 Laredo Ln.
Box 1261
Sebastian, FL 32958

Jewelry:

Lotus
532 San Anselmo Avenue
San Anselmo, CA 94960 $2

Tiffany's
Fifth Ave. & 57th Street
New York, NY 10022 $3

Cartier
2 East 52nd Street
New York, NY 10022 $5

Jenny B. Goode
1194 Lexington Avenue
New York, NY 10028

Ambassador
711 W. Broadway
Tempe, AZ 85282

M. & I. Haberman, Inc.
122 E. 42nd Street
New York, NY 10168

Large Sizes:

Great Impressions
720 Anderson Road
St. Cloud, MN 56340

Old Pueblo Traders
600 S. Country Club Road
Tucson, AZ 85726 $1

Nancy's Choice
Indianapolis, IN 46201

The Avenue
310 Madison Avenue
New York, NY 10017

Half Sizes:

Roaman's
Saddle Brook, NJ 07662

Lingerie:

Victoria's Secret
Box 31442
San Francisco, CA 94131 $2

Bare Necessities
12372 Olive Boulevard
St. Louis, MO 63141 $1.50

Frederick's of Hollywood
6608 Hollywood Boulevard
Hollywood, CA 90028 $2

Intimique
1 Eastwood Drive
Dept. 182
Cincinnati, OH 45227 $2

Intimate Boutique
P.O. Box F
Wheeling, FL 60090

Petites:

Unique Petites
Plaza Petites Mail Order Co.
5625 N. 19th Avenue
Phoenix, AZ 85015

Piaffe
1500 Broadway
Suite 812
New York, NY 10036

LP For Short
2300 Southeastern Avenue
Indianapolis, IN 46201

Maternity:

Mothers Work
P.O. Box 40121
Philadelphia, PA 19106 $2

Thelma Lager Assoc.
Dept. WD, The Complex 100F
3015 Glendale Blvd.
Los Angeles CA 90039
(exercise wear)

(See also ethnic clothing catalogs)

Nursing/Postpartum:

Mamamade Nursing Fashions
110 Idlewild Lane
Media, PA 19063 $1

Designer Series
3015 Glendale Blvd.
Los Angeles, CA 90039
(Mary Jane Maternity &
nursing apparel)

Talls:

Lane Bryant Tall Collection
2300 Southeastern Avenue
Indianapolis, IN 46201

Shelly's Tall American Beauties
747 Towne Avenue
Los Angeles, CA 90021

Miscellaneous:

Crate & Barrel
195 Northfield Road
Northfield, IL 60093

Bill Tosetti's
17632 Chatsworth Street
Granada Hills, CA 91344
(Pendleton sportswear)

Ken Nolan
16901-D
Box C-19555
Irvine, CA 92713 $1
(military surplus)

Professional Uniforms & Accessories
19 Booker Street
Westwood, NJ 07675

Shoes:

Barry Collection
Box 1150
Auburn, ME 04210

Hill Brothers
99 Ninth Street
Lynchburg, VA 24504

Mason Shoe Mfg. Co.
Chippewa Falls, WI 54774

Mooney & Gilbert, Inc.
5th Floor, 31 West 57th Street
New York, NY 10019
(long and narrow shoes)

Nierman's
17 N. State Street
Stevens Building 12th Floor
Chicago, IL 60602
(narrow, wide and long)

Lawson Hill Shoe Co.
Old Sanford Mills
61A Emery Street
Sanford, ME 04073
(smalls to long; narrow to extra-wide)

Recommended Reading

The following is a list of recommended books that complement the *Chic on a Shoestring* philosophy and/or offer an in-depth discussion on a particular fashion topic.

Style and Proportion
The Complete Bonnie August Dress Thin System, Bonnie August with Ellen Count. Rawson, Wade Publishers. New York, 1981.
The Fashion Survival Manual, Judith H. McQuown and Odile Laugier. Everest House. New York, 1981.
Short Chic, Allison Kyle Leopold and Anne Marie Cloutier. Bantam Books. New York, 1983.
Womanstyle: Your Personal Guide to Timeless Fashion, Leah Feldon. Clarkson N. Potter. New York, 1979.

Antique and Eclectic Style
Cheap Chic Update, Caterine Milinaire and Carol Troy. Harmony Books. New York, 1978.
Harriet Love's Guide to Vintage Chic, Harriet Love. Holt, Rinehart & Winston. New York, 1982.

Care and Closets
The Closet Book, Elin Schoen. Harmony Books. New York, 1982.
How to Organize Your Closet and Your Life!, Crislynne Evatt. Ballantine Books. New York, 1980.
Taking Care of Clothes, Mablen Jones. St. Martin's Press. New York, 1982.

Fashion Reference

Fairchild's Dictionary of Fashion, Dr. Charlotte Calasibetta. Fairchild Publications, Inc. New York, 1975.

The Fashion Encyclopedia, Catherine Houck. St. Martin's Press. New York, 1982.

Individuality in Clothing Selection and Personal Appearance: A Guide for the Consumer, fourth edition, Mary Kefgen and Phyllis Touchie-Specht. Macmillan Publishing Co. New York, 1984.

Shopping

Clothing By-Mail Catalogue, Sarah Gallick. New American Library. New York, 1982.

The Savvy Shopper, Judy Young Ocko and Larry Goodman. Ballantine Books. New York, 1982.

Secondhand Super Shopper, Ellen Weiss. M. Evans and Company. New York, 1981.

S.O.S.: Save On Shopping, ninth edition, Iris Ellis. SOS Directory Inc. Jacksonville, Florida, 1983.

The Underground Shopper, Sue Goldstein. Andrews and McMeel. Kansas City, 1983.

Fashion History and Aesthetics

The Collector's Book of Fashion, Frances Kennett. Crown Publishers. New York, 1983.

The Fashionable Mind, Kennedy Fraser. Alfred A. Knopf. New York, 1981.

The Language of Clothes, Alison Lurie. Random House. New York, 1981.

What We Wore: An Offbeat Social History of Women's Clothing, 1950–1980, Ellen Melinkoff. Quill. New York, 1984.

The Women We Wanted to Look Like, Brigid Keenan. St. Martin's Press. New York, 1977.

If any of these books are out of print or unavailable at bookstores, check your library.

Chic on a Shoestring Models:

Blake Dillard	Cathy Naples
Suzanne Dillard	Lornay Gealer
Kim Robinson	Milca Melano
Anastacia Blaisdell	Kathryn Gates
Monica Magnus	Lesley Charlton
Cindy Morris	Marilyn Clark
Karen Hahn	Maureen Strange
Tracy Hayakawa	Viki King
Jeanette Reiko	Tong Su Kim
Chai Lee	Gretchen DeBoer
Yoko Cato	Siri Pinter
Linda Pierce	Megan Diamond
Carol Austin	Jacquie Dedona
Lisa Maniboc	Ann Mace
Candace Lee	Bette Cunningham
Cindy Delpit	Linda Spencer
Frankie Slater	Terri Culiner
Stevie Ellison	Linda Hanafee
Glenda Toni	Janella Robinson

Chic on a Shoestring cover credits:

Photography by Leigh Charlton
Model: Cindy Morris, Wilhimena West
Stylist: Annette Swanberg
Hair and Makeup: Marla Quincy
Assistant: Lauranne Herwegh
Clothes courtesy Alan G, Tarzana, California

Index

A

Accent colors, 21, 51, 82
Accessories, 34, 35, 37, 49, 58, 67–72, 84, 120
   chain store, 166
   construction checks, 128
   day/evening changes, 93–96
   discounters, 172
   men's, 76
   travel, 86
Acetate, 131
Acrilan, 131
Acrylic, 129, 131, 141, 142
Action wear, 97, 166, 192
   double duty with sports wear, 97, 100
Adolfo (designer), 94, 97
Adzer, Laise, 106
Alakazia, A'lone, 133–35
Aldens chain stores, 100
Allard, Linda, 89
American Silk Mills, 141
Ameritone Paint Corp., 19
   pocket dictionary paint chip samples, 21, 24

B

Andrews, Julie, 73
Antique and vintage clothing, 77, 142, 180–82
Antron, 130, 131
Armani, Giorgio, 114
Arnel, 131

Ballet shoes, 63, 97
Bargain huntress, 149, 152
Basics, wardrobe. *See* Classics.
Bean, L. L., 100
Beene, Geoffrey, 11
   label, 171
   on seasonless dressing, 83
Belts, 15, 34, 57, 58, 68, 94
Bermuda shorts, 115
Big, Beautiful Woman magazine, 12
Black, 22, 30, 42, 85
Blass, Bill, 103, 104
   label, 171
Blazer, boys' size, 73, 74
Blouses, 34

Body (figure). *See* Figure
Body wear, 97
Bonwit Teller, 159
Boots, 58, 63, 64, 65
Boutiques, 161, 163, 177, 179
Boys' clothes, 73–74
Bracelet, 89, 95
Brannan discount chain, 171
Brooks Brothers, 74
Buck, Genevieve, on fashion trends, 123–25
Bust, 30, 34
   measurement, 28

C

Caftan, 57, 116
California Apparel News, 13
California Fashion Publications, 12–13
Camisole, silk, 83, 86, 92, 93
Cape, 102, 104, 105
Cardigan, 83
Cardin, Pierre, 73

Care instruction labels, 129, 131, 141
Carnaby Street designers, 123
Cashin, Bonnie, 117
  label, 171
Cashmere, 129, 130, 141
  dress coat, 104
Catalogs, mail-order, 165–66
Caulfield, Loré, 141
Cautious shopper, 150–51, 153
Chain stores, 71, 73, 100, 165–67
Chanel, Coco, 97
  on jewelry, 68
  suit, 116, 123, 124
  on trends, 123
Charity bazaars, 184
Charlton, Leigh
  basics in personal wardrobe, 113–14
  Italian shoe boots, 65
  Tsu silk chemise, 54
Chemise, silk, 54
Chicago *Tribune*, 124
Church rummage sales, 184
Claiborne, Liz, 9, 17
  label, 171
  on proportion, 36–39
  travel advice, 89
Classics (basics), 13, 14, 15, 53, 54, 81, 82, 113–27
  accessories, 120
  best buys, 121–22
  blouses and shirts, 118
  coats and jackets, 119
  dresses, 119
  evening wear, 119
  shoes and boots, 119
  slacks and pants, 119
  sports gear, 120
  suits and separates, 118
  sweaters, 120

Closet, cleaning out, 48–53
  clothes to discard, 48, 50
  clothes to keep, 48, 50
  organizing new, 51–53
Closet management, 55–59
Clothing, one-size-fits-all concept (Fragments), 39
Clothing Selection and Personal Appearance: A Guide for the Consumer (Kefgen and Touchie-Specht), 23
Coat wardrobe, 101–4
  from authors' closets, 103–4
  basics required, 101
  down, 101, 103, 104
  figure considerations, 101–2
  fur, 103, 104
  hemlines, 102
  high-fashion wool, 104
  men's, 75, 76, 104
  princess-style dress-length, 101, 102, 103
  shopping for, 103
  styles, 102–3
  travel, 86
  trench coat with removable lining, 101, 102
  See also Raincoats
Cocktail dress, 115
Cohen, Lois, 165
Colorfast fabric, 131
Color Key Corporation, 19
Color Key Program, 19–25
  accent, 21
  cool, 19, 22, 23
  eyes, 21, 24
  fabrics, 20
  key 1 colors (cool), 19
  key 2 colors (warm), 19
  makeup, 20, 23, 24
  shoes, 61

Color Key Program—*Cont.*
  skin tone, 19–21, 24
  solid, 21
  summer, 25
  warm, 19, 22, 23
Colors, 34, 38
  accent, 51, 82
  bright, 51
  cool, 19, 22, 23
  dark (slenderizing), 29
  evening wear, 93
  figure proportions and, 30, 42
  neutral, 51, 82
  seasonal dressing, 81, 82, 83–84
  summer, 25
  warm, 19, 22, 23
Comfort, 11, 16, 39, 118
Communication, dress as form of, 23
Consignment shops, 50, 177, 179
Construction, 134
Cosmopolitan magazine, 12
Cotton fabric, 130
  care, 141
  transseasonal, 82
  travel, 85
Cotton gauze, 85
Counterculture, 123
Courrèges (designer), 123, 159
Crawford, Joan, 103, 118
Crease-resistant fabric, 131
Creslan, 131
Crisp, Quentin, on fashion, 123

D

Dacron, 130, 131
Dance wear, 16, 97, 192

Index • 201

Day to evening chic, 91–96
Dayton Hudson Corp., 171
De la Renta, Oscar, 37, 97
Design, Mary Kefgen on, 116–18
Designer clothes, 154, 157
Designer discount stores, 171
Designers, menswear styling in women's clothes, 73
  transseasonal dressing, 83–84
Detail, 34
Devoe and Raynolds Co., 19
Diagonal lines, 30, 31
Diamond, Megan, 70
Diana, Princess, 105
Dietrich, Marlene, 73
Dior, Christian, 123
  label, 171
Discount shopping, 165–67, 169–76
  advantages, 171
  chain stores, 71, 73, 100, 165–67, 171–72
  directories, 175–76
  disadvantages, 171
  myths, 169–70
  outlet stores, 167
  seconds and irregulars, 174–75
  shopping tips, 172–74
  spotting forgeries, 174
Dress, communication, 23
Dress codes, 24
Drip-dry fabric, 131–32
Dry cleaning, 137–38
Durable-press fabric, 132

E

Early Winters catalog, 100
Earrings, 95

Ellis, Perry, 8
  label, 171
Equivalent size charts, women's and boys',
  jeans, 74
  pants, 74
  shirts, 74
Essence magazine, 12
Ethnic dressing, 116, 192
Evening wear, 14, 51
  colors, 93
  maternity clothes, 106
  metallics, 93
  resale shop, 180
  texture, 93
  travel, 86
Eyes, color key program, 21, 24

F

Fabrics, 38, 129, 134
  color key program, 20
  matching pattern at seams, 128
  menswear for women's clothes, 73
  natural fibers, 85, 129–30
  patterns, 33, 38, 128
  prints, 21, 22, 85
  seasonless dressing, 81, 82
  solid colors, 22
  synthetics, 129, 130–31
  travel wardrobe, 85–86
Faddist shopper, 150, 152
Fads, 16, 122–23, 124
Fairchild Publications, 12, 13
Family Circle magazine, 12
Fashion classics. *See* Classics
Fashion identity, 114
Fashion photography, 124

Fashion magazines, 11–12, 14, 124, 125
  trade, 12
Fashion shows, 10
  retail stores, 165
Fashion-watch, 9
Feet. *See* Shoes
Feraud, Louis, 104
Fiber content, 129
Fibers. *See* Natural fibers; Synthetics
Figure, body know-how and attitude, 39–43
  diagonal lines for, 30, 31
  half sizes, 154
  horizontal lines (stripes) for, 30, 31, 34
  how to look taller and slimmer, 29, 30, 38
  importance of properly fitted clothes, 16, 37, 132–33, 135
  long-waisted, 28, 101, 154
  maximizing (minimizing) flaws, 43
  measurements, 27–28
  petite, 154
  short, 154
  short-waisted, 28, 101–2
  slenderizing, 29, 30, 31
  tall, 154
  vertical lines for, 30, 38
Finity, 17
Fit, 16, 37, 132–33, 135
Flea markets, 184
Fortrel, 131
Fox, Patti, on retail shopping, 163–65
Fox label, 166
Fragments (one-size-fits-all clothes concept), 39
Fuchsia, 23
Fullness, 32, 34, 37

Fur coat, 103
    1940s style full length, 104
Furs, 129
    care, 142–44

G

Garage sales, 184
Gernreich, Rudy, 117
Givenchy, Hubert, on couture, 123
Glad Rags and *Glad Rags II* directories, 1, 50, 176
Glamour magazine, 12
Gloves, 58, 71, 72, 95, 145
Good Housekeeping magazine, 12
Goodwill Industries, 182
Goolagong, Evonne, 166

H

Hair, 21, 22, 40, 42
Half sizes, 154, 193
Halston, 166
    labels, 171
Handbags, 57, 58, 69–70, 95, 145, 172
Harper's Bazaar magazine, 11
Head, Edith, on classics, 122
Hats, 57, 58, 71, 72, 95, 145
    men's, 76
Hemline, 15, 38
    coat, 102
    maternity clothes, 105–6
Hepburn, Katharine, 73
Hips, 30, 34, 37
    measurement, 28

Horizontal lines, 30, 31, 34
Horn, Carol, 9
Hosiery, 71, 94, 166
How to look taller and slimmer, 29, 30, 38
Hunt Club label, 166

I

Impulsive shopper, 151, 153
Indecisive shopper, 149–50, 152
Instinctive shopper, 151, 153
Investment dressing, 115, 116, 123, 124, 125
Ironing, 140–41
It's Me magazine, 12

J

Jackets, 38, 83, 103, 104, 181
    sleeve length, 37
Jeans, boys' sizes, 74
Jet pack dressing, 84
Jewelry, 57, 58, 70–71, 93–95
    where to buy, 71, 192, 193
Job hunting, 14–15
Jock chic (survival dressing for the 1980s), 97–100
Jogging outfits, 100
Jogging shoes, 97
Jones, Gwen, on classic styles, 13–17
Jones New York, 17
Jumpers, 105, 106
Jumpsuits, 38, 57, 83, 86, 99
Junior League, 182–83
Junior sizes, 37

K

Kamali, Norma, 16, 97, 113
Karan, Donna, on seasonal dressing, 84
    travel advice, 89
Keaton, Diane, 73
Kefgen, Mary
    on color, 23–25
    on timeless chic, 116–18
    with Phyllis Touchie-Specht *Individuality in Clothing Selection and Personal Appearance,* 23
Key 1 colors (cool), 19–25
Key 2 colors (warm), 19–25
Killough, Walter, 185
Klein, Anne, 84, 89, 161
    label, 170
Klein, Calvin, 11, 16, 161
    label, 171
K Mart stores, 100
Knits, 30, 82, 83, 94
Kodel, 131
Krizia (designer), 7

L

Labels care instructions, 129, 131, 141
    designer's and manufacturer's, 170–71
Ladies' Home Journal, 12
Lady Madonna stores, 107
Lands' End catalog, 100
Large sizes, 193
Laundering, 138
    hand washing, 138

Laundering—*Cont.*
  ironing, 140–41
  machine washing, 139
Lauren, Ralph, 73, 74, 124–25, 182
  label, 171
Laver, James, 122
Layering (layered dressing), 82, 85, 86, 87, 93, 117
Leather, 134, 142, 143
Lee, Lina, 17
Leg warmers, 54
Leotards, 83, 86, 97, 98, 100
Lesso, Elke, 107–10
Levi label, 73
Lilli, Ann, label, 171, 181, 182
Line (stripes), 34, 35, 38
  diagonal, 30, 31
  horizontal, 30, 31, 34
  proportion and, 30
  vertical, 30, 38
Linen, 130
Lingerie, 96, 141, 192, 193
Linings, 128–29, 134
Lipstick, 23, 24
Lister, Sara, 115
Little, Carole, 22
  sale outfit, 173
  travel advice, 89
Loehmann's discount store, 17, 170
Long johns, 100
Long-waisted figure, 28, 101, 154
Lord & Taylor Creative Design award, 39
Loré Lingerie, 141
Los Angeles *Herald Examiner*, 13
Loungewear, 166
Lycra, 131, 141

M

McCall's magazine, 12
Mademoiselle magazine, 12
Mail-order shopping, 165–66, 185–94
  catalog ordering, 189
  catalogs listed by categories, 189–94
  cons, 186
  pros, 185–86
  shopping tips, 186–87
Makeup, 20, 23, 24, 192
Mamamade Nursing Fashions, 107
Mandelli, Mariuceia, 7
Marcus, Stanley, 127
Marshall Field & Company, 115
Marshalls discount chain, 100, 171
Maternity clothes, 105–10, 154, 156, 194
  dropped waist, 108
  postpartum and nursing needs, 107, 110, 194
Maxwell, Vera, on fashionable women, 114
Measurements, 27–28
  bust, 28
  hips, 27, 28
  shoulders, 27–28
  waist, 28
Menswear, 73–77
Merchandising, 135
Mervyn's, 172
Metallics, 93
Military gear, 76–77
Miller Shoes, I., 159
Mirror, full length, 56
Mix and match, 19, 23, 49, 85, 87
Models, 197
Monroe, Marilyn, 40
Montgomery Ward, 71, 100, 189
Motherhood Maternity stores, 107
Mugler, Thierry, 13
Muir, Jean, on seasonless dressing, 83
Mulqueen, Jack, 166

N

Nail polish, 23, 24
Nast publications, Condé, 12
Natural fibers, 85, 129–30, 192
Neiman-Marcus stores, 127, 159
Nylon, 130, 131, 141

O

Off-price buying, 169
Orange, 23
Orlon, 129, 131
Outlet stores, 167

P

Packing, 87–89
Pants, 38, 74
Pantsuit, 115
Paper Tiger (movie), 53
Pappagallo chain stores, 159
Parnis, Mollie, on quality, 127
Parton, Dolly, 42
Pattern, 33, 38, 128
Pearls, 95
Penney, J. C., 71, 73, 100, 107, 125, 165–67

Penny, J. C.—*Cont.*
  catalogs, 165, 167, 189
  Fox and Hunt Club labels, 166
  outlet stores, 167
Permanent finish fabric, 132
Permanent press fabric, 132
Personal shopping, 163–64
Petite figure, 154, 193
Pic-a-dilly chain, 100, 171
Picone, Evan, 17
  label, 170
Polyester, 130, 131, 141–42
Poncho, 102
Posture, 37
Prints, 21, 22, 85
Proportion, 27–43
  accessories, 67
  color and, 30, 42
  detail, 34
  experimenting, 36, 37
  fullness, 32, 37
  how to look taller and slimmer, 29, 30, 38
  lines and, 30
  Liz Claiborne on, 36–39
  rear-view perspective, 37
  scale, 37–38
  shoes and, 61
  silhouette (shape), 30, 32
  texture and, 30
  tips on, 37
  two-thirds ratio, 38
  women's sizes, 37–38
Pumps, 62, 63

Q

Quality, 127–35, 182
  construction, 128–29
  fabric, 129–31

R

Raincoats, 74, 86, 88, 96, 102, 103
Rayon, 82, 131, 141
Reagan, Nancy, 51
Recommended reading, 195
Retail shopping, 159–67
  boutiques, 161, 163, 177, 179
  chain stores, 165–67
  cons, 157–60
  guerrilla tactics for, 160–61
  markdowns, 161
  personal shoppers, 164
  pros, 159
  resale stores, 50, 177, 179, 180
  specialty stores, 161, 163, 177, 179
Rykiel, Sonia, on seasonless dressing, 83–84

S

St. Laurent, Yves, 16–17, 159
  on classics, 122
Saint Tropez West, 89
  label, 171
Saks Fifth Avenue, 117, 157
Saks Fifth Avenue, Beverly Hills, 163
Salvation Army, 182
Sarong, 86
Savvy magazine, 12
Scarves, 34, 57, 58, 68, 69, 95, 145
Sears, Roebuck & Co., 71, 73, 100, 107, 125, 165–67
  catalogs, 165, 167, 189

Sears, Roebuck & Co.—*Cont.*
  outlet stores, 167
  Silver Unicorn insignia, 165
Seasonless (transseasonal) chic, 81–84
Secondhand shopping, 177–84
  best buys, 180, 182, 184
Self magazine, 12
Selwyn, Harriet, on body know-how and attitude, 39–43
Separates, 86, 87, 89
Shamask, Ronaldus, on simplicity, 116
Shape. *See* Silhouette
Shawl, 69, 102, 105
Shoes, 34, 39, 40, 49, 53–54, 57, 58, 61–66, 69, 95
  ballet flat, 63
  boots, 58, 63, 64, 65
  care, 144
  chain store, 166
  color, 61
  construction checks, 128
  day into evening, 93–94
  discounters, 172
  flats, 64
  mail order, 194
  penny loafers, 63
  price ranges, 64
  proportion, 61
  pumps, 61, 62, 63
  shopping for, 64, 65–66
  style, 63–64
  tips, 64–65
  travel wardrobe, 86
Shoes, B. F. discount chain, 171
Shopping, 8, 81–84, 127, 149–53, 177–84
  European/American differences, 107
  planning your shopping trip, 154–57, 160

Shopping—*Cont.*
See also Discount shopping; Mail order shopping; Retail shopping
Shoulders, 34, 37
    coat styles for, 101
    measurements, 27–28
Shrink-resistant fabric, 132
Short figure, 154
Short-waisted figure, 28, 101–02
Shy shopper, 150, 152
Silhouette, 30, 32, 36, 38, 73
    A-line, 102, 105
    seasonless dressing, 81, 82
Silk, 82, 85, 130, 141
Silver Unicorn insignia, 165
Simpson, Jack, 165
Skin tone, color key program, 19–21, 24
Skirts, 37, 38, 62, 82, 83, 123–25, 161
    hemlines, 15
Slacks, 34
Sleepwear, 166
Soil-release fabric, 132
Spandex, 123, 131, 141
Sperry Top-Siders, 74
Spiegel catalog, 185, 189
Sportpages sale catalog, 100
Sportswear, 166
    double duty with action wear, 97, 100
Spot-and-stain-resistant fabric, 132
Stain removal booklets, 144
Status shopper, 150, 153
Stole, 102, 103
Storage tips, 145
Suede, cleaning, 142
Suits, 13, 15, 16
    appropriate to living area, 25
    hand tailoring, 129

Suits—*Cont.*
    knits, 83
    transseasonal, 82
    travel, 86
Suit vest, men's, 76
Swanberg, Annette, 10
    basics in personal wardrobe, 113–14, 166
        3-day travel wardrobe, 86–87
Swap meets, 184
Sweaters, 30, 83, 141
Sweatsuit, 86, 97, 99, 100, 166
Swimsuit, 86, 97
Synthetics, 129, 130–31, 131–32
    pills, 131, 145
    scrunch test, 131

T

Tailoring, 73
Tall figure, 154, 194
Tandy Leather Co., 142
Target, 100, 172
Taylor, Ann, 159
Tent dresses, 105, 106
Texture, 30, 34, 93
Thrift shops, 182–84
Tiegs, Cheryl, 166
Tights, 97, 100
Touchie-Specht, Phyllis with Mary Kefgen, *Individuality in Clothing Selection and Personal Appearance*, 23
Tracy, Ellen, 89
Travel wardrobe, 85–89
Trends, 15, 16, 122–24, 125
Trigere, Pauline, 103, 120
Tsu, Irene, on building a wardrobe, 53–54, 86

Tunics, 38, 115
Tuxedo, 73, 76
Twiggy, 40
Two-piece dress, 115
Two-thirds ratio, 38

U

Underwear, 86, 100, 166
Ungaro, Emanuel, 104

V

Valentino (designer), 159
Vertical lines, 30, 38
Victor/Victoria (movie), 73
Vintage clothes, 142
V-neckline, 30, 39
Vogue magazine, 11, 12
Vreeland, Diana, 42

W

Waist, 28, 34
    dropped, 108
Wardrobe, authors' personal, 113–14
    care, 137–45
    classics. *See* Classics
    color, 19–25
    day-to-evening transition, 91–96
    experimenting with your own, 9, 36, 37, 39–40, 42, 48, 51
    fabrics. *See* Fabrics

Wardrobe—*Cont.*
  men's and boys' clothes for, 73–77
  organizing new, 51–53
  seasonless, 81–84
  survival dressing for the 1980s, 97–100
  travel, 85–89
  what to borrow from a man, 75
  your own personal fashion, 7–18
Wash-and-wear garments, 132

Waterproof fabric, 132
Water-repellent fabric, 132
Water resistant fabric, 132
White, 22, 24, 85
Winter leisure activities coat, 101, 102
Woman's Day magazine, 12
Women's Wear Daily, 12, 13
Wool, 82, 85, 130, 141
Woolite, 141
W publication, 13
Wrangler label, 73

Y

Youth-quakers, 123

Z

Zoe label, 107, 108
Zoran, 118
  on seasonless dressing, 84

Notes

Notes

Notes

NOTES